Never Stop Looking
Down the Road

Praise for Novels by Sherman Smith

The Honeysuckle Rose Hotel

"Full disclosure: I did not buy the book, it was given to me by the author. I was with my family in Bellingham WA eating Christmas dinner at a hotel. I didn't notice the gentleman eating alone at the next table until he arose and introduced himself. "I couldn't help but overhear your discussion about historical fiction. Perhaps you would do me the honor of reading my latest book." There was no quid pro quo, I didn't even tell him I'd written a historical fiction book myself. I assured him that yes, the subject was intriguing and I would be happy to read it. Now, writers are the most severe literary critics, at least until they can afford to be generous, which I cannot. So when I say this book is well written, that I found myself immersed to the point where I was no longer editing as I read, then you can trust me that it's a good read. The Honeysuckle Rose Hotel is especially delightful for those of us with connections to both San Francisco and musicians. I learned something, I felt something. I never did see Mr. Sherman again, I'm sure he's not usually alone at Christmas, but I am happy that he had the chuzpah to introduce himself. Thank you, Sherman Smith, wherever you are, and happy writing."

~5 Star Amazon Review

Silencing the Blues Man

"Wow—finished it in one night. Mr. Smith's handling of the intricacies of each character shows personal depth. Feels like I know each of the characters like good acquaintances or really good friends. It made we want to be part of this ragtag family. The book made a run of my emotions and that, to me, signals awesome writing. The fact that it drew me in to the point that I couldn't put it down to sleep made me smile. He just keeps getting better and better, Well done."

~CJK

"Silencing the Blues Man is the third book in the Poets Can't Sing series featuring amazing characters including the Blues Man himself, Earl Crier and his Lady Stella. The story of a quirky set of misfits, mostly musicians, takes place in post WWII San Francisco. The story illuminates some of the racism and fanaticism of the time, challenging us to think about we face today. The story within the story and the characters are compelling. I wanted the group experiences at the Honeysuckle Rose Hotel to continue. The author's work helps keep our faith in humanity."

~RH

Novels by Sherman Smith

Previous Books in the Poets Can't Sing Series

Poets Can't Sing
The Honeysuckle Rose Hotel
Sausalito Night Music
Silencing the Blue Man

Other Titles by Sherman Smith

Golden City on Fire

For information on the author and all his writings go to:
Shermansmithauthor.com

Special thanks to the team at FPW Media
for the cover design and irreplaceable editing support.

This book is a work of fiction. Any references to historical events, real people, or real places are used fictionally. Other names, characters, places and events are products of the author's imagination, and any resemblance to actual events or persons, living or dead, are entirely coincidental.

Never Stop Looking Down the Road © Sherman Smith

© Without limiting the rights under copyright reserved above, no part of this publication may be reproduced, stored in or introduced into a retrieval system, or transmitted, in any form or by any means (electronic, mechanical, photographing, recording or otherwise), without the prior written permission of the publisher.

I

April 18, 1906
San Francisco, California

"Fire is both a terrible and wonderous thing," Huckleberry Freeman whispered, almost reverently, as he watched a fire burn on the far side of the city.

"I've got a bad feeling…" Bojan murmured to the waning night sky.

The old man ignored the man who set beside him.

The flames, though distant, raged high into the night sky its smoke devouring the stars. "Fire," he continued, "is the great leveler of humankind. When the fire is finished kings and paupers stand equal in the ashes." The old buffalo soldier took a deep breath as he shook away the memory of the great forest fire in Skagway that he had once fought.

He clicked at their mule team to keep moving up the steep hill.

Bojan was a man of few words, mostly because his English was poor. When he spoke Huck almost leapt at the chance to chastise his fellow cesspool engineer. Huck glanced at Bojan who just stared ahead at a mule's tail as it flicked at flies—flies they had plenty of. "You've got a bad feeling about what, in particular? Shit, you've got a bad notion bout most everything one day or another."

Bojan spat as if the next word he spoke might come out foul. "Won't know until the sun comes up."

Huck mumbled to himself glad that the nightshift was nearly over. He knew from experience that the few words Bojan had spoken was the beginning and the end of their conversation, at least until the sun came up. That was okay by him being that the Albanian immigrant didn't make much sense most of the time anyway.

Huckleberry Freeman regretted most moments of each day since he had retired. He had once been a proud Buffalo Soldier, an ordinance sergeant, 9th Calvary, Troop M, 24th Infantry. That was as high as a black man could go in the army; something he had been proud of. He and his men had fought Indians on the frontier, helped tame Alaska, survived the Skagway River Flood, a forest fire that had burned down their barracks and nearly roasted them all alive. His proudest moment had been when they had helped build the first roads into Sequoia National Park. It had been hard, difficult work. Those were the good old days before he grew too old to do the work. He did not consider himself to be old, just worn out and troubled by the aches that were the souvenirs of his younger days. Now he drove a *honey-wagon,* where he and a moronic Slavic imbecile under the cloak of darkness collected and took away their shit, so polite society would not be offended by its stench. He would have worked alone, except for his lumbago and the arthritis in his knees, which forced him to walk with a cane. He had tried riding without a partner, but after spilling a barrel or two, he finally accepted the cards he had been dealt.

Working on a night-soil wagon was not an idyllic job, but he been forced to retire just short of the thirty years required for full retirement because of the arthritis and his retirement pay fell short of what he needed. His retirement pay should have been $42.50 a month minus a twelve and a half cent tax for the old soldier's home but because he had not put in his thirty years—two years short. Now he took home less than $33.00, not nearly enough to live out his so-called golden years in a big city. The night wagon paid $2.50 a week, minus the four bucks he paid for an old horse stall he had managed to make into a room. After almost thirty years of honest soldering, he hadn't much to show for his labors. A can of beans and an old soldier's memories did not give you much to count your blessings on.

He had thought about packing up and moving back to Texas. He did not have any kin back there, if he did not know where to find them. He had been born and raised a slave, sold twice, finally to a white family just outside Galveston, Texas. It wasn't until June 19th, 1865, months after the war was over, that he had learned that he was a free man. He changed his name from Jonah Number Three to Huckleberry Freeman, turned his back on the cotton fields he had labored on, and looked for honest work, the gift God gave to every free man.

He did not find any.

In 1866 he signed up with the army, became a buffalo soldier, and the army had been his home ever since. That was, until he was forced to retire.

There are days, he thought, *this being one of them, when I wish that fire would burn the whole place down. Yes sir, that would be a sweet thing to see; then there would be no one left around here no more shit to burden my day.* He rubbed his chin, wishing that he had shaved before putting on his uniform.

On the first and third Wednesday of each month he wore his old uniform when he made the trek out to the Presidio cemetery. It was April 18th, the third Wednesday and the ache in his knees reminded him that it was going to be a long day.

Night was fading with a crescent moon. The weather not unusual for springtime. The low hanging smoke that blanked San Francisco in winter had been absent for a week now. It hadn't been much of a fire, quick to rise and roar, now whimpering its last gasp as the firemen beat it to death. The smoke from the fire blowing out towards the bay.

San Francisco was an industrial city where most of the factories were steam powered, the steam powered by coal. There were giants here, great men who carved the earth into their own image. Men who lived in great redwood mansions perched atop the city's iconic hills. Below that, men with lesser dreams, as there were those who did not know that they could dream at all. The streets were covered by the droppings from thousands of horses, horses that pulled street cars, horses that pulled carriages, dray horses that pulled the night wagons. The bay was an open sewer. The fabled city of San Francisco was smoggy, the air far from the freshness of the Sierra Nevada's he longed for.

It was dirty and corrupt.

The city's reputation for tolerance was a fairy tale with its largest racial minority—the Chinese—crowded into a ghetto. The only black men Huckleberry Freeman knew where buried in a segregated cemetery at the Presidio.

Those old black soldiers, lifers like himself, had held a powerful sway, and when the time came, he planned on joining them there.

Huckleberry Freeman glanced back as the fire flickered its last promise—the great equalizer.

Not today.

II

Leah could not sleep.

It was almost daybreak, as she hid beneath her comforter, afraid of something she did not understand. She had not had this sense of foreboding since the day her parents had died in a horrible accident. It was her birthday, a special day she had been looking forward to.

III

Grazia whisked the cake batter until the stiffness in her hands no longer allowed her to hold the spoon. She looked at the batter as she set the bowl on the counter. She hoped that her frenzied whisking would chase away her tears—it had not. Crying was an emotion she thought she had left behind her years ago. It was early in the morning and the sun was about to rise, as she quietly wept, a single tear falling unseen into the cake batter that she vigorously whisked while trying to hide her pain.

Alphonso, her husband of thirty-one years, had sat in his chair throughout the night, the bottle of wine on the table next to him untouched as he sat wordlessly chewing on whatever thoughts tore at his soul. They had slept in separate beds for many years, but this was the first time in many years that he had not slept in his bed across from hers, which is why she knew that whatever disturbed him was as grievous as the day they had lost their only child. For that she had never forgiven him.

That had been twenty-nine years ago when she had last wept knowingly; tears that had not come back until now. She knew their son's death had broken his heart; at least that was partial payment. Her heart had been hardened since.

She stepped to the kitchen door and looked at her husband while letting out a long-exaggerated sigh. Alphonso has never been a handsome man. He was short, barely five foot three, lean—bordering on scrawny—pale, his skin translucent. He has a thin semi-circle of feathery thin white hair. His ears hadn't looked quite so large when he had been younger with a thick crown of black hair. His bifocals. Perpetually smudged, sat perched precariously on the tip of his nose, looking as if they might slip off with his next breath, but never did. He looked much older than his fifty-four years. To say that he is not a handsome man is not fair, for she knew that she was no longer a woman that can spark a man's interest; never was. His eyes had not changed. They were the only things she still loved about the man. Despite her scorn she loved his eyes; his most beautiful eyes, deep gray mostly, which would transform to turquoise, with little golden specks that seem to dance in correspondence to his mood. Alphonso seldom smiled with his face, but rather it was his eyes that smiled, for this smiling of his eyes was the most sincere and pure emotion that her husband could show. His eyes never lied, and while she could not see them from where she stood now, she knew that at this moment her husband's eyes would be the color of a tombstone in deep December. When his eyes went to December his heart was as dead as hers.

Alphonso was a watch repairman. It was not an easy job, laborious in small detail with uncounted hours looking through a magnifying glass at tiny gears & screws, things that make other tiny things spin in uniform circles. At the end of the day, when her husband came home Grazia would greet him at the door. She would stand there silently, inspecting his shoes for dirt before he came into the house. She did not ask how his day had been.

Alphonso had learned to tell her about something he had seen or heard on his walk home—often just made up to fill that awkward moment. If he didn't, he might as well walk back out into the cold San Francisco wind for the chill in the house would be unbearable. The meaningless, one-side exchange of words done, he would fall quietly into his chair until he had a couple of glasses of wine, and then they would chat over dinner. In truth, it was mostly Grazia who talked. He listened, nodding at the appropriate moments. He is careful not to say anything that might anger his quick tongued wife—if he did, he would never hear the end of it, and all the unforgiven transgressions she would sling like so much muck from a pigsty.

Yesterday he had come home with steel gray eyes, oblivious to the world, nothing said of his walk home. Her deliberate scowl at his silence hadn't phased him. At first, she was angry, then she had wondered if the steep climb up the hill had tired him; he was no longer a young man. That wasn't it. She knew him to be a quiet man of few words, but this silence unsettled her more than anything she could remember. Her husband was troubled, and it sent a shiver through her bones. He left his meal untouched, never coming to the table, just sitting, and staring at nothing through his smudged spectacles.

Unable to sleep, Grazia quietly got out of bed, his side empty. She said nothing as she placed a blanket over her husband's lap. His eyes were open, he neither blinked nor smiled acknowledging her presence. With an open sigh, she left him alone to wrestle with his demons. Busying herself she began to make a cake. The cake was to be for Leah, the granddaughter of her dearest friend Maud, who lived two houses up the hill. Leah was to be ten. Grazia and Maud did not have much in common. She was kind and willing to chat about little nothings over a cup of coffee. The other neighbors avoided Grazia as if she were a snarling dog. That was all right by her, she did not care what the neighbors thought, she had her anger as her constant companion.

"Alphonso," she started to ask, but put her finger to her lips to silence herself instead. He would tell her when he was ready, and not a moment before. After all their years of marriage she really did not know much about her husband's inner emotions. She did not ask about what she didn't need to know, only that which she could use to keep him under her thumb.

Alphonso was Italian, and wine was in his blood, never-the-less, this long night he had not drunk a drop. The previous day had brought such tragedy that deep down he wanted to drink copious amounts of it until he was so drunk no thoughts would be left in his head to be worth the pity.

He had not. His thoughts, just this side of anguished self-pity.

Yesterday he had been a watchmaker, and he had rightfully thought that when his employer, Anton Jacobi, retired the business would be his. It had been spoken about, never promised. Yesterday had been his employer's sixtieth birthday and he had gleefully gone to work thinking that this would be the day.

He hadn't seen it coming.

Anton Jacobi, his employer, and once-upon-a-time friend announced that he had sold the business. Impatient to break the news the new owner, with glass raised high, divulged that the shop would be merged with his own, and since there was not enough work for everyone the younger men with children still in the nest would keep their jobs. Alphonso, and Isaak Lapin, a watchmaker two years older than he, were to be let go with thanks for their many years of loyalty and craftsmanship. There were no benefits, no gold watch to tick away their last days, their final paychecks reflecting only the time punched on their timecard.*

Alphonso quietly stepped away, knowing that his continued presence made everyone uncomfortable. He certainly was. Jacobi lent him a tight-lipped sad smile as their eyes briefly met. Once Alphonso and Isaak Lapin were out of sight, and out of mind, Jacobi raised his glass to his birthday, his retirement, and to everyone's bright future.

Now, at age 54, with only a week's pay in his pocket, what was he to do? He had been a fool to trust in Anton Jacobi's promises. *A fool.* A fool, which was what his wife would hiss as she quickly became angry and vindictive. He shook his head regretfully. Grazia was no fool, the least he could do was to tell her the awful truth. He closed his eyes for just a moment as he prepared himself to confront Grazia with what he had been dwelling on through the long dark hours of the night.

He listened to the click-click-click of the wooden spoon in the batter bowl as he saw her in his mind's eye. She was a smallish woman, all of five feet three. She had plumped out with age, as many Italian women do. She was still very much the way she was the day he had asked her father for her hand in marriage.

---

*Time cards have been used since 1868.

She had never been a beautiful woman, but she had been his first kiss, and thus his first love. Her once black hair, now streaked with gray, would be tied-up tight in a bun. She had smallish buttercup blue eyes. Now he found something else buried deep in her eyes, a hard frost that warned him that she was deceitful, self-righteous, superstitious, and emotionally unstable. His wife, his partner in life, was unforgiving, manipulative, and frigid. These are not things one would want to find in the gateway to your wife's soul. Whether it was her scolding tongue, the bitter cold ice in her soul, or life's experience, he had learned to avoid looking into her eyes whenever possible.

When they were young it had been her smile that brought out that turquoise with golden specks in his eyes, and it was that smile he needed most—now. Try as he might he could not remember what that smile had been like.

Alphonso knew that Grazia did not take bad news well. If an egg were to be dropped on the floor, she would not see just the broken egg, she would see all the dust bunnies that now ran rabid, carnivorous, and plotting to turn her kitchen into an abominable garbage dump. And he, her loving husband, had brought the damn rabbits home.

If there was a way to not tell her, then surely, he would choose that route. But this was something he could not hide. He wasn't sure which he feared the worst, that he no longer had a job, or telling her.

"Grazia," his voice, dry and emotional, sounded as if it was coming from a much older man, "I have something to say."

She put the bowl of cake batter on the kitchen counter as she turned towards the sound of his voice.

IV

Hattie Poirier was a demimonde—a courtesan, and every-
one in the ballroom knew it. She was a rare jewel in a city
overflowing with strumpets, harlots, whores- all collectively
classified as seamstresses regardless of what crib, alleyway,
or hotel room they plied their trade. Hattie was one of a kind
and could easily earn as much as one hundred of these seamstresses in a single night. Her company alone was worth the
price without necessitating the presumed sexual favors. Sometimes all she needed to do was smile. Some of her wealthy
patrons understood this, favoring the smile and the jealousy
of other men, holding themselves back from a more intimate
liaison least they embarrass themselves. No man would dare
define Hattie as merely a beautiful woman—few managed to
untie their tongues when she passes by, her long blond hair
cascading down her statuesque back like so many golden rays
of sunshine.* Her figure, temptation beyond imagination. Her
gown, fit like a second skin, waiting to be stripped away—the
serpent from the Garden of Eden cloaked as Venus, a goddess
of sexual presence, no man can resist. At five feet five inches
tall—in bare feet—when she enters a room, she makes all
other women seem insignificant.

It's the way she smiles.

---

*Most women wore their hair tied up. Hats were worn not just for fashion's sake but for good grooming. In 1906 there was no shampoo, there was lye soap, wash- ing one's hair was not something most women looked forward to.

She wore the same sequined, delicate lilac gown, she had worn to the opera, with a string of opulent pearls her gentleman of the evening had bestowed upon her. No hat, which made her scintillating hair that more enticing.

What had made her night was that she had met the Great Caruso. He had bowed and kissed her hand, all the while his eyes never leaving hers, except for that stolen glance at the burgeoning swell of her breasts. She knew how men looked at her—that way. She likes the way another man's gaze digs at the ego of the man she is with.

She smiled.

As did the mighty Caruso.

There had been a late-night party where the privileged and wealthy had gathered to greet the Great Caruso. She, and James, her escort on the best of occasions, had danced, and drank champagne, filling themselves with caviar, salmon, and pastries as the hour hand moved all to quickly around the clock. The promise of her feminine charms became mere wishful thinking with each glass he consumed. Until finally, weary of his public pawing, she took leave, her pay having been discreetly placed in her purse at the beginning of the evening.

James kept a room on the fourth floor where she planned to catch a couple of hours sleep. He had basked in the glow of her feminine spender and was now content to gloat over a game of cards, cigars, and brandy, with men sharing boyish chuckles. She wasn't worried about James having any amorous intentions, the sun was just waking, nothing with her escort would rise this night.

The sun yawned, its first morning light peaking over the hills on the east side of the bay. The morning was unusually quiet.

V

Francis DeGeorgie was a contradiction. Born to a wealthy family in Budapest, he was high-browed, and somewhat of a dilettante, he was a spoiled, foolish young man, always knocking on trouble's front door. He is tall, with pale bloodless skin, eyes the color of glacial water, his hair, and eyebrows raven dark. Often, he will wear spectacles, not for vision's sake, but to look the intellectual. Beneath his suave manners, he is gentile, persuasive, high-strung, quick to anger, and a self-described anarchist. Fluent in languages, and somewhat of a thespian who can easily manipulate others with his choice of words and flamboyant tongue. Humor seems to come easy, but that is a fraud, for he never truly laughs. In a world so much in need of earthshaking change he finds little to laugh about. A spirited agitator, he is a fraud seeking attention.

In December 1904, reading of a strike that had occurred at a railway and artillery factory in St. Petersburg, Russia, Francis left Budapest to see for himself what a real revolution was about. He and his father argued, Francis was adamant, and his father closed the door saying that he was never to come home again. His mother could never close that door sending her love, and just enough cash to support his idealistic wonderings whenever he had an address to forward.

He was soon caught, hook, line, and sinker, into both the chaos and the cause of the revolution, the chance for the average person to rise-up against the wealthy and industrialists of the world. In St. Petersburg sympathy strikes in other parts of the city raised the number of strikers to 150,000 workers in hundreds of factories until in 1905 the St. Petersburg had reached a volatile short fuse -the city had no electricity or essential services, and all public areas were declared closed.

The strike spread and culminated with the march on the Winter Palace and the delivery of the petition to the Tsar. Francis DeGeorgie marched at the head of the strike, both vocal and aggressive. The Okhrana's undercover agents had already identified the young Hungarian as a foreign instigator to be watched, and if possible, to be turned as a double agent. Francis did not know it at the time, but he was getting too close to a revolution that was threatening the very power of the Tsar.

Father Gapon, the Orthodox Priest that had rallied the legions of the unemployed, was not anti-Tsar. Indeed, dressed in their Sunday best, they bore banners and portraits of the Tsar, carried icons while singing hymns and songs proclaiming their support for him, whom they affectionately called their 'little father'. They believed, essentially, that the Tsar was a good man who had their best interests at heart and that once he knew the extent of the workers' discontent, he would put in place the means to address their grievances.

Francis had a different message; he wanted the Tsar to fall. He joined the march as it neared the Winter Palace just as they found their way barred by thousands of armed troops. The troops fired a few warning shots, then fired directly into the dense crowd. Cossacks on horseback charged, galloping through the terrified protesters, slashing lethally at people with their Sabers. Because of the sign Francis carried and his loud voice he was targeted by two horsemen who charged through the crowd to silence to him. He quickly retreated through an alley. The cries of the men, women, and children as they were slaughtered, the sound of the charging Cossacks, echoed throughout the city. Elsewhere a canon was used against the helpless hordes. The pools of blood on the white snow, the whips, the whooping of the gendarmes, the dead, the injured, the children shot were something Francis would never forget. Nearly 200 people were killed, and many more wounded.

Francis had tested his limits and was now afraid for his life. He was 19 years of age and wanted by the Tsar's all-powerful political police.

With his mother's help, and an uncle who worked for the Hungarian Embassy in Moscow, he escaped from Russia with his life, making his way to America where he soon found a new cause with the *Wobblies*, the *Industrial Workers of the World.*

He took on the guise of a working man, a foreigner with no skills other than the labor of his back and calloused hands. There was nothing about him that might suggest that he was uneducated, riffraff, poorly suited for anything but common labor. He needed to blend in with the emigrant poor who worked long hours for little pay on the docks and in the factories along the waterfront in San Francisco. He played the simpleton getting a job as a night janitor at the California Wine Association's massive warehouse not far from the waterfront and an industrial area called Butcher Town. At night he pushed a broom, and during the day he spread the word of the *Wobblies* sowing discontent, revolution, and anarchy.

VI

Alphonso rose from his chair looking down at the floor, never at her. "Grazia, I have something to say. I want you to hear me out before you…"

The floor lurched!

He felt suddenly dizzy as the floor rose, then twisted beneath his feet. Beams groaned, cracked, as glass shattered, one wall collapsing as a mighty earthquake woke the city of San Francisco.

Grazia screamed as she fell to her knees the very floor beneath her pulled apart, the darkened basement yawning up before her. "Madre di Dio quello che sta succedendo?" Mother of God, what is happening?

VII

Half-way up the hill the old buffalo sergeant had had enough. As far as he was concerned San Francisco had too many steep hills. The bumping and jarring of the wagon were too hard on his ass. It did not matter whether it be up or down both aggravated his arthritis to no end, but a bruised ass was something else. He told Bojan that he would be getting off and to take the wagon down to the waterfront at China Basin where it would be unloaded.

He did not look back as Bojan cursed at being left to finish the shift alone. Smiling to himself he thought about the hot coffee and breakfast biscuits he would be given at the back door of the Presidio Commissary.

At 5:13 A.M. that thought was erased from his mind as he was thrown painfully to his knees as many of the wooden houses around him splintered, cracked, and collapsed, while poorly reinforced brick buildings tumbled to the ground. Bleary residents scurried into streets that were rippling like waves and firing off cobblestones. Stunned by the suddenness of it all he braced for the worst as trees whipsawed and telephone poles snapped. Amidst the noise, all of San Francisco's church-tower bells rang, sounding an eerie alarm that lasted until the shaking stopped nearly a minute after it had begun. He knew that he wasn't addled, this was bad, and most likely going to get worse.

VIII

Unable to sleep Leah climbed out of bed. It was her tenth birthday and seemed as if she had been nine for almost half of her life. The house was quiet, the sun just peeking at the early morning sky. The aroma of fresh baked wheat cakes and sausage waffled up from grandma's coal stove. The clop-clop-clop of two mules and the grate of heavy wooden wheels as they pulled a wagon echoed up Rincon Hill on the cobbled street below—comforting and familiar. The morning seemed unusually silent, the normal sounds of a bustling city somehow held at bay, a precursor to something pending. There were no birds chirping to greet the day. There were no clouds, fog, or morning breeze. Oddly, she thought of a Mother Goose rhyme, recited it, as the curious silence drew her:

> *'The birds go fluttering in the air.*
> *The rabbits run and skip.*
> *Brown squirrels race along the bough,*
> *But while these creatures play and leap,*
> *The silent snake goes creepy-creep.'*

She went to the window, stumbled over nothing, or so she thought, as she grasped the window frame. Outside the horse reared, the whites of its eyes bulging white; terrified. She quickly looked across the street, expecting to see a wild dog, something that might have spooked it.

The snake, she thought.
The birds sing and whistle loud,
The busy insects hum.
The squirrels chat, the frog says "Crook!"
But the snake is always dumb.
With not a sound through grasses deep
The silent snake goes creepy—creep.

Seeing nothing she leaned out the window to get a closer look.

All at once, the house began to rumble and shake. Outside the street ruptured; a giant crack opened causing houses on both sides to lean precariously towards the chasm. Inside the chasm she thought she saw the eyes of the snake…its flickering serpent's tongue…huge, searching for its prey. The chasm widened as if reaching out for a night service wagon which turned over, its team of mules terrified, their hooves kicked stones into the fissure. The poor creatures pulled free dragging part of the wagon down the hill, the stench of the upturned barrels immediate. The driver man did not have a chance flying head over heels landing hard on the street. A brick chimney crashed down off Mrs. Cassidy's boarding house burying him.

Leah's breath caught in her throat as she blinked away a tear at what she had just seen, a lone wheel wobbled like a top as it rolled down the hill. She turned back from to the window as she heard grandma call out her name. "LEAH!" Just once. The sound of fear in her voice caused her to turn and run towards the sound of her voice. Then the house took a terrible jolt.

It sounded as if the world was ending. A wall, near where she stood ripped free, the floor beneath her tilted, everything rose, then fell, the world suddenly topsy-turvy, the furniture sliding every which way, as she clung to her bed as it was thrown out into the street. "Grandma!"

The gas streetlight on the corner shattered, its small flame suddenly a gigantic dancing genie. The house behind it, a Queen Ann crumbled, falling forward, it's beautiful woodwork instant fuel for the fire. People, in all arrays of dress made their way to the street. The hillside above Leah, crowded with boarding houses, surrounded by smaller stately Victorians, and shanties, perilously close to the fire.

"Grandma!" Leah screamed. With tear-clouded eyes she searched the wreckage of what once had been Grandma's house. She reached into the rubble, groping, hoping, finally finding her grandma's hand. A pool of blood slowly oozed from beneath the shattered cottage. Through a small crack Leah could see her eyes. The sparkle was gone. Grandma wasn't there anymore. A fire spread around her, the heat and smoke finally pushed the little girl away.

"It's time to go, little one, she's gone." She heard someone say, not knowing who.

"No, I can't leave her," she cried as she felt herself being pulled away. She looked into the frightened eyes of the old man who tried to pull her away, a stranger whose appearance frightened her even more. Then she saw her doll* which she had been given by an uncle she had never met. The doll had been in her room, it now lay in the street, its bisque head now separated from its rod. It's one black face seemed to cry and was as dark as the man's face who now tried to help her.

Alphonso and Grazia fled their home moments before it crashed down. The ground still roiling like an ocean beneath them as they saw more houses around them succumb to the earth's shaking. Just two houses further up the hill they could see a little girl trying to pull someone from the rubble as what remained of the house teetered precariously above her.

---

*Several 19th-century European doll companies preceded American doll companies in manufacturing Black dolls. These predecessors include Carl Bergner of Germany, who made a three-faced doll with one face a crying Black child and the other two, happier white faces. In 1892, Jumeau of Paris advertised Black and mixed race dolls with bisque heads. Gebruder Heubach of Germany made character faces in bisque. Other European doll makers include Bru Jne. & Cie of Paris, Steiner, Danel, Société Française de Fabrication de Bébés et Jouets (S.F.B.J.), and Kestner of Germany.

IX

"Azt a leborult szivarvegit!" Francis DeGeorgie cursed in Hungarian as he heard a bottle shatter somewhere towards the back of the warehouse. By the sound, it had been a full bottle of wine, perhaps more, being readied for shipment. Now he would have to go back and clean it up. Before he could finish the thought, he felt unsteady on his feet as he heard another bottle fall, and another…

The warehouse shelves, reaching eight feet in height, gave way one after another under the weight of the glass, wine, and violent shaking, he was being buried alive in a sea of glass.[*]

---

[*] The California Wine Association in its San Francisco cellars lost 4,750,000 gallons of wine.

X

Katie McGillicutty, with bread in the oven, coffee on the stove did not bother to call upstairs. Her one tenant, Morgan Piff, was old and like many of his age group was usually early to rise. Once the aroma of fresh baked bread reached upstairs, he'd be down just as sure as the sun was to rise. She gathered some clothes pins and a basket of laundry and headed out the back door to hang some laundry for the morning sun. In another couple of hours, the back side of the house would be in shade the rest of the day.

The early morning was quiet.

The fog horns were silent, even the birds seemed to be dozing, the usual noise of a waking city the size of San Francisco eerily absent. She noted the muffled day but did not pay much heed other than glancing out of her backyard fence towards the end of the block where she had a little view of the city and distant bay. The morning wasn't just quiet; it seemed to be waiting.

Katie felt a sudden chill as she bent down to get some laundry from her basket. The pressure in her inner ears rose just as every dog in the neighborhood yelped and the gulls and garden birds alike took flight with a turbulent whoosh.

The eerie silence was instantly replaced by a grinding and banging followed by a boom that seemed to be made up of every sort of sound mixed up in a great stirring pot.

Knocked to the ground she grabbed hold of the laundry basket as if its soft contents might protect her from worse things to come. The earth beneath her rolled and inundated for several long moments before quieting.

The world around her was no longer silent as she put her hands over her ears adjusting the unexpected pressure that now also seemed to have passed. The sounds that echoed from the earthquake and its aftermath seemed distant. Her house still stood as did her immediate neighbors'.

Morgan Piff leaned out an open second floor window.

"Woo…wee, that one was a lollapalooza!" Bracing himself in case of a second shock, he hurriedly scanned what he could see of the city from his perch. "It looks like Market Street over by the Palace Hotel might have taken some damage. I don't see no fires yet. "You, okay?"

Katie nodded that she was as she dusted off her dress and apron.

"I do smell some smoke though," Piff added.

Seeing no smoke in the sky Katie immediately thought of her bread baking in the oven and hurried back inside.

Piff lingered for a few moments as he watched his view of the city begin to change with dust clouds and tendrils of smoke beginning to rise. "Yes, sir, that was one lollapalooza…one for the books."

The yawling of the dogs agreed.

XI

Alphonso found standing difficult, walking impossible, so he ran, much like a drunken jack rabbit, in his stocking feet until he arrived at Leah's side. It was obvious that the old woman was dead. "We've got to go now, darling, the fires are growing." He hadn't noticed the fires until that moment. While small, they were numerous, driven by a finicky morning breeze.

As abruptly as it has started the violent shaking had stopped. His fear did not as he came eye to eye with a Black person—a black man. He had seen a few at a distance, mostly on ships as they passed through the bay. This one seemed just as startled by Alphonso's pale face as Alphonso was his black one. The blue uniform he wore reminded him that he had heard at one time that there were a company of black soldiers stationed at the Presidio army base; Buffalo Soldiers they were called, or something like that.

The black hand on Leah's shoulder was replaced by Alphonso's. It wasn't as strong but felt more reassuring for such a small man. "Grandma, please don't go…" she cried as she looked up at Alphonso. It was then that she got scared. Her grandma was dead, and she had no one else in the world. Her vision blurred with tears as she looked down towards the bay where tendrils of smoke were beginning to rise from the devastated city below. "What happened?" Her voice small and confused.

Grazia came to her side, taking her hand as the groaning of timber caused her to slowly look up the hill towards where a huge mansion clung precariously to the hillside. It's intricate redwood woodwork seemed to be in motion as it threatened to slide down upon its neighbors in a massive avalanche. She gave a troubled nod to her husband that they had best leave while they still could. Grazia quickly turning her attention back to where Leah's eyes could not turn away from where her grandma lay buried, the fire beginning to consume the shattered home.

Now, too stupefied to cry, Leah sat on her knees, frozen in fear. At the sight of the black soldier Grazia stepped away, her hands to her mouth as if to stifle a scream. The earth shook just a little, the house shifted. The roaring gas consuming the streetlight nearby instantly shut off leaving a long stuttering hiss. She turned towards Alphonso, not trusting Grazia who had always been mean and snoopy. Why her grandma had been friends with the woman Leah had never understood; perhaps it was just because they were both old.

They were all shaken from their despair as the front of a house above them slid into the street with a terrible crash, exploding in an instant into a gas fed fire.

Huckleberry Freeman wasn't sure whether to stay and try to help or move on. He looked back at the over-turned wagon where Bojan had simply disappeared. The horses had fled. Fortunately, he was able to retrieve his cane. He tested his weight guessing that it would become powerfully handy in the near future.

Leah wanted to run but couldn't.

The earthquake that had just changed all their lives had lasted less than two minutes. It was the impact of the fallen house, not an aftershock, which shook them back to their senses.

One of the lenses in Huckleberry Freeman's glasses had cracked when he had fallen to the sidewalk. The good news was that it was the one covering his bad eye, the one with a problematic cataract that only grew worse with time. Cleaning his good lens and placing his spectacles back where they belonged, he was not surprised at the look he saw on the white woman's face.

Fires were breaking out all over town. He turned, thinking that this was as good a time as any to get back to his room to see if he had anything left. What few medals he had earned as a soldier over the years he wore proudly anytime he paid a visit to the old buffalo soldier's cemetery. His stomach rumbled reminding him of the breakfast biscuits he had been looking forward to. The clacking of a few bricks as they slid from the chimney gave him pause to think that breakfast was not about to happen anytime soon."

"We going to spit into the wind or at each other?" The black soldier challenged in a low voice. Alphonso wasn't quite sure how to take it, one thing for sure was that the man was a heap bigger than himself and his weathered featured showed a history of hard living. A retired watchmaker should be careful where he spat especially when the man was as dark as a Barbary Coast alley at night. Still, there was something about the man that he sensed he could trust.

Alphonso cupped his hand to his brow as he looked at the rising sun from their once majestic view from Rincon Hill. He could see buildings down or shattered across much of the city. The great dome of City Hall hung precariously on steel ribs, the brick facade beneath now rubble. For the moment, there was more dust than smoke, but he knew that would change as he counted the many small fires taking hold in the ruins below. The ones that concerned him the most were taking hold in the ruins above them. The twisted wooded ruins of the shanties, boarding houses, and small homes in the working man's neighborhood of Rincon Hill made for easy fuel. As were the lofty mansions that topped the hill.

The morning breeze came from the west.

His feet suddenly felt as if they were caught in a deep primordial bog, his limbs fused knowing that he and Grazia were too old to fight their way on foot through the ruins of San Francisco to the Presidio and presumed safety. Grazia loved her bread and pasta, and the weight showed its unkindness as each year passed. Another gas streetlight exploded into a flaming Whirling Dervish on the hillside telling him that despite his age, aches, and pains, it was time to go.

He lowered his hand extending it towards the old soldier. "I can't say spitting one way, or another, would be a good use of either of our limited resources. May I suggest that we head down the hill towards the old winery where we might wet our whistles and discuss our options further?" It was decided that they should head down towards the California Wine Association's massive winery, the hill less steep, where they might latch onto a couple of draft horses and a delivery wagon. He scratched his unshaved chin as he looked at his wife, then back up to the fires building above them. *What was it he had been about to tell his Grazia?* For the life of him he could not remember what it had been. *Well, if it had been important, it would come back to me. Right now, there were more important things. The little girl was barefoot. He in his stocking feet. Their trek was not going to be easy.* The old soldier appeared to have a limp, and Grazia would do her best to make life more miserable every step along the way.

"Alphonso Paluso," he said.

Huckleberry Freeman slowly smiled as he spat into his hand the way an old soldier might as he extended his in return. "Huckleberry Freeman, just call me Sarge; friends, few that are, do."

An aftershock nipped at their already frayed nerves as the mansion above them slipped one more notch towards collapsing on its neighbors below. He looked back at their house which was damaged, but not beyond hope. He needed to get his shoes which should be right where he left them beside his chair. A loud crash and groan from the mansion above them warned that it was too damn risky.

Leah pulling back from Grazia's grasp, wanting desperately for her grandma to rise from the flames, sniffling her name, followed.

There had been no vote electing the old sergeant as their leader. He just took the role knowing that harm was in the air, and they needed to find safe ground. The aches and pains of his age making no-never mind. "This way and be quick about it." Sarge took the lead, his voice confident, a man who was used to giving orders.

Time seemed to be out of kilter, a second seeming like a minute, a minute only a few short seconds. A collapsed building blocked the street no more than half a block down from where they had once stood. The ruins of a brick chimney was blocking their way. Climbing over the least steep side of the pile of broken and unsteady bricks they could see three great plumes of brooding smoke snaking into the sky that came together like a colossal hungry beast above the city. A breeze fanning life into what would become a fiery colossus.

A sharp crack followed by a thunderous roar sounding from somewhere behind them. Leah, slowest to make her way through the bricks, turned to see what it was as the mansion at the top of the hill gave way in an avalanche of redwood, brick, fire, furniture, plumbing, and debris. A massive bonfire instantly crowning what was left.

Canyons of rubble blocked their way as the sarge struggled to find a way through. Alphonso a few steps behind was grateful the old soldier was the one breaking trail. The buildings on all four corners of Folsom Street had collapsed into a mountain of brick, wood, and shattered glass. Sarge was struggling to find his footing searching for an easier way; there wasn't one.

In her bare feet, Leah struggled to keep up. She was more a little princess than a tom-boy type of girl. Being raised by her grandma since the death of her parents had left her home bound and home educated. She had never ventured far from home—now—suddenly she had no home.

Time seemed pointless. Two hours, two days, who remembered how long it had been since the earthquake had shaken their lives to the point where they had to wonder if they were going to live to see another day. Climbing over and through the rubble seemed to take forever. They hadn't really traveled far—at least not far enough—as the unfolding disaster seemed to close in on them. Smoke, fire, fear, exhaustion, all buried within an overwhelming sense of loss, bleeding feet, and hunger were pushing ten-year-old Leah to the edge of her ability to cope.

Alphonso's feet were not faring better.

Grazia tried to follow but exhaustion soon began to take its toll. Her breathing became labored as her heart felt heavy in her chest. Her steps slowed. She climbed over a collapsed wall into a narrow alley, the walls on both sides ready to crumble with the next aftershock. "I…I can't go another step," she gasped as she looked ahead to where Alphonso and the black soldier stood on top of a partially collapsed wall gazing down towards what they saw on the other side.

Ahead lay a vast purple swamp, where millions of gallons of wine had spilt from where the California Wine Association's huge warehouse now lay shattered, fingers of hungry flames snaking their way through its collapsed roof. The dark purple sludge covered a vast boneyard of twisted cooperage, brick, iron, and glass from a million shattered bottles. The air pungent with the sweet smell of fermented grape and smoke from the fires that seemed to sprout like weeds everywhere about them, black smoke crowded the sun from the sky. The heat from the fires made each breath taste of charred wood, scorched paint, burnt hair and roast beast that came from the stockyards just a few blocks away.

Sweat dripped from their brows and soaked their clothes as the fires ravaged the hillside from where they had just escaped. While the sarge tried not to show his own limitations his knees had moved from annoying to downright painful; his cane becoming more of a hindrance than an aid in the rough terrain. Needing a moment to catch his own breath Alphonso stepped down to the edge of the pond, knelt and tasted the wine. Just below the thin film of ash and debris it wasn't bad. Good, it wasn't, considering the circumstances. He looked back to see if the sergeant was watching, then took a second taste.

Grazia looked ahead to where Alphonso had disappeared beyond the mountain of bricks she was not prepared to surmount. She shook her head, muttering beneath her breath, that the *black bastard* was leading them further into harm's way. If they managed to find horses and a wagon what good would they do in this rubble? Her anger rose as she prepared to lambast her husband for being a fool and for becoming subservient to a niggerman. They needed to turn towards Market Street, where no doubt the proper soldiers would be gathering to rescue them.

The sarge shared a slight knowing smile as Alphonso stumbled back to the top of the debris pile with something in his hands, and a sheepish grin that a child might have when caught with his hand in a cookie jar.

When Grazia saw what he had she lambasted him with words

no little girl should hear. To her consternation he ignored her as if she weren't even there as he passed her taking his gift to Leah.

Leah's eyes, red-rimmed with salty tears, mixed with gray from the soot in the air, lit up with the innocent joy of Christmas morning as she took the granite light gray Abyssinian kitten from his hands. It was scrawny, thin-haired—practically bald—just old enough to be free from its mother's tits. Shivering, hungry and scared, its golden eyes beamed with mischief and a desperate need for attention. Its *meow*, a sharp tiny squeak, the older adults couldn't even hear. Leah did, meowed back, letting the kitten know that it had a new mama. It was love at first nuzzle.

Leah was no longer alone in the world.

As Alphonso watched, his eyes quickly changing from the dark winter squall gray they had been a moment before to an early evening turquoise with twinkling golden stars. "You take good care of it; she'll never survive all this alone."

"Oh, I will. I will! Thank you." Leah looked at her new best friend who now purred contentedly on her lap. "I'm going to call you *Purplepaws*. Yes, that's it, *Purplepaws*." It was an ugly little cat whose four feet, paws, and tail were stained a deep purple from the river of wine it had almost drowned in. Hunger its middle name.

Grazia looked as if she might drown the helpless kitten just for spite.

XII

The violent shaking of the earth knocked Francis DeGeor-gie from his feet rendering him helpless against the oncoming avalanche of glass. Bottles pummeled his flesh as he covered his head with his arms and rolled into a ball to protect himself. His eyes wide, he could not help but look up as he heard a loud crack as a section of the ceiling gave way.

The noise was beyond anything he had ever before or would want to hear again—if he lived beyond the immediate moment. Certain that he was about to be crushed to death he tried to find the faith he had grown up with as a child—but came up short. The intellectual and revolutionary in him had turned away any notion that there was a God a long time ago—that the church and its false gods held man down not lifted them up. None of that mattered now as he faced death alone, no God to beg or seek forgiveness from. No angels calling from the heavens, only a burning roof and the weight of thousands of bottles holding him down.

XIII

The Palace Hotel, located at the SW corner of Market and New Montgomery Streets, was more than majestic. That it was over-built and of the highest quality of construction proved its worthiness. The earthquake that did so much damage across the city broke a few windows, a few chandeliers had come down, and the power went out. Those who had been trapped in over-sized redwood-crafted elevators soon knew exactly what was happening as they were thrown around the suspended 'rising rooms' as if they were rag dolls.

Hattie Poirier was one of those trapped. When the shaking stopped, try as she might, she couldn't find her smile.

XIV

Pummeled and properly bruised, Francis felt like he had just been run over by a column of Cossack Horsemen. The collapsed section of shelving, landing with the grace of God—not that he believed in one—barely covered him, the weight of the bottles on top causing it to creak and groan, threatening to further collapse at any moment. With less than six inches of clearance above his head, all he could see was glass, both shattered and whole bottles, which appeared to have buried him deep. There had been close to two million bottles in the warehouse. *Two Million! Jesus, how am I to dig myself out of this?* He thought, his sense of doom almost as heavy as the glass, as both panic and claustrophobia began to set in. He could not rise, nor could he crawl. He dared not try to move from beneath the wooden shield that both protected and threatened him with immediate death. Surrounded by the broken glass he had no doubt that he had been hurt somewhere. In places, he felt wet. Running he hands slowly along his body, then bringing his hand hesitantly up to taste, he found wine, not blood. The next sound he heard was the slow hiss of his own breath in relief. Twisting his body with bone straining efforts he tried to touch his lower legs and feet. Each movement caused his protective shell to groan as it shifted under its burdensome weight, the tinkle of glass always present. Somehow, he had come out with nothing more than a few small cuts on his scalp, wrists, and hands; nothing broken, everything bruised.

For the moment it seemed that the earthquake had ended but the sea of glass continued to shift, a crystal surf lapping at his door. *Perhaps he should just stay where he was; surely someone would come?* He called out, his voice at first timid, afraid that his voice might bring down a bone crushing avalanche of glass. Finally, with more force and desperation he called out, his cry masked by the shrill bell tones of settling glass, creaking timbers, and the sound of a rapidly flowing river caring with it a multitude of glass buoys.

And crackling?

He could not tell how far, or how bad the fire was, he could only see its flickering reflection in the glass prisms. With the growing fire, his desperation became paramount, his breathing became exaggerated, his heart pounding as his sense of being trapped crowded his every thought. Each movement caused bottles around him and above his flimsy shelter to move. The clink-clink-clinking sounds that marked the bottles movements sounded like ten thousand erratic crickets. He pushed with his fingers at the glass just in front of his face. Sweat ran down his brow, the salt stung irritating his eyes. He struggled to catch his breath; his lungs unable to pull in enough. He tried to scream but could not. Cutting two fingers, he pulled them back, brought them to his lips, tasting salt, the coppery taste of his own blood. The cuts stung but were shallow, the paper cut like pain bringing him back to his senses.

As he wiped the blood on his shirt, he remembered his broom. Slowly extending his wrist and fingers he found it and began to use the straw brush end to push at the glass which caused more shards of glass to slide into his tiny space than he could push away. Crickets driven mad by the crackling of flames drawing closer.

The air around him, harder to breath, grew uncomfortably hotter by the minute. The unnerving stench of scorched wood and smoke motivated his efforts. If he did not do something he would be roasted alive, and time was running out. With effort, he managed to turn the broom around using the handle to bore into the mountain of glass that imprisoned him. The glass shifted, small crickets, all with sharp bites, slid into his enclosure as he angled the broom handle up—twisting—prodding—heart pounding—dripping sweat stung his eyes as he carefully testing and turning until a little better than half of the broom stick had bored into the glass before finally breaking surface.

It took fifteen minutes, give, or take an hour, to finally secure a clear hole from which he could make out a little of what was happening around him. While hot and smoky the small draft of fresh air felt good. The room was filled with glass dunes, three to five feet tall, mixed with broken beams, fallen walls, shelving, and a slumped ceiling that was close to being fully ablaze. When, not if, it came down, he would be grilled alive like a poor Hungarian peasant under glass. Getting out from where he was seemed an impossible task. So far, what little he had managed to dig out had caused more glass to slide into his space making it harder to move. Death by a thousand cuts was one of two thoughts foremost in his mind. How to get through the glass dunes that waited outside the second. His mind raced as he tried to find and hope. What choice did he have? He knew that he was trapped somewhere near the middle of the gigantic warehouse. With a sea of glass all around and fire above he had little time; odds against him were overwhelming.

XV

Katie had been through an earthquake or two before but nothing like this. When it hit, she just held on. Afterwards, as her heatbeat slowed she had a chance to put everything into perspective. At first glance no real harm done other than a few broken dishes and a nasty looking crack in the wall near enough to the stairwell to cause her some concern. She was surprised to find that the biscuits in her oven had not fallen even though the stove pipe had come loose. As she took them out of the oven setting them on the kitchen table, she thought about taking a short walk to see what damage the quake had done elsewhere. All-in all she thought herself lucky.

XVI

"**Segítség! Van ott valaki? Segítség. Én DeGeorgie Ferenc. Bárki hall engem?**" Forgetting himself, he tried again in English, "Help, is anyone out there? Hello, I am Francis DeGeorgie, can anyone hear me?" His Hungarian accent, while not thick, only hindered his plea. The morbid thought that he might be the only survivor in a city where hundreds of thousands had once lived crossed his mind.

Shaking off this thought he twisted and contorted his body until he was able to pull off first one, then both of his boots. Placing them over his hands they came up over a foot on his forearms offering some cover. He worked the toe of a boot into his small hole slowly pushing everything up like a mole breaking ground. When he had pushed as far as he could he removed the boot leaving it to cap the enlarged tunnel. Putting his other boot back on he pushed the straw end of the broom into the boot he had jammed into the hole and once again began to work it forward. As it broke surface, a section of glass slipped filling half his tunnel; not unexpected, never-the-less exasperating.

After ten minutes of tedious labor, using both broom and boot, he finally opened a tunnel large enough for him to crawl up through. His tunneling had caused much of the broken glass to settle beneath the thousands of whole bottles. Carefully putting his boot back on, then, holding his breath, he carefully slid out. His movements were now agonizingly slow, especially since he desperately wanted to bolt and run. Getting to his feet on this shifting sea of bottles was not an easy feat as his feet slipped down deep enough to be caught in the underlaying glass shards.

He could feel the nearness of the fire as he looked up from the glass sea that engulfed him to the burning roof above. By now most of what remained of the ceiling was ablaze, which would soon come down as the fire continued to weaken it. It did not matter if it was 30 feet or three hundred yards it was a goodly distance to the nearest doorway. The way was blocked by what looked to be mountains of glass that were at best insurmountable.

He stopped, listening intently, something had changed. The faint sound of rushing water had been replaced by the crackling of flames. *Rushing water?* It didn't make any sense, but that was no longer relevant, the sound was gone. The fires spreading. Multitudes of crickets warned each other of eminent doom. He had to concentrate…there had to be away out.

His eyes settled for a second on the collapsed shelving which had been burning at the far end of the warehouse, now burning frightening closer to where he was trapped. *How long did he have?* That same collapsed shelving just might be his lifeline. The nearest was only a few feet away but not near enough to reach, nor could he climb over or through the glass without cutting himself to shreds.

The shelving that had once stood eight feet tall, supporting hundreds of pounds of wine bottles, looked like capsized ships.

During the earthquake, the weight had shifted, the wooden shelving collapsing like dominoes filling the aisles with bottles and shattered glass. The closest unit to him had slid into the center aisle, its front buried in glistening shattered debris. Then it struck him, if he could push enough of the glass off the collapsed shelf and out of the way, he could use it to climb up to the top of the long line of collapsed shelving. If lucky, he might find a way to pass over most of the glass. A slight smile crossed his lips as he thought, *like finding a shiny new penny, there wasn't much value, but there was promise.*

His moment of fleeting hope was stripped away as an aftershock shifted everything. An avalanche of rolling bottles crushed his former shelter. He felt the glass beneath him shift, drawing him dangerously down. He swore loudly as he suffered numerous cuts on his legs above his boots. To add to his troubles a large section of the burning ceiling and roof collapsed at the rear of the gigantic warehouse quickly adding more fuel to the fires. His raw terror was that he would not be able to pull himself free from where he was now buried waist deep in the glass that still shifted around him. A section of a wall at the front of the warehouse groaned as it bent outwards before collapsing, the remaining roof above visibly sagging. Luck laughed in his favor as enough glass slid away from him towards the front of the warehouse, his view opened to where a flash flood of wine had cleared a wide swath leaving a bare purple floor where thousands of gallons of wine had come through when the giant vats had split open under their own weight when the earthquake had brought everything down. A small stream still flowed freely out of the ruined warehouse towards San Francisco Bay.

As the mountain of glass moved, the bottles on the partially buried shelf began to slide down burying him deeper. A few seconds prior he had not been able to see that the corner of the collapsed shelf—now he could see that it was actuality only a few feet away. He pushed the broom handle down until he felt it touch bottom. Using it to leverage his weight, he pulled himself free. The cantered shelf now clear of bottles had left hundreds of sharp glass shards behind. Using the straw end of the broom, he brushed these aside as he propelled himself onto the shelf. He did not know how many cuts he had received but at least now he was free. His heart stopped in his chest as the shelf tore away under his sudden weight. If he slid back, there would not be a second chance. The sound of the fires around him now louder than the crickets. Bottles shattered from the heat. Wind outside the building fed the inferno. Supported by the glass beneath, the shelf had nowhere to go. As more bottles shifted around him, he flung himself to the next collapsed shelf, and then the next, praying all the while that they were stable enough to support his weight.

They weren't.

XVII

Sarge shook his head slowly from side to side. The way forward promised to be a risky decision, one he was not willing to make. They might be able to wade through the purple swamp, but he had no idea what hazards lay beneath. The once massive warehouse on the far side had partially collapsed and most likely would be a huge bonfire before they even reached it, if he were stupid enough to try. From where he stood, he could see little if any chance of rescue. He turned back towards Alphonso pointing towards the city's center. "That way." His aches and pains were not going to forgive him for some time to come.

XVIII

No sooner had DeGeorgie reached the top shelf it slid to the left carrying him across the aisle, and its lethal glass, until it was stopped by the next row of shelving. He climbed up, prying, and kicking at the loose top section until it too slid taking him across the next aisle. The top of the next shelving unit was as solid as the day it was built.

The next moment a larger section of the ceiling gave way, a swarm of glowing embers and sparks filled the air around him—stinging hornets—which he slapped at as he felt his clothes and hair start to ignite. He ducked as the ceiling immediately above him burst into roiling flame. His singed hair leaving him with no choice but to jump. Landing hard on the purple stained floor, he rolled back onto his feet, slipped, then fell back into the purple stream bed. The vibration of his landing started the bottles on both sides to slide, soon becoming an avalanche, which if he didn't hurry would block his escape route.

Crickets!

Millions of dying crickets. Their dying voices fading as much of what remained of the warehouse exploded into flame. Outside he stopped for a second to catch his breath and to make sure he was not bleeding or on fire. He had dozens of cuts, none fatal, most not hurting much but he knew that they would be screaming at him later. He turned, gasping at his fortune, as the rest of the ceiling of the giant warehouse caved in, the supporting walls collapsing, as flames leapt a hundred feet... and more.

XIX

Alphonso could see where the wine had come from, how much there had been he could not fathom. They were two blocks away from where the California Wine Association's massive warehouses had been, a firestorm would soon engulf the entire neighborhood. Their way to the waterfront was blocked by flames, rubble, and a pond of Zinfandel. He blindly followed the old buffalo soldier as he struggled to find a path through the ruins towards Market Street. Grazia, Leah, and little Purplepaws not far behind. The closer they got to Market Street the easier their travel.

Damage to buildings was nothing like what they had experienced, most were still upright and relatively whole. Some residents remained in their homes and apartments gawking out their windows at the stream of refugees as they fled from the fires that now torched Rincon Hill.

Even with Purplepaws cuddled in her arms Leah was miserable almost distraught. Her grandma was dead. Her home and everything she knew had burned. She cried, "Grazia," she said with an embarrassed whisper of a voice, "I have to go."

"You what?"

"I have to go."

The little girl's urgency reminded Grazia that she did to.

"What's the problem now?" Alphonso asked when he saw that Leah and Grazia had come to a complete stop. The answer was not easy. There were now plenty of distressed people around them who had much the same needs—and no public facilities. Alphonso had stepped behind a broken garden wall. What were the women going to do? The sarge understood, if he were caught taking a piss where he ought not to, someone just might lynch him. Adjusting his spectacles, he told them to wait where they were while he explored a nearby alley. Alphonso followed, soon taking the lead, glad to finally be on flat land. Half-way down the alley he found an open gate, inside a good old-fashioned outhouse, which many of the homes in this neighborhood had. This one served a two-story apartment building and came with two stalls. He quickly returned to the alley showing the ladies their way towards some relief.

An urgent need to piss overtook the old soldier, his urgency taking second place as Grazia slammed the door in his face, the other stuck shut. Sarge moved behind the outhouse unbuttoning himself before he might piss himself.

Leah handed Alphonso her frantic kitten as she yanked open the johnnie. Little hands can be mighty when nature calls. Not wanting to leave Leah the kitten, barely old enough to squeak out a hiss, protested greeting the old watchmaker with her small but sharp claws. That was all it took, the cat was dropped, the old man shooed it with his foot least the misbehaving feline try to climb his pants. Kicked, hard enough, it scurried first into a nearby garden, then into an open back door to the house.

Alphonso lost sight of it.

When Leah came out, she broke into tears at the news that Purplepaws had run away. She called frantically for her lost kitten as she crawled through the garden looking everywhere in the cabbage patch. Searching for a lost watch widget might have proven easier for the remorseful old man as he started to do the same when he was waylaid by Grazia who berated him unmercifully for his carelessness.

Sarge, baffled as to what was going on, stepped out from behind the Johnnie.

"Here, here, what's all this ruckus?" A woman said as she leaned out of a window tisk-tisking at the outrageous behavior of Grazia. Her accent told of her distant homeland of Scotland. "You there, blackie, get out of my yard before I sic the dog on you. McGonagall," she called, "come here."

The sarge braced as he grabbed a nearby garden hoe as a defensive weapon, half-expecting an over-sized Scottish Deerhound to come bounding out the door.

Leah was the only one who answered. "I've lost Purplepaws." She wept.

"Purplepaws, is it now?" The woman left the window returning a moment later with a saucer of cream and a hungry kitten setting both on the windowsill.

"Purplepaws!" Squeaked Leah with unbridled joy as she got to her feet and ran towards the purring kitten as it happily lapped the cream. "Ouch!" She screamed as her foot squared down on a wicked thistle weed.

Leah's scream silenced Grazia as she looked to see what caused the child's despair.

The woman left the kitten in the window as she came out into her backyard to help the little girl remove the thistles from her bare feet. The sarge had beaten her to the punch having discarded the hoe for a pocketknife that he had unfolded to pry the thistle from the little girl's foot.

Alphonso moved towards the windowsill meekly seeking forgiveness from the kitten which all but ignored him.

Leah watched Purplepaws as the sarge carefully picked and removed the thistles from her foot.

The woman, who had a moment before had threatened to let loose a vicious dog on sarge because he was black, and thus not to be trusted watched intently, admiring the gentleness the rough-looking black soldier dealt with the sticker that had attached itself to the little girl. She did make eye contact with Grazia, which Grazia pretended to not notice. Neither exchanged the typical familiarities that women do as strangers who might be interested in each other. Grazia looked ready to explode, she had had it with her husband's idiotic notions and she had plenty of anger stored in her hat.

"Purplepaws will be wanting a nap soon as she has finished her cream. I'll fetch you a small basket for you to carry her as you flee the devil's work this day." The woman stopped, smiling apologetically at the once offending black man. Alphonso stood before her in greeting. "Katie McGillicuddy, if you please—and you, sir?"

The woman was just a touch taller than he, wearing a tight bun of silver hair. She wore a flowered patchwork house dress that brought out the rose in her cheeks, and the sparkle of humor that seemed to dance in her round green speckled eyes. She wiped her hands on a brownish apron that was several days passed cleaning.

"Alphonso Giuseppe Peluso," he responded, pleasured by the geniality in her voice.

"This a sad day we all must get through, tis it not?"

The world outside that yard, noisy with dread, was not as loud as the cold silence Grazia and Alphonso shared as they waited.

"Here you go, darling, a basket with a lid for your Purplepaws." She held out a second gift, a boy's used roughneck trousers, and a dark red long-sleeved shirt; more importantly a pair of shoes. "Come inside and try these on, a young lady shouldn't be running around in broad daylight in her sleepwear." A last-minute pink ribbon was added to Leah's light brown shoulder length hair.

"Enough small talk, if you please," snapped Grazia. "There is a great calamity knocking at our door and we have no time for tea and biscotti."

The sarge stood by the weathered old gate to the alley

waiting—for what he did not know. The foul-tempered old witch was right. The acrid smoke now pervasive in the air, warned that the fires were near, and none of them were fit enough to run a footrace against it.

The pleasant woman said that she had to gather up a few things and that she would be along in short time. The goodbyes were brief with only Grazia's glare to dirty the pleasantries.

Leah was the only one to look back giving a small thank-you wave with the fingers of her left hand.

Katie McGillicutty took out her spectacles from an apron pocket, cleaning them with a touch of her breath and a rub of cloth. She shook her head; the fires were too damn close. She had hoped to wait and see, but now there was little doubt that once the fires reached her block they had better be long gone. She turned back from the doorway and hollered up a flight of service stairs that ran off the kitchen. "Mr. Morgan, its best you be coming down now. It's time to go, a gentleman your age won't be outrunning the flames this day." She moved his wheelchair close to the base of the stairs and waited for the old man to descend. He was proud and would not allow her to raise a hand to help him down the stairs. She listened to his progress as she made sandwiches while keeping an eye on the fires as they neared.

XX

Having survived the warehouse Francis was not out of harm's way. The flash flood that had cleared a way for his escape had formed a lake when it had crashed into a brick building. The building, already damaged by the earthquake, was undermined by the tidal wave of wine and glass, which brought the rest down creating a dam. He desperately needed a drink. Failing to see the wine for what it was, his adrenaline drove him forward. There was no way around except for a beam that had fallen across the burgundy swamp. With hesitation he stepped out onto the beam, finding it unsteady with his first step, it twisted a little to the right. Unnerved by the sudden pitch he nearly froze in place with the thought that he had already gone too far. His sense of balance had never been good which challenged his self-confidence from the get-go. Backing off, he carefully dropped to his hands and knees. The hot wind of the fire pushed against him. The smoke made it hard to breath. Shards of glass shimmered in the purple pool below as he slowly crawled, the millions of shards of glass gleamed like so many diamonds caught in the light.

He thought he was going to make it when the beam suddenly rolled dropping him the short two feet into the edge of the pool. He managed to land on his feet but was forced to keep his balance by grasping a broken pipe from which a hissing jet of flame made the gas line impossible to touch. The roar of the fires that consumed the old warehouse was nothing compared to his blood-curding scream as the red-hot pipe burned into the soft flesh of his hand. Pulling his seared flesh from the pipe he rose, stumbled back a step, before steading himself with his good hand on the beam from which he had fallen. His grasp became more precarious as he began to feel dizzy from the loss of blood as well as a highly stressed morning.

With more determination than guts, he made it over the remains of the brick wall that proved to be no steadier than the beam. Tears from the pain blinding him, not knowing where he was, or where he was going, he stumbled down a pile of bricks towards a maze of ruins that took him back towards the waterfront.

Climbing atop the last pile of timber and bricks he could see that he had reached the industrial section. In front of him were the piers and warehouses, all broken and torn asunder. To his left was the Ferry Terminal, to the right an ominous trench, eight inches to a foot wide, filled with a mixture of muddy water and wine which ran from underneath the bricks he stood on, to a pier across the way. The pier had been a loading dock for the slaughterhouses and the stockyards. The quake had liquified the ground and the slaughterhouses had been sucked into the mud. Hundreds of carcasses, sides of beef, body parts floated in the surf; the stench, not yet potent, wouldn't be long to come. The damage to Butcher Town stunned him. Up until now he had been focused on his own survival, his burned hand, as well as his multiple lacerations. *Death by a thousand cuts, close, but I'm still walking.* He had no laugh to stifle. His view, limited, prevented him from seeing much of the rest of the city. *Workers of the world unite. What the hell? the slate has now been wiped clean, there isn't much left to fight for.*

On the far side of Butcher Town there had been a row of cheap boarding houses where he had a room. Had. He could only see a few roof tops, the rest sucked down into the mud. The ground was soft, his feet sinking deeper into the muck with each step, if he went any further his boots might be sucked right off his feet. He felt a kindred unimpeachable fondness for those boots. There was no sense in trying to reach his boarding house; if it was still there, it was too dangerous to enter. The truth was that he lacked the courage to try.

He looked back towards the ferry building. On the bay beyond, an armada of tall ships were setting sail amongst a developing storm of glowing sparks carried in the wind. He could just make out what might be a ferry idling offshore. There were none taking on any passengers where thousands were already gathered.

His hand hurt like hell as he sat uncomfortably on some brick. With some difficulty he ripped a sleeve from his shirt wrapping it tightly around his wounded palm. *Damn, that hurts!* The shirt was far from clean, still wet in places with wine and sweat, but at least for the moment it was something. He needed a doctor, clean clothes, and some food. His father, if they were on speaking terms, would recommend a tall brandy and for once he wouldn't argue with him.

He took a moment to think. If he went to the ferry, he would be one of who knows how many thousands looking for safe passage across the bay. It looked like the whole city might burn. There were three large plumes of smoke and a dozen more waiting to become one major firestorm. The smoke, a black ominous beast bullied the sun from the sky.

Perhaps, he thought, *he should try his luck with the ferry.* On the other hand, the *Wobblies** had recently instigated a labor riot on the Oakland docks and the police would be looking for him as one of the instigators. It wasn't jail time he feared, it was what would happen if the cops got hold of him. More than a few had been injured in the skirmish, few had any kind thoughts regarding the *Wobblies,* and they would be looking for some payback.

He opted to turn back towards the city center. With some clothes he could steal. He wished he had had enough time to drink some of that wine. His vision swam, just a bit and he retched as he tried to stand up.

As he approached Market Street things were less chaotic, the earthquake damage less severe. Just ahead was a corner store which was being looted. It was a liquor store. With his good hand he pushed his way through the crowd of looters to latch onto the last bottle of rye whiskey, which he cradled in the crook of his arm as he pushed his way back out into the street. He had never tasted rye whiskey, but it was what he was able to grab.

Three gunshots followed by two more.

---

* The Industrial Workers of the World (IWW), members of which are commonly termed "Wobblies", is an international labor union that was founded in 1905 in Chicago, Illinois in the United States of America. The union combines general unionism with industrial unionism, as it is a general union whose members are further organized within the industry of their employment. The philosophy and tactics of the IWW are described as "revolutionary industrial unionism", with ties to both socialist and anarchist labor movements.

Panic!

Another shot.

A scream. Somewhere up ahead, someone had been shot. He was caught in a crowd of looters. Someone crashed into his right arm; the pain momentarily blinded him. He was no match for the crowd, dropping the rye, he was carried by the crowd against his will back towards the waterfront. He stumbled over a body. Soldiers were shooting at the looters; at him.

XXI

Sarge, Alphonso, Grazia, and Leah slowly made their way through the crowds and damaged neighborhoods until they found Market Street where hundreds of people were pouring out of the blazing hills. The sarge had seen it all before when he had been stationed at Skagway, Alaska. The gold rush town had been surrounded on three sides by fire—tall trees a blazing. Most of the town folk had gotten out, those that were left, including the Buffalo Soldiers, made a heroic stand to save the town. Skagway, as well as the military camp were destroyed as the fire won the day.

Now, as he looked out over the city, the air thick with smoke, cannon-like booms resounding as walls and buildings collapsed across the city. A fire storm consumed all the buildings on the surrounding hills threatening everything between it and the bay. Sarge did not have to second guess what disaster was headed their way. The mighty ache in his knees screamed at him that enough was enough, but he knew they had to keep going, even if it was only one step at a time.

When they found themselves across the street from the Palace Hotel Leah could go no further. She collapsed on the front steps of a large building that was mostly intact. "Grandma," she sobbed.

Alphonso plopped down next to her, gave her head a gentle

pat as she cried. *What do you say to a little girl who has just lost everything?* He looked briefly towards his wife. *What can I tell Grazia, that we too have lost everything, including my work?* He looked up at Grazia, then patted the ground—"Sit, time for some rest. Just rest, no words, not now."

"I'll sit when I am ready to sit," she snapped as if the words could fix blame. She stood because she was afraid that if she sat, she would never get up again. Her world had just been turned upside down and she had no one to blame but her lazy, no-good husband. Her house dress covered her swollen ankles, but she couldn't cover the pain in her chest which made it hard for her to catch her breath.

Alphonso turned away from her brittle words. One thing he had learned over the many years of their marriage was that when her words grew caustic, he should look away and become a smaller man than he already was. At home he would look at the floor. Here he looked at the street, curiosity slowly drawing his eyes to the front of the majestic Palace Hotel.

"I need something to drink. Hot tea would be nice," she said to her husband, her voice suggesting that she might look past his transgression, if he was quick about getting her some tea, forgiveness never in the cards. "Do you have a coin in your pocket to buy your ailing wife some tea, or did you forget that along with your shoes.?" Her husband made no motion that he had heard her.

Leah cried.

Grazia gave her worthless husband the evil eye.

The sarge had seen women like Grazia before and knew that they could often be worse than white men when it came to looking down on people of color. Black, red, or yellow he suspected the Chinese got the worse of it, at least here on the west coast of the land of the free. On behalf of the white man, he had fought the Indians until there were not enough left to stand and fight; but damn, if he had not learned to respect a few. He did not dwell on the notion that the old woman had a cold heart and that she would never change her ways.

Most of the crowd in front of the hotel were still dressed in their fancy evening cloths, a few in their night clothes. There was one man who for some reason seemed to stand out above all the rest.

Grazia paid little attention to the urgent needs of the rich and powerful across the way. Her attention had landed on a pathetic miserable-looking young man who at first glance looked like he was bathed in blood. He was holding one hand with the other. The hand he was holding was wrapped in a patch of cloth the same color his shirt. She did not take him for a beggar, but rather someone who had taken some of the worst God had to test us with this day. As she looked at this pathetic creature, for a moment she wondered if it was God or the Devil who had brought this on. She though it was God, knowing that the devil had a sense of humor and there was nothing funny about this. She looked around for a doctor or a nurse, finding none she decided that the self-important barons of the world across the way had no time for a poor laborer, who had no money, no family, and nothing to offer the world besides his own sweat, and weary bones that would only take him to an early grave. Her thoughts, a little dramatic were, none the less real, having grown up in a poor village in Italy where the only hope a young man had was to find a way to emigrate to America—of those that did many fared less well than the Irish. The thought put a half ounce of forgiveness back in her heart. At least her husband, a small man with small dreams, was a craftsman who always managed to keep a roof over their heads. She looked back towards the fires that engulfed the hilltop where their home had once been. "So, God what are we to do now?"

There was no answer.

An explosion somewhere off in the distance reminded her that God was having a busy day with far more important things to focus his attention on. "Forgive my asking, we'll talk another day." She said in Italian as she gestured towards the smoke smothered sky.

Francis DeGeorgie winched, too weak to do anything else, as she slowly unwrapped the filthy cloth from his palm. She could almost feel his pain when she saw the wound that crossed his palm like a brand, its external layer of skin split open and partially separated away from the layers beneath it. The top layer was pale and papery, while the skin underneath looked raw, shiny, and splotchy. The skin surrounding it was painfully red and blistered, the stench unpleasant. Afraid that she might retch she looked away. She immediately understood that the wound might become infected unless he got medical attention. Wrapping the wound once again with the filthy wine-soaked cloth, she pulled it tight enough to cause the young man to scream. Taking his other hand, she told him to keep the pressure as tight as he could stand it. "Sarò di ritorno, avete bisogno di un medico." She often spoke in Italian when she was harried.

Francis nodded. He understood a little Italian, though. it would be easier if she didn't say everything so fast.

She grabbed the hem of her house dress as she crossed the street. "Un medico, abbiamo bisogno di un medico qui."

To her surprise five people immediately answered in her harried tongue. None were doctors. One man she thought she recognized.

XXII

When the earthquake struck the power went out stopping the elevator between the third and fourth floors.

The plush redwood paneled chamber became instantly dark except for a thin line of feeble light that barely penetrated the closed doors. An elevator does not move the way it had unless something major has happened.

The passengers hollered and banged on the door for twenty minutes before they realized that no one was coming to their aid, at least not for a while. A burly man dressed in an ill-fitting tux Hatti had noticed when she first got on board lifted another man on his shoulders long enough to pry the 4th floor door open. Thanking the gentlemen, she was the first to exit using them as a makeshift ladder to climb up and out of the elevator, very much aware of their grins and eyeballs as she climbed over their heads and inquisitive eyes into the better lit hallway.

When she reached her room, she found that her evening purse, with the room key, had been left in the elevator. An aftershock brought down some plaster from the hallway's ceiling was enough to convince her that staying any longer in the hotel was not the ideal thing to do. *Best to go home,* she thought. Hattie kept an apartment, the nearest thing she had that might be called home, at the Martinet Residency Hotel at the southwest corner of Broadway and Van Ness. With the electricity out the cable cars and trolleys were not working, carriages for hire would be at a premium, and couples who had had a big night at the opera were not about to pick up a working girl; even one with her lofty reputation. She needed to find James. It was his responsibility to see that she got home safe with appropriate transportation. There were just too many hills to cross, and after the earthquake who knew what dangers. Regardless of what he was doing she would demand his immediate attention.

The stairwell was dark and crowded as she fought her way down to the lobby then to the ballroom where she had left her date. To her surprise, the room was mostly empty, even the waiters had abandoned their posts. She was baffled as to where to start. She knew that he was married and had a grand house up on Russian Hill. *Had he gone there, abandoning her in a city where civility was breaking down?* She fumed knowing the answer.

It wasn't until that moment that she realized that she had always taken the opulence of the Palace Hotel for granted. It was advertised as the largest and most luxurious hotel in the world. With 755 giant rooms, each with its own private toilet, in addition to a fireplace in every room. Its decor, intricate woodwork, all up to the highest standards. That it had suffered so little visible damage did not surprise her.

The *Men's Bar* had been dubbed the *unofficial capital of California* since many of the state's most powerful men spent their evenings there. On any given evening she knew that many of her gentlemen friends could be found there. While she wasn't allowed in, a note delivered by a diligent waiter would bring her chosen gentleman to the door. Now she stood well inside the mostly empty *'Men Only'* room with chandeliers still swinging high over-head. Plaster that had fallen from the ceiling covered the floor and billiard tables, the smell of liquor heavy in the air from countless bottles that fallen from a well-stocked bar. The room was smokier than the rest of the hotel where smoke from the fires outside drifted through broken and open hotel windows. The few men who remained savored their cigars as they watched her with curiosity. The drinks they held more important than this gorgeous morsel who had just violated their private realm. There seemed to be no urgency in their deliberations, the world outside not much concern. The sound of silver chips signaling that another bet had been matched or made.

In the lobby she overheard that while the hotel was thought to be essentially "fireproof" because of its extensive standpipe system which was attached to and fed by water kept on site in a massive cistern located in the building's basement, it would burn. The firestorm raging towards them was simply too powerful, nothing was expected to survive it. As guests checked out their golden room keys were given as parting souvenirs. The smell of smoke, and the dazed look in many of the hotel's guest's eyes convinced her that she was simply going to have to walk. It wasn't that far, was it?

When she stepped outside the doors, she knew the distance would be too great. The front doors to the hotel were jammed with people, most with bags, or trunks quickly packed, most too large to carry, and few if any wagons or carriages to tote them. To her left was a growing mountain of luggage belonging to the Metropolitan Opera. What caught her eye was not the famous opera tenor Enrico Caruso[*] who stood not six feet from her clutching a framed portrait of President Roosevelt the president had given him—it was a little girl dressed in boy's clothes, two sizes too large for her tiny frame, who sat on the steps to a building across the street holding a kitten and crying. There was an old man sitting on the steps nearby but to Hattie it looked as if the little girl was all alone surrounded by all the misery this dying town could heap on her tiny shoulders.

Caruso watched as the beautiful woman he had met the night before crossed the street and knelt next the traumatized child, one of those moments that would always live in his memory. He wished that he could hear what she was saying.

Alphonso noticed the amazing woman who now knelt beside Leah. His eyes moved to that of his wife who was crossing the street looking as if she were on an urgent mission. He glanced at the injured man she had just visited and suspected that his wife was seeking help for this injured stranger—an action not found often in her unkind heart. He rose, following slowly, his tattered and blood-stained socks evidence of his cruel morning's trek.

Hattie took Leah's tear-streaked face in her hands using a handkerchief she had tucked inside the bodice of her gown to dry her tears. "Are you alone?" She asked.

---

*Enrico Caruso (February 25, 1873–August 2, 1921) was an Italian opera singer of the verismo style, and one of the most famous tenors in history. Caruso was also the most popular singer in any genre in the first 20 years of the twentieth century and one of the pioneers of recorded music. Caruso's popular recordings and his extraordinary voice, known for its range, power, and beauty, made him one of the best-known stars of his time.

Leah nodded.

"Alone?" Leah looked at Purplepaws. I suppose I am. My grandmother is dead. Our house fell on her." The little girl said as if her words weren't making any sense.

"Your parents?"

"Gone, all I have is grandma and…and…she's…"

Leah said, but the thought of the last moment she had seen her grandma brought her to tears again. The cat meowed sympathetically. The Abyssinian kitten, all the little girl had left, was pathetically ugly.

"I'm Hattie, what is your name sweetheart?"

"Leah. And…and this is Purplepaws. Would you like to hold her?"

Without knowing why, she asked, "Leah, do you like to sing?"

"Yes," Leah managed to answer between sniffles.

"Sing little bird," Hattie whispered.

"Sing?" She looked up with small eyes.

"Yes, your heart needs lightness, sing to your grandma, as she rises to the heavens."

A little smile came to Leah's trembling lips. She liked to sing.

Her grandma had a gramophone with four records, and she had memorized them—all recordings of Enrico Caruso.

Odd how little things get stuck in one's mind. Grazia had seen his picture somewhere. Where, she wasn't quite sure? But she had, and amongst all these strangers, the harsh moments of the day, she could not get him out of her mind. He was of medium height, stocky, with a chubby face, with a well-manicured upturned mustache, well dressed, and stood a confident individual, with a worldly uncommon air.

The well-heeled Caruso stood apart in the crowd. Many were from the Metropolitan Opera and were used to the maestro's presence. "Mario, how many more?" He yelled back through the doors of the Palace Hotel. Mario, his valet appeared, having drug yet another large trunk, one of a dozen, down several flights of stair, and out of the hotel. Suddenly, Caruso turned, looking past Grazia as he followed the sound of a child singing, her voice distant, almost lost against the hubbub of chaos, dust, and smoke, surrounding them. A whispering angel beckoning towards a celestial place:

> *'Per me pari sono*
> *Questa o quella A quant'altre d'intorno mi vedo,'*

Caruso heard this child's voice sing as sweetly as he had ever heard *Questo O Quella* sung. Then he saw her, a little waif of a girl, dressed oddly in boy's clothes stained with dirt and soot. Next to her was that beautiful woman of his dreams. From where he stood it seemed as if the child was staring straight across the street at him.

Awe-struck, the crowd momentarily parted, as Enrico Caruso answered this child's song with his own rich voice, both manly and powerful, sweet, and lyrical:

> *'Del mio core l'impero non cedo Meglio ad una che ad altre beltà . . .'*

When the famous tenor began to sing, his voice rich as rare velvet, Grazia knew who he was. She had heard several of his records at Leah's grandma's house. Now, there was little Leah singing with the great Caruso.

The crowd parted as Caruso, hands raised theatrically, crossed the street, until he reached her as their voices came together, a mighty giant and a fragile little songbird.

> *'La costoro avvenenza è qual dono Di que il fato ne infiora la vita . . .'*

Even the flames towering above them on Rincon Hill seemed to stop in place, as indeed did the world, as their voices spun a special magic into the winds that blew harshly through the devastated streets of San Francisco. For one moment everyone forgot the tragedy that gripped the world around them, the power of that moment lifting their hearts as Enrico Caruso finished the song with an astonishing flair that even the members of the Metropolitan Opera had never heard before.

A man next to Grazia exclaimed: "Bravo, il grande Caruso ha alzato la sua voce al cielo e il fumo da questi grandi incendi si è separato." For a moment, as Grazia heard his words, *"Bravo, the great Caruso has lifted his voice to the heavens and the smoke from these great fires has parted."* The smoke did part.

The wind shifted blowing hot sparks rallying the firestorm's hunger pangs. The time for singing had passed, the time for fleeing urgent.

—

In the army Sergeant Freeman had known his place. He had been a top-ranking sergeant. His had been a firm hand, his orders to be obeyed, his look not to be challenged. He had been the link between the black soldiers and their white officers.

The officers needed his experience and the respect the black soldiers gave him. And if, now and then, an arrogant white officer came onto the field, who felt himself to be superior to the soldiers beneath him because he was white Sergeant Freemen kept the men in line while protecting them from the Jim Crowism manners of the officer. He was the buffer. The army needed the Buffalo Soldiers just as it needed the sergeant to stand in the way of an incompetent officer who might think it proper to lord himself above the mostly illiterate hard working black men who had been born into slavery, displaced by the civil war, and now served the country that had once enslaved them.

Retired from the army, regardless of the uniform he occasionally wore, Huckleberry Freeman knew that now he was just an old black man, who had no say; no longer a buffer, better to remain in the shadows. Across from the Palace Hotel he watched as the rich and all-powerful white men and women pretended to be above what was happening all around them.

My, oh my, how the mighty have fallen. His eyes flickering with the humor, his heart acknowledging the height of the hills they would all have to climb. Then the fat white man sang with Leah and that touched his heart.

—

While Caruso's valet was back in the hotel retrieving yet more pieces of luggage, Alphonso quickly opened and searched one of The Great Caruso's trunks until he found a pair of shoes and fresh socks. The maestro had small feet for a man of his girth; they were a reasonable fit though a bit large. He pocketed a couple of fine linen handkerchiefs that he wrapped around his feet to take up the excess space. A moment prior he had felt exhausted beyond his years, now he flushed with unexpected energy. He felt impish having stolen the shoes. He hadn't knowingly stolen anything since he and two childhood friends had stolen sweet pastries from a bakery shop's window. He might have asked for the shoes but doubted the charity. At this moment it was survival of the fittest, he had never been fit, but intended to survive.

Grazia saw her husband take the shoes opting to say nothing for the moment. Her little mouse might just have a shadow of a lion in him. Finding a woman who seemed to oversee the wardrobes and costumes for the Metropolitan Opera she asked for spare clean cloth for a bandage for the young man's wound. She was not one to ask for charity, her request more of a demand landed on deaf ears. The seamstress' response was just as brisk. Grazia looked like an old street woman "Go away you old cow, I have nothing for you.

While she and Grazia argued Alphonso absconded with a small bag the woman kept close at hand which held patches of cloth, multiple needles, and threads to patch the costumes under her charge. There were plenty of eyes, but no one thought this insignificant older man was doing anything that he wasn't supposed to—which made it that much easier.

Grazia left the seamstress without either a needle or thread to show for her efforts, or a winning word, her victory a rare smile. For some reason, unknown to her, her husband had changed, no longer a mouse he had become a rapscallion, a purloiner of little necessities—which just might come in handy now that they were pauperized and threadbare. All those years of tedious work repairing watches had made his fingers sensitive and dexterous.

Her overwhelming sense of helplessness began to slide away—just a little.

Caution to virtue, Alphonso did not give his purloined bag to Grazia but went to the young man's side and knelt beside him. The truth was that he hadn't a clue on how to help with the man's wound. He was embarrassed to ask strangers for their help, and it galled him to ask Grazia. Unwrapping the wound while looking into the young man's face as he grimaced from the pain, he knew he had no choice. "Who I am is not important, that you need help is. A woman will come, and she will know what to do. Be careful what you say to her for she is not a kind woman."

He stood and waved in Grazia's direction.

The sarge was standing close enough to hear. As a small boy he had tended to the wounds and scrapes of the other children as his parents worked in the fields. As a soldier he had dealt with broken bones, burns and arrows, wounds suffered in combat with the noble red man. "Here, give me that," he ordered as he searched the bag for what might be needed. "I have dealt with many a wound in my day, son, and yours ain't as bad as it looks," he said. He corrected himself, no longer being in the regular army. "Huckleberry Freeman, at your service."

"Francis DeGeorgie," Francis answered, surprised with being helped by a Black person, one of the first he had ever seen this close.

"You stay here with Purplepaws," Hattie said to Leah, "I'll be right back. I promise." She rose speaking to sarge just as if he were the same as everyone else. "I think some brandy will do the job."

Helen Gilson was a white nurse during the American Civil War which caused her to become a controversial character and a pioneer for the rights of injured black soldiers. When Gilson first heard about the plight of wounded black troops engaged on the front line, she vowed to take-action but was counseled against it. Nevertheless, Gilson was undeterred—even though none of her co-workers agreed to help her. Determined to succeed, Gilson used her feminine wiles to persuade Major General Ambrose Burnside to help her overcome the prejudice of the medical profession. Her hospital for black soldiers was eventually set up, consisting of a square mile of tents. Often, she treated the soldiers in temperatures of over 100 degrees. Aged 29, Gilson wrote about how tired and ill she was becoming. She was suffering from malaria but remained in her post until the fall of Richmond on April 2, 1865. Because of her weakened condition she died at childbirth in 1868.

The sarge smiled, re-wrapping the wound in the filthy cloth to help staunch the bleeding.

Tired, emotionally confused, and hungry, Leah had a tiny grasp on her *everything will be all right* good luck stone as she peeked into her basket where little Purplepaws cautiously explored a piece of cheese—solid food still very much the mystery. The taste brought a purr, the purr brought a happy glint to Leah's eyes as she quietly watched.

From the stack of luggage near the hotel's front door Caruso turned, smiled, and tipped his hat to a remarkable little girl. Behind that smile he knew that everything would not be all right, that Leah was going to have a hard time of it as the firestorm gathered nearby. He would gather his resources promising to leave the city he once admired to never return.*

No one cared if hotel property was stolen or damaged, it was going to all burn anyway. What was important was the hotel's reputation. Once one of the finest hotels in the world management wanted the guests to remember her as dignified and a lady. Her last hours were to be treated in keeping with good taste and propriety.

Alphonso quickly joined Hattie. "You stay here and help keep Mr. DeGeorgie comfortable. I know where to get what we need."

---

*The fires merged becoming one ferocious beast descending on the Palace Hotel. By mid-afternoon it was gone. The Metropolitan Opera lost most of their staging, costumes, and personal luggage. Caruso, who had left earlier, lost little, and never returned to the city.

No one noticed as the quiet, unobtrusive older man pinched a small leather valise, dumping its contents behind a chaise lounge—all accept a package of six fine Cuban cigars. Finding himself outside the *Men's Bar* he donned a waiter's service jacket and an apron that he found on a chair near the entrance and entered the bar under guise of a waiter.

Upon his entrance one of the card-playing gentlemen raised an eyebrow in his direction. Alphonso gave him a responsive nod, went to the bar where he left his valise, returning a moment later with a tray carrying a bottle of the hotel's best brandy, a pitcher of fresh branch water, four fresh glasses, eight cigars, and a small box of stick matches. "Compliments of the house, Sirs. Will there be anything else?" Two silver chips were dropped onto his service tray as he backed away leaving the gentlemen to their game.

"Oh waiter, how goes it out there? The fires, I mean."

It was the gentleman who had first bid for his attention.

"Not well…not well at all. You might want to move your game to the St. Francis, or perhaps the Bohemia Club* if you are a member."

No further discussion was made as their game of Faro—Bucking the Tiger—continued. The glass ceiling in the *Men's Bar* allowed enough light to continue the game.

With the electricity out there would be no light at the Bohemia Club. The thick smoke overhead would soon finish their game for them.

An invisible servant, Alphonso filled his valise with two bottles of brandy, one bottle of vino, six settings of plates and silverware, and eight coffee cups which seemed less fragile than any of the bar glasses. An icebox, with half a block of ice still intact contained an assortment of exotic cheeses and sliced dried sausages which he wrapped in a napkin. He wished he could take more of the ice for it would become a commodity more valuable than gold in the near future. However, anything more and the little man would have trouble carrying the valise. Exiting as quietly as he had entered, he left the apron where he had found it retaining the coat which he knew he would need. The smoke was much thicker than he remembered it to be as he exited the hotel. The air tasted hot.

Outside the hotel scavenger wagons, drays, hay-wagons, milk carts, loaded with every sort of furniture and valuables someone might seek to save, or plain junk, pending the state of an irrational mind under stress, a torrent of humanity clogged Market Street—all headed one direction, towards the waterfront.

It began snowing gray and white ash as the firestorm on Rincon Hill became ominously real. Red hot fireflies played in the dry

---

*The Bohemian Club, an elite invitation-only social club founded in San Francisco in 1872 by a group of male artists, writers, actors, lawyers, and journalists, all of means and interested in arts and culture. Since its founding, the club has expanded to include politicians and affluent businesspeople. The club is known especially for its annual summer retreat at what is known as Bohemian Grove in the redwood forest of California's Sonoma county, an event that continued into the 21st century. Notable members over the years have included Clint Eastwood, Henry Kissinger, Walter Cronkite, Richard Nixon, Ronald Reagan, Charles Schwab, Ambrose Bierce, Bret Harte, Mark Twain, and Jack London.

hot wind being generated by the fire, which blew stronger the minute he stepped away from the hotel.

There were thousands of people, some wearing three or four layers of clothing, some in their night clothes, a few babies cried, otherwise most passed with an eerie silence.

Silence?

If someone had spoken to him, he would not have heard them. The noise was stunning. Multitudes of frightened dogs barked, steamer trucks scrapped along the street, buildings collapsed, deep throated explosions resounded across the city. Bells rang as fire engines hurried to fight fires that soon would become one thunderous bonfire. Windows crashed. Here and there people screamed, parrots squawked, and the voices that stood out against the din were Irish, Italian, German, Spanish, Russian, Chinese, a tower of babel he could not understand. Even the earth beneath his feet was not silent.

Shots fired.

The shots came from the direction of the Financial District, far enough away to not be an immediate threat, but close enough to raise the hair on the back of his neck. The crowd he fought his way through didn't seem to care. His eyes trained on a platoon of soldiers that had come to a halt in the middle of Market Street a full block ahead. Four of the soldiers had dropped to firing positions on their knees with rifles aimed at a crowd of civilians packed in front of a collapsed store front. Looters! No sooner than he had thought the word, the soldiers fired, followed by four more soldiers who fired from a standing position as the first rank reloaded. In a panic the looters dispersed, swallowed up into the crowd, leaving six or seven of their number dead or mortally wounded in front of the store front. The soldiers didn't wait to see if anyone needed medical attention.

He pushed his way through the mob until he finally reached the far side of Market Street where he found Leah with her cat, and Grazia, along with the young woman who for some reason had attached herself to their lot, tending to the injured man—the sarge in charge. He had no doubt that he too would add his name to their growing caravan. *How many more?* He thought, *how many more?*

Nailed to a door immediately behind them was an ominous warning:

> *Marshall Law has been declared.*
> *All looters will be shot.*

That was all the news that mattered. His valise felt twice… three times as heavy in his hand.

The masses were all heading down Market Street towards the waterfront. No doubt the army would follow them as the fires reached Market Street with its towering buildings, the city's center of commerce with its theaters and grand hotels. He looked North, up the hill, past where he knew Chinatown to be, Little Italy, and the Barbary Coast. Instinct guided him to find his own kind. They would go to little Italy.

One look affirmed that the brandy would be both vilified and a blessing. He introduced himself to Hatti as he opened his new valise pulling out a full and expensive bottle of brandy and one of the coffee cups. The cup he filled half-way.

"Francis DeGeorgie," the young man answered through a teeth-clinched grimace as the sarge held his wrist firm. "That for me?" He asked, seeing his burned palm as if for the first time.

"It is, with moderation, my young friend." Alphonso said as he held up the cup. "Just enough to help with the pain, but not enough to stupefy you. It won't be long until the fires are nipping at our heels, and you've got to be able to walk on your own. DeGeorgie gulped the fiery nectar as the sarge signaled with his eyes that it was time. Alphonso seized him by the shoulders as the sarge poured the brandy straight on the weeping burn.

"Mi az istenért csinálsz?—What in God's name are you doing?" He shrieked in Magyar, screamed loud enough to turn everyone's heads across the way; then passed out, his neck and face rigid with agony.

The sarge shook his head. I do not give him much chance if it gets infected. We have done the best we can do. Now we must wake him back to his pain and somehow get him back to his feet. He then slapped his unwitting patient with a firm slap across the face followed by a second which caused Alphonso to winch from the sound and sight of it.

Francis DeGeorgie stirred, then opened his eyes wide immediately after a third whack.

Alphonso took a solid slug of the brandy before saying, "Here, drink some of this.

The sarge rose and stepped away not wanting him to associate the agony he had just experienced with a black face.

Seeing his discomfort Alphonso poured some of the brandy into a cup placing it in DeGeorgie's uninjured hand. His lips quivering, eyes glazed, he held the cup, not comprehending what to do with it.

The sarge had had enough, it was time to go. Two large gulps went down the young Hungarian's throat before the sarge could pull it away. "Easy, you must walk, remember."

Francis swore that the old soldier was getting some perverse thrill out of his pain. He hated soldiers and this was not meant as a compliment.

Alphonso took a sip of the brandy before offering the cup to the young woman. "Alphonso Giuseppe Peluso, and you are?"

Hattie gladly took the brandy draining much of what was left in the cup. She waited a moment while the warmth settled. "Hattie Poirier, pleased to meet you," she answered with an eyebrow raised towards the bottle.

"Young Mr. DeGeorgie has had enough, I think." Alphonso responded as he took the cup from Francis's trembling hand pouring a pinch of it into the Hattie's empty cup.

She started to offer some to Grazia but saw the look in

Alphonso's eyes.

He plucked a second cup from the valise pouring a good measure for himself. He knew that Grazia would be full of questions about the sudden appearance of his gift bearing valise. That would have to wait, the normal westerly winds had changed and were now blowing from the East. While there were many fires, the three major ones were now all roaring towards the Financial Center and when they met, they would become one monstrous firestorm beyond comprehension.

"How long until he is fit to travel?" Alphonso asked the sarge.

Grazia scowled. "What obligation do we have to this stranger to tote him to God knows where?" She looked at Hatti, then back again towards Leah. *A child, a prostitute, and two old people who are already bone tired...* she thought as her eyes turned back to gaze down at the DeGeorgie's hand that Hatti had just wrapped.

Everyone's head turned abruptly, "Stop, thief!" as a woman's voice rose from somewhere nearby.

Alphonso cradled the valise with both hands as he felt the first pangs of fear.

"There, over there." An older man dressed in a tuxedo and top hat raised his arm pointing an elegant walking stick towards two young men—teenagers really—who were running east in the middle of Market Street, laughing hysterically, as they absconded with a woman's purse. Others pointed, though no one tried to intercede.

The two thieves chose the wrong direction as soldiers appeared in front of them, knelt, and fired without warning.

"Looters will be shot," A.B. said matter-of-factly, his words directed towards no one.

"Yes, they will," said the sarge, adding his experience. "As will idiots and those who are vain." He continued as he took a little of the brandy for himself. His patient stiffened as a sharp surge of pain flushed through his hand. He swore then stole the bottle back, guzzling as much as he could before he gagged.

"That's enough," barked Alphonso as he took the bottle back, corked it, placing it back in the valise.

"He will be ready as soon as he can get to his feet," Hattie said as she raised his eyes momentarily towards Alphonso. "And thank you for this," her eyes pointing towards the bag Alphonso had stolen from the seamstress across the way. "And you had best be careful with those cups, we will be needing them for some time to come."

Supporting him by his elbows Alphonso guided DeGeorgie to his feet. "Everyone seems to be going towards the waterfront. The ferries must be working." He thought about the soldiers guarding the waterfront, the tens of thousands of people all wanting to get on the few ferries that could only hold a hundred to two hundred passengers at a time, and the fires that would soon be closing in on them. "There is nothing for us there," he said to everyone, and no one in particular. "I think that we should go to Little Italy where we will find refuge for the night, then try for the Presidio in the morning."

The sarge nodded, enough said, the decision made.

Grazia didn't mind. She did not realize that she found Alphonso's new confidence exciting—that was something she had not felt in a good many years. She stood, still not feeling right in her chest, took a breath, gathered the seamstress bag saying. "I'll get Leah" Then, pausing for just a second as she turned back towards Hattie. "Will you be joining us." This a confirmation, not an invitation.

Hattie smiled in with acknowledgment.

Grazia bristled back with her smile.

Under normal conditions the hike to Little Italy would only take an hour or so. Conditions were far from normal—age, bad shoes, injuries, hunger, collapsed buildings, fires, and a bevy of unknown obstacles—would make it a whole day's effort, and the day was already half-way done. And that did not take into consideration what they would do once they got there?

Not being either Italian or Catholic Sergeant Huckleberry Freeman had never been to Little Italy.

XXIII

No one spoke as they slowly began their trek east on Market Street towards Washington Square. The crowd was as thick as a herd of buffalo and just as ungainly. No one gave way. The noise, loud enough that any conversation seemed impossible. People dragged streamer trunks loaded down with all their earthly goods, odd things that one would normally not think of when a disaster forced you to flee from your home. Just ahead of them a brilliant orange and red plumed parrot squawked in its cage as it sat on top of a dining room table and chairs piled on top of a three wheeled wagon that was in pitiful need of a horse. This weighty, broken wagon was pushed and pulled by six young boys, the youngest perhaps fourteen. An old woman sat in her rocking chair amongst the kitchen furniture as the wagon bounced and jarred as they slowly made its way through a river of humanity. The old woman appeared small and insignificant, even though she was dressed in multiple layers of clothing; perhaps all she had. The old woman wagged a finger at the distraught parrot. The bird scolded her back. Two heavy trunks were being drug behind the wagon by the mother and father who pleaded loudly in their native German[*] at the boys to be careful not to break another wheel. They too were dressed in two, three, more layers of clothing. The fire blew hot, the clothes heavy and uncomfortable. This story was repeated in multiple ways, multiple times, in different languages as the flood of refugees made their way East towards the waterfront.

---

[*] In 1900, the percentage of San Francisco's foreign-born population totaled 116,885, of whom about 35,000 were from Germany.

A dark plumb of broiling smoke, bellowed up a thousand feet, darkened the sky above them, while hot glowing embers darted about seeking refuse in anything that might burn. Behind them a wall of flame, licked at the bottom of this cloud as it consumed buildings, whole neighborhoods. Where there had been no fire an hour earlier the fierceness and viciousness of those flames roaring like a blast furnace, their steady crackle a great unforgiving forest fire. The upward draft of the fires was terrific, the air rushing in from all sides to a common center where it was being sucked upward towards a blood red sun barely visible, the smoke rising to a height of a thousand feet or more. The tremendous power of the draft spinning great pieces of sheet iron roofing ten feet square upward into the air, out of sight like Kansas cornstalks drawn in by the mighty winds of a late summer tornado.

In the blink of an eye a three-story building would catch from the explosive flames consuming the next. In twenty minutes only the cellar remained; nothing more—not even charred and blackened timbers. Combustion was complete and absolute. This was the firestorm, one of three that drove this river of refugees towards the waterfront and whatever safety there might be.

Firefighters stood helpless, their hoses screwed to hydrants that ran dry because the cisterns and plumbing beneath the streets had been rendered useless by the quake. Pumps were brought in to draw what they could from the sewers; this proving to be too little too late.

Colorful hats of all sizes and fancy plumage tumbled down the street like so many panicked exotic birds as they were torn from women's heads by the hot stiff wind generated by the massive firestorm.

While this trek was astonishing and hearts-breaking, in most cases the refugees were calm and civil to each other. It was the military that brought a dangerous tension as they threatened, bullied, and ordered the civilian population about. The Indian wars over, the remaining troops, under-educated, rough men, more used to harsh living on the plains, understood little of big city ways.

At Kearney Street they left behind the river of refugees chancing their luck by turning north. Kearney was a straight shot to Washington Square. While there was plenty of smoke, crumbled buildings blocked their way, bricks and glass continuing to rain without warning, the greatest danger seemed to be behind them—fewer hot angry sparks drifted around them.

There were fewer soldiers to turn them away. The closer they got to Washington Square the less panic seemed to be in the air. The quake had happened. The city was on fire—nothing could change that. People seemed to have accepted this, gathered what they could, thinking that the fires wouldn't reach this part of town.

One place Alphonso felt uncomfortable was when they passed by the Eastern edge of Chinatown. There were soldiers patrolling with rifles topped with long sharp-pointed bayonets to ensure that the Chinese did not go other than where they were told. From Chinatown itself came the blare of Chinese horns, bells, and odd musical instruments as the Chinese flocked to their churches to pray, fearful that the mighty *Earth Dragon* had risen angry and avenging of mankind's many sins against Mother Earth.

They hadn't intended on stopping at Portsmouth Square, but its relative calm proved more than enticing. There were plenty of people standing around, content for an elusive moment away from the combustible world surrounding them. If one did not look out and beyond the square you were in a tiny pocket of relative sanity which was shrinking by the moment. They were in front of The Hall of Justice, one of the newest, if not the newest public buildings in the city. It was situated on the east side of Kearny Street between Washington and Merchant streets, opposite Portsmouth Square. It contained police headquarters, the police courts, and the criminal departments of the Superior Court. If there was a safe place in the city, it should be there.

There were some fires in Chinatown which was only a few blocks away—most on the Southeastern edge of the ghetto. While they weren't that far from Market Street they stopped by silent if not spontaneous agreement. Sanity in an insane world. There were people sitting. While the stench of fire and destruction was still there, the sky still enveloped in a brooding cloud of smoke and toxic gases, there were people having what appeared to be picnic lunches. They stood there, stomachs growling, trying to understand what they were seeing until Alphonso remembered the sausage and cheese wrapped in his valise. The only one in their band who had eaten anything all morning was little Purplepaws.

Francis suffered from acute dyspepsia as well as a throbbing palm. The truth was, that despite being a risk taker, an avant-garde radical without fear, his tolerance for pain fell far short of his self-indulged reputation, with no stomach for the sight of blood, especially his own. He was fairing the worst of the lot, his melancholy eyes, with sweat on the brow, seeking as much commiseration and sympathy as he could reap from the very air around him. The sarge had seen to his wound, and that was enough. Francis was a young man, supposed to be viral and strong—a visionary who spouted words he could not explain.

Grazia did not have much use for words, what few she had she spat. There was nothing good about this day. Wasn't it enough she had a ten-year old and a dammed cat to look after? Look after; she hadn't the time. She still had not been able to release herself of the pain in her chest—heartburn most likely—since she had escaped from their ruined home earlier in the morning. At least, her husband was beginning to act as a man ought to. She looked on, caring little for her husband's own miseries as she watched him unpack his valise.

Hattie had on her best evening shoes and long day's night blisters to match, add to her great frustration her evening gown was filthy and torn. The one thing that did not seem to tire or ache was her smile.

While Leah didn't complain, Purplepaws basket was a bit much for her to handle. Leah had been the only one who had gotten any sleep the night before; now exhausted; she was ready for a nap. She looked hungrily at the cheese and sausage as Alphonso plated and measured out the shares.

Alphonso was glad for the break, however, instead of taking in the relative quiet of the parklike square he looked back in the direction they had come. It seemed to him that with each step forward everything left behind would be lost to this all-hungry maelstrom. That troubled him, leaving him with the feeling that he had left something important behind. What? He had lost everything, his home, job, identity; everything. If he didn't go back before the fires expanded any further, it would be too late. What had he left behind that mattered?

"You stay here and rest. I will go and see if I can find some water." He said, not looking at Grazia as he spoke.

Grazia always knew when he was lying and could see that he was lying, but she did not have enough energy to argue. While they needed water—she knew that this was not what her husband was after. She would get the truth from him later, right now all she wanted to do was eat something and rest. With nothing else to drink but brandy she poured everyone except for Leah a half measure to go with their meal.

Alphonso pocketed some of the cheese and sausage in a greasy paper wrapper, took one swig straight from the bottle, gave a generous smile to everyone—except for his wife—left his valise by the sergeant as he turned back towards the direction they had come from.

The sarge gave him a look, not sure of what he was doing or if his intentions were good.

Leah nibbled on her food, sharing little bits and pieces with her kitten. "Hattie," she squeaked, just short of tears, "there is something wrong with Purplepaws. She's not eating and won't purr when I pet her." She took the docile kitten out of her basket cradling her, nuzzling the tiny feline with her own nose, singing softly, part of the opera song she had sung with Caruso.

Grazia ate a small amount without much relish. She was glad to be lost in her thoughts, away from her husband for a few moments, needing some time to think and not worry about him. Secretly she hoped the cat would die a quick and quiet death. The damn thing was just holding everyone up. If they came across a supply of food, which they needed, the basket had better use than a cat bed. When she coughed on a spicy piece of pepper in the sausage the annoying pressure in her chest become a brief sharp pain. She spat the sausage out as she closed her eyes measuring her breath until the pain gradually went away.

Hattie went to Leah taking Purplepaws into her own hands. "Hello, little one." After a moment she tenderly passed the kitten back to Leah's caring hands. "I wouldn't worry too much," she said to Leah whose eyes told all. "It's been a long grueling day for all of us. Purplepaws is incredibly young and misses her mother, brothers, and sisters, very much. She needs her mother's milk, and we haven't even water."

Hattie looked towards Grazia about to ask how long until Alphonso returned. The older woman sat silently, her eyes closed, the look on her face not one you would want to disturb. "I'll go and see if I can find some water and something for little Purplepaws to nurse on," she whispered.

While still in pain, Francis DeGeorgie had to admit that as

he watched Hattie walk away, her sway was more than just enticing.

XXIV

Alphonso walked as fast as his scrawny old man legs would allow him towards Hillock Alley off Sansome Street. Once there he barely recognized the watchmaker's shop as the building, and the two adjoining had partially collapsed. The buildings had been four story masonry, three of the four stories had succumbed to the shake leaving one wall remaining. The first floor, where the watchmaker's shop had been, with a mountain of bricks, filing cabinets, assorted bric-a-brac, and a dental chair from the dental office on the third floor, obstructed where the front door to the shop had once been.

Remembering the stern warning posters announcing that looters would be shot he had taken special care to avoid the looting on Sansome Street. He felt his heart beating triple time in his chest from the fear that gripped him as he carefully brushed away shards of glass in what remained of the large street front display window. As he cautiously climbed through the window, he did not see nor hear the soldiers as they arrived at the intersections at both ends of the block. His attention was focused on the caved in ceiling, small debris sifting down, which supported too much brick and debris to remain in place much longer. Thick dust hung in the air dramatized by the multiple groaning and ominous creaking of the strained remnants of the weakened beams above. Only a fourth of the room remained open enough for him to squeeze into which was barely big enough for him to reach a multi-drawer tool cabinet where the watchmakers kept their tools.

He had emptied his drawer the morning that he had been let go. The drawer in the middle of the cabinet, was jammed shut by a long narrow pipe that had come down like a javelin spearing the wooden cabinet through and through blocking his drawer from ever being opened. If that weren't enough, he could see the debris above the cabinet visually shift as it continued to sag under the massive weight. Outside, explosions, distant, but still too close for comfort, the shock wave rattling everything around him, the explosive echoes a hundred drums beating down on an unnerved populace. Two close ear-thumping explosive bangs caused his heart to skip three beats as he ducked raising his hands above his head as if his puny old man shoulders might be strong as Hercules when the building came down on him. The bangs came from the rifles of soldiers as they chased looters on the street outside. "Halt or I'll shoot," barked one from just outside the window above him.

"Shoot, private, shoot! Don't give them any god-damned warning. Our orders are to shoot to kill any and all looters." A sharp *BANG* caused more dust to settle around him as one of the soldiers took lethal aim at the fleeing looters. "You never killed no one have you son?" A grizzled sergeant reminisced as he looked for a target. Once you done it a couple of times, it ain't no never mind. Back in 1890 I rode with an outfit up South Dakota way. We were keeping an eye on the Lakota. They had this here Ghost dance, which when done got them all steamed up for another fight. We had orders to go on their reservation and put a stop to this Ghost Dance ritual. Once we got there a fight broke out, gunfire erupted, and we kilt up to 300 Indians. I must have kilt me five or six of them that day.*"

The clatter of a large slide of bricks across the street caused both soldiers to look momentarily away from their intended targets. Their backs to the watch shop, Alphonso quickly reached up testing the drawer that he wanted, it belonged to Anton Jacobi his former employer. Alphonso had to smile. Jacobi had the best tools money could buy. Had, now they were his. He took a jeweler' apron with all the tools attached, not bothering to close the drawer as he ducked down into a dark shadow as the burly sergeant now pointed directly through the window, less than two feet from Alphonso's head and fired. The *BANG,* loud enough to stun, caused him to gasp aloud as he brought his hands up to cover the immediate pain and ringing in his ears.

The open drawer barely hid Alphonso from view as the sergeant leaned in through the window to see if he had a better target. He had aimed into the rear of the ruined shop where he thought he had seen movement. The impact of the bullet brought down a thick dust cloud along with rubble that immediately filled the rear of the shop obscuring his view. The sergeant spat some tobacco through the open window as he eyed the dust as it quickly filled the rest of the space. Satisfied that it was only falling rubble the sergeant turned quickly away seeing no reason for any further inspection. "Dang it, private, didn't I just tell you to shoot their hairy asses." Both soldiers fired more shots as they scurried after more looters who were just as afraid of the crumbling buildings as they were the soldiers aim.

A short but strong aftershock validated their uneasiness.

---

*On December 29, 1890, a Ghost Dance ritual on the Northern Lakota reservation at Wounded Knee, South Dakota, Soldiers killed up to 300 Indians, mostly old men, women, and children in the Wounded Knee Massacre.

Alphonso could barely hear his own cough as the dust and debris enveloped him as it fell and was drawn to the street outside. For the moment he did not know if he had been shot or not. If he had, it must have been a head shot, he thought as he brought one of his hands down to see if there was any blood. He tried to stand. Unsteady on his feet, he desperately wanted to hide, but there was no safe place, and not sure. Not sure the soldiers were, he sat down hard, placed his head in his lap and waited for the dizziness and the pain in his head to pass. From where he sat, he felt the aftershock which gave him every motivation to throw himself out the window as fast as he could manage A thick cloud of dust raced him to the outside.

XXV

Hattie asked a young mother with three small children in tow where she had gotten a milk pale filled with water the children now shared.

The woman gave her a reproachful look as she pulled her children near, certain that even breathing the same air as a woman of ill-repute might scar the children for life. Somehow, they always knew which always surprised her. It wasn't immediately clear whether the woman understood or spoke English until she said something in German or Austrian, a harsh language Hattie always found hard on the nerves. The steep hills of San Francisco created their own tower of babel with ethnic neighborhoods where many stayed close to their native languages and customs.

Portsmouth Square was boarded by Italian, Chinese, the Barbary Coast, and a small German neighborhood that persisted, despite the growth of the Italian. The Italians she liked, *Amore*. It had only been luck that had kept her from plying her trade in the Barbary—or perhaps it was her smile.

Angered, Hattie hiked her evening dress, as she turned, edging just close enough to overturn the bucket.

The water a loss, the woman crossed herself, saying something to her children about a witch. Hattie half-turned, glancing back, her lips spelling out *BITCH*. Others watched as the offended woman's evil eye did its best to keep this gorgeous but obviously evil witch at bay. Men parted, tipping their hats as Hattie passed through the park; now there goes a lady.

No water was to be found.

Across the street a lone soldier stood guard in front of a street that led to Chinatown. The street was empty. Several blocks up she could see that the street was clogged by hundreds of Chinese who had gathered to stare towards the far western edge of their community which was now ablaze, the fire spreading quickly as explosions sent flaming debris high into the air igniting more fires wherever it landed. She could hear their strange whistles and bells which they played to keep evil demons away.

"You can't go that way, miss," the soldier cautioned. He had orders not to let anyone go into the Chinese Ghetto, nor let anyone out. It was obvious the young man was thrilled, his blushing cheeks a dead giveaway, to be speaking with a woman of this grandeur and sex appeal.

"Is there any water to be had?" She asked with a just a hint of a lascivious smile.

"No…no Miss, the water mains are all broke." He stuttered nervously as he turned his head slightly towards the fires in Chinatown before fixing his gaze back on Hattie. "The firemen are just going to let Chink-town burn. I suspect it's them who are using the black powder."

Hattie looked inquisitive.

"Yes, Miss, black powder. I've worked with dynamite, and they aren't using it. The explosions are too haphazard blowing everything every which-ah-way spreading the fire without plan or reason. If I were you, Miss, I'd be getting out of here before the fires drive the chinks this way."

XXVI

After sucking in a lungful of dust and smoke Alphonso reared back releasing a thunderous sneeze. Struggling to breath, knowing that sneezes often come in threes and that the next just might launch a mouthful of teeth, his nose dripping, blurry puffy eyes stinging, he slowly got to his feet in the dust and soot cloud. Now he was truly scared, if there were soldiers, they would shoot before he had a chance to explain that he worked there—or did. The aftershock had left him no choice. He threw himself out the window then rolled and crawled out of the shadow of the building as everything, but that one wall came down. The debris and dust cloud so thick he was not certain that he had survived. His ears rang, his brain rattled, not sure what was up or down, left, or right, as he just sat waiting for something normal to show itself.

XXVII

Earlier that morning, the sun about to rise, the first forty head of long horn cattle were herded into a narrow fenced in chute in Butchertown. The steer nearest the execution run, sensing something, snorted at the gate, primal fear spreading from beast to beast. The smell of humans, blood, and death hanging in the air. The steer had part of a horn broken off, its hide marked with ugly scars from battles long won. He was an old bull, not one to be tested. He was a loner, preferring to remain separate from the herd, the crush of cattle around him bringing his temperamental side to an easy boil.

"What the hell," screamed a cowhand who had been sitting on the fence readying to open the gate. Three others, all armed with rifles for the kill, lost their perch, as the ground beneath Butchertown shifted in several directions at the same time. The slaughterhouses and corrals leaned, some breaking apart as the ground liquified trapping men and cattle alike.

A dozen—or more—of the steers made it to firmer ground. Their sharp horns prodding the others forward as instinctive panic drove them forward onto the waterfront and up merging streets as the momentous earthquake ripped the city apart.

The loner slashed his one sharp long horn at another steer as he broke free of the stampede running into a side street because it offered a path less crowded. While the earthquake had momentarily ceased the ground still shook as buildings crumbled around him, the chaos driving him further away from the herd and deeper into the city where no one expected to confront a distraught beast both scared and defensive.

It did not understand mercy.

XXVIII

The dust cloud slowly lifted allowing Alphonso some air and the simple realization that he had survived. He was coated in a cloak of gray, char, fine grit from head to toe, his face a mask so complete that until he opened his eyes you wouldn't have known he had any. He coughed—much more a retch—tried to spit but found his mouth was dust bowl dry—as two little tears etched a track through the filth on his cheeks until they were absorbed.

He sat in the street only a few feet from where the rubble had fallen, an avalanche that had nearly killed him, suffering an uncontrollable urge to laugh…to root-roar with a laugh just short of insanity. What tickled his funny-bone was that he had spent the entire night fretting about how to tell Grazia that he had lost his job—and now the building he had worked in had nearly squashed him like a bug. His outburst did not last long, his throat being dry, muddy perhaps; never-the-less he cackled until his tears could no longer flow. Finally, his vision restored, though his eyes stung like all hell, he remembered that he had told Grazia that he had gone for water. Water he now needed to flush the stinging away. But from where he sat there was no water was to be found. He was so thirsty he could have drunk from the River Styx, his thirst an illusion of forsaken hope.

Without rising he looked up and down the street. No soldiers, which was a good thing. There were a few people, refugees like himself, who had stopped for the moment to gape at the madman cackling in the middle of the street.

"Mr. Peluso, is that you?" A voice called from across the street. It took him a moment to recognize that it was the kind woman who had helped them earlier in the morning providing milk for a hungry kitten, and proper clothes for Leah. To his embarrassment he couldn't remember her name.

"It's Katie McGillicutty, are you all right?" A concerned expression animated her face as she tried to peer into the still settling dust cloud. "Where is the little girl…and her kitten?" She couldn't immediately remember Leah's name.

He nodded as he started to rise, a cloud of gray dust rising around him as he tried to dust himself off.

"You wait right here, Morgan. I know this man."

The old man looked up from his rickety wheelchair and smiled with only his two lower front teeth showing. "Won't be go'en nowhere cept with you—but Katie don't you be long, those buildings behind us just took fire."

Katie McGillicutty looked back to where they had just been, and sure enough there was fire where there hadn't been a few moments before. "Leah, now I remember, the little girl's name, I mean. It's Leah, and she has that pathetically ugly kitten with the purple stained paws. They're…they're not…?"

Alphonso saw the almost panicked expression on her face as

he met her halfway. "Leah is fine, everyone is at Portsmouth Square taking a break." His voice sounding as might a man drowning in quicksand, and almost under. I came in search of water."

She looked at the apron balled up in her hand, all that she had brought with her, "No water?" She shook her head. "I hadn't thought of that." She looked around, to the old man in her care, to the street and the chaos that surrounded them. Her eyes taking on her concern and regret in being unable to relieve his suffering, and her regret in having not thought to bring something as necessary and import as water.

With skin wrinkled and dried as thin old leather Morgan Piff waved a pint bottle of whiskey in their direction. "Come and take this woman before I actually die of old age. He took a sip, "Damn, if I am going to give it all away."

With a joyous expression and all the gratitude that could pass through her lips Katie took the whiskey as if it were the last communion offered by Christ pressing into Alphonso's hands.

The potent drink cleared his throat as water was never meant to do. The first sip he spat out mud vomited from a dry well. A second more serious sip clearing his gullet leaving him breathlessly grateful.

Seeing his relief, Katie greeted him as if they were lifelong friends, not strangers as they had been a few hours prior, as she hugged him long and hard. She did not ask about his wife.

"Now ain't that something." Piff commented to himself.

"I came to find water," he started to explain still a bit befuddled from his near-death experience.

She shook her head with bemusement. "You are a bit far from Portsmouth Square. I doubt there is any water between here and there, Mr. Peluso?"

"Alphonso, please." He answered as he unconsciously tried to brush the dust and filth from his being. Some of the dust settled on Ms. McGillicutty's hat, dulling the colorful red, yellow, and blue straw flowers, Alphonso stopped, smiling sheepishly.

That was when she saw his eyes change. While lined with tiny red veins they changed from ash gray to a deep late afternoon autumn sky blue, a kind she had never seen before in a man's eyes. *Oh my,* she thought, saying nothing more as two explosions broke the moment visibly sending flaming debris above where they knew Chinatown to be.

"Excuse me," the old man said, "I think…"

"It's time to go." She finished for him. "Portsmouth Square is near Chinatown, we had best go." Without pause or an extra breath she changed the conversation.

I've been rude," she was now flustered. "This is Mr. Piff, he was a border, and—well—as you can see, I couldn't very well leave him behind."

The old man looked as though a puff of wind could blow him like a tumbleweed straight out of his wheelchair. He had a hand tremor and constant waggling and bobbing of the head.

The old man's deep wrinkles seemed to carve a map of his life on his surprisingly still agile and mobile facial features. His eye lines told of laughter, of warm smiles and affection. His forehead told of worries past and worries present. But mostly they were so deeply ingrained they told of a man who had traveled through many decades—not to be dismissed as *old* when he was so much more than the sum of his years. His twinkling eyes were framed by thick white eyebrows and on his stubbled chin were white whiskers, thin and sparse, resistant to a razor's edge. When he opened his mouth there were two front teeth in the center of the lower jaw, nothing above, and not much more in the gap that surrounded his tongue which at times peeked out as might a wooden bird in an old musical clock. At first glance one did not expect much but a dried-out crackle with mumbled bits and pieces of words struggling to connect to anything meaningful. What came out were words carefully pronounced by a master poet, deep and rich as a slowly played viola.

"Most folks call me Morgan, Morgan Piff." He reached out a liver-spotted, thin skinned, wrinkled old hand. "Some folks tend to spit when they try to pronounce my last name; so, if it's all no never-mind its Morgan, if you please."

Alphonso took it, surprised to find the strength in the old man's grip.

"I'd get up from this here thing," Morgan said as he took back his hand and tapped the arm of his wheelchair, but that would be a waste of time. Ms. McGillicuddy, here, would just push me back down. Oh, I can still walk, just as good as the next man." He gave a sly smile exposing his two remaining teeth.

"Now, if it came to a race between an old mule and me, I'd be putting money on the mule. My legs in their old age have taken on a stubbornness of their own. Not to change the subject, if you don't mind holding the conversation, I think we had best get a move on before I'm forced to walk."

"Katie?" It was the first time Alphonso had caught her first name. "I'll show you the way."

"Katie." Her voice giving permission. "Thank you, A-L-P-H-O-N-S-O."

XXIX

Grazia heard the rustle of Hattie's dress preferring to ignore her approach. Grazia, bone-tired, was totally caught off guard by the collapse of her own strength, she felt like an old balloon gone flat. She didn't care about Washington Square, or why they might be going there—nor anything that was happening around them on Portsmouth Square. All she wanted to do was rest.

Leah, thirsty, watched Hattie approach with hopeful eyes.

Francis held his wounded hand on his lap as he lay with his head rested on Alphonso's valise. The center of his palm where the burn was worse was numb with little pain, the rest of his palm suffered sharp almost electric shocks of shooting pain with the slightest movement.

Purplepaws' meow was the only sound any of them made as the relative calm in Portsmouth Square changed to abrupt chaos in an instant.

Buffalo? No, it can't be, the sarge thought as his senses alerted him that in a world gone wrong somehow it was about to get worse.

—

The steer wandered farther and deeper into the city than any other member of the herd. Most had been cut down by rifle fire less than a mile from the devastated slaughterhouses.

Exhausted and terrified almost to the point of insanity the steer stood with its back to a wall in a narrow alley on the southeastern edge of Chinatown. Collapsing buildings, fire, explosions, and man, surrounded it. Its head lowered, horns ready for battle, eyes bulged, with rapid breath blowing out in great snorting sounds, it braced for mortal battle.

A few blocks away two simultaneous explosions blew apart a burning wood framed building as firemen sought to build a firebreak in the wooden ghetto that made up Chinatown. Rolls of flaming cloth from a sewing factory spread fire in every direction. Caught in a fire-driven wind some landed in the alley where the steer stood its ground, a piece of the burning cloth caught on the steer's undamaged horn. It violently shook its head, the heat, smoke, and brilliant flame perilously close to its eye; it's one instinctive reaction to run; everyone and everything a threat. The harder it ran, the closer the flames appeared to its terrified eyes. While the cloth quickly burned away, blind panic controlled its every move. This panic growing with every sound, sight, smell, and threat that blocked its way. It ran away from the direction it had come, away from the sound of the explosions and fires, until the alley met Washington Street, which was filled with hundreds of Chinese, many ringing bells and banging gongs to keep the evil earth demons at bay. The steer charged straight into their mass, skewering and trampling those in its way. The terrified Chinese scattered chaotically; the majority driven by the bull straight towards Portsmouth Square.

The soldier that Hattie had spoken with turned towards the stampede as it was practically on him. He had been told the Chinese would not dare come this way. The police station and government buildings that lined the square emblematic of the forces that kept the Chinese people down, isolating Chinatown into a festering ghetto. The white men who filled the park, many armed, most of whom thought the Chinese to be disease ridden and less worthy than a mongrel dog. Caught between a killer bull and the bone-marrow deep prejudice before them in the park the Chinese had no choice but to fight.

The soldier did not see the bull, only the wild-eyed horde of disease-ridden little yellow men. He fired a shot in warning. The panic was whipped by the first explosions from a fireworks factory that had caught fire on the far side of Chinatown.

A small handful of the Chinese heeded the warning shot, most were driven forward by those behind them.

Single Chinese men led the charge, many of the women children, elderly, extended family now trailed behind the bull, Chinatown in flames behind them.

The few soldiers stationed around the square rushed towards the sound of the shot. The explosive fireworks caused some to think that they were under attack.

The German woman with the three small children fled in panic as the first of the Chinese flooded out of Washington Street. Every head in Portsmouth Square turned in unison to see the soldier, over-run by their sheer numbers, fall beneath their feet, followed by the horrifying sight of his body being flung above their heads, by the deadly force of a berserk longhorn bull that appeared to be much larger than its actual size—this backlit by the brilliant violence of the fireworks caught beneath a massive brooding black smoke plume.

XXX

Li Fengzhang was a man of purposeful intent.

In 1906 San Francisco that was not an easy task. His father, Li Hanzhang, had come from Quinchi Village, in the Anhui Province in China in the year of Fengzhang's birth. His father's work in the gold fields had given him bitter memories of the coolie life. What meager wealth he acquired he used to open *'Paper Dreams Bazaar'*, a general store that served the Chinese miners. In time he opened a second and then a third store in other mining camps. Often these camps were destroyed by white miners, out of necessity his father had moved to San Francisco where he opened a bazaar in Chinatown.

When Fengzhang was fourteen his father sent for him. As the elder son he was expected to go. Saying good-by to his mother Zhou Xiaolian, his brothers, and sisters, he booked a ticket on an old tramp steamer and set sail for America knowing he would never see any of them again. That was 1883, a year after the Anti-Chinese Exclusion Act made it all but impossible for common Chinese laborers to set foot on American soil. His English schooling, he had gotten at a Missionary School in Shanghai, and his natural inclination for mathematics allowed him to upgrade is identity papers from coolie to merchant.

At 37, Li Fengzhang had grown from being a book-keeper at his father's store to that of an accomplished businessman in his own right owning a garment factory, along with three laundries. Because of his obsessive hours he never married. He preferred wearing western suits, black and exquisitely tailored, always accompanied by a shiny black top hat. He wore a cloak of dignity as if it were a well-tailored suit, and while he would tip his hat as a white man passed by, he would not step off the sidewalk to let the white man pass. After years of painful trial and error he had mastered this art of self-determination without much more bruising.

Besides his western attire he stood out because he had no pigtail—no *queue*. For those who hailed from Manchuria and associated with the imperial family, the queue symbolized personal pride and a keeping with tradition. For many westernized Chinese men, the queue meant defeat and humiliation. Fengzhang, who never planned on returning to China, had cut off his queue as the ship he was on sailed through the golden gate.

Li Fengzhang looked out the window of his third-floor apartment, its glass cracked in three places at the scene so many saw that dreadful morning—the city of San Francisco burning. More importantly, the explosions that vomited both man and debris into the smoke-filled air, spreading the fires that would turn the largest enclave of Chinese outside of main-land China to ashes. The fires were already near his factory, and there was nothing he could do as he watched his wealth and good fortune burn before his eyes. Below, filling the four-corner intersection, a large crowd had gathered, mostly single men, uneducated laborers, whose future were severely threatened by the fires, and the hatred of the white men who surrounded their ghetto. The bells, gongs, drums, and chimes they beat spoke volumes of their tragedy. Cries and pleas for aid in the

Cantonese dialect rose. *'Aeeya! Dai loong jen!'* They screamed. *'The earth dragon is wriggling!'* More frightened residents ran out of the damaged buildings. Chinatown's picturesque narrow streets and alleys were potential deathtraps from falling cornices and other debris.

Li Fengzhang knew that this day would come; that it was inevitable. You cannot have this much superstition, illiteracy, hatred, and poverty all but fenced in in a city as rich as San Francisco. He did not know how it would come, the end of Chinatown but it was just a question of time. That Chinatown would be scorched from the face of the earth along with the mansions and the towers, he symbols of wealth that surrounded it came as a surprise.

At first, he hadn't determined the cause of the stampede—then he saw the enraged steer as it drove hundreds of Chinese towards the relative safety of Portsmouth Square. Fengzhang stood helpless as their hue and cry rose outside his window. A single tear rolled silently down his cheek. He knew it was too late for them. The fireworks behind brought a Wagnerian stagecraft to the tragic opera.

XXXI

There is a sound, a sound once heard you can never forget. It is a primordial sound, archaic, as old as humankind that comes from the deepest, most frightening side of our basic instincts. A sound that does not come from any one language, culture, or belief system. It comes from the blind rage that drives men to hack each other to death as they did in days of the knights of old, Bull Run in the American Civil War, a Japanese *Banzai* attack, or the battle of the Somme where more than 19,240 died in a single day as they charged across no man's land directly into deadly mortar and machine gun fire. They all heard this sound because it came from them as they charged their enemy wanting to kill or be killed.

On Portsmouth Square the panic was instantaneous and beyond description. The Chinese had limited space to run. They came out of their underground burrows like rats and tumbled into Portsmouth Square. No one knew how many Chinese there were, perhaps a thousand or more. With their backs to the firestorm, they ran straight into thousands of Italians, Spaniards, Germans. It seemed as every one of these, along with the riffraff of Barbary Coast, made for that one block of open land. The two uncontrolled streams met in the center of the square and piled up on the edges.

Hatred and madness.

It was the sound that woke Francis from his stupor. Francis De Georgie had first heard that sound in St. Petersburg, Russia. It had come from the Cossack Calvary as they charged into the massive protest ranks of the unemployed their swords striking men, women, and children alike. Their intent was to kill, not warn.

While the Germans Spanish, and the Italians in Portsmouth Square, did not care much for each other, they were adamant that the modest safety provided by the square was not to be shared with the Chinese.

The Chinese were caught between the fires and the soldiers behind them as they faced the hatred and blood lust of the men the stood in their way—that primordial sound now coming from both. Both dangerous and deadly the bull was no longer the threat as both sides went after each other with bare hands, knives, clubs, any makeshift weapon that could be found.

Francis rose, launching himself at Hattie, knocking her to the ground as the bull passed her with inches to spare.

Its hooves shredding the kitten's basket Leah had so lovingly carried. Purplepaws, who was on Leah's lap bolted, prepared to run blindly from dangers it could not comprehend only to be caught by Grazia's quick hands as she rolled out of harm's way.

Francis's landed roughly on his hand the pain sucking his breath away, but neither the blood or pain would stop him as he gathered Leah and Hattie. Holding them close, as he searched for a safe exit from the square as the fighting spread around them. The terrifying noise fed Francis's instinct to survive, knowing that if they did not get out, they would all fall victim to man's worst folly within moments.

Grazia grabbed Alphonso's valise, shoving the kitten inside as she slammed it shut, following Francis so close she was protected from rocks and flying projectiles as they fled the battle for Portsmouth Square.*

Sergeant Freeman had stood up against stampeding buffalo, elk, and bear. He had fought against Indians who would not give ground. It did not take any real thinking to know what he had to do. The thundering of the steer's rampage practically rattled his teeth as he grabbed the rifle from the fallen soldier and fired from almost point-blank range the bullet striking straight through to its' brain. Not seeing the sarge or who had fired the shot a soldier thought that he alone had stopped the enraged beast with a determined thrust with his bayonet.

Without comment Sergeant Freeman joined them as they passed the lone steer, still twitching, blood pouring from its two wounds. The soldier, alone, backed away. His rifle's bayonet still dripping from the steer's blood. The stories he would tell for years to come on how he alone had brought the fearsome animal to ground.

The mindless mayhem continued until a platoon of army troops restored order with their bayonets.

---

*The battle of Portsmouth Square is the only documented race riot in San Francisco on the first day of the turbulent earthquake and fire. A rogue steer had indeed driven the Chinese from their burning ghetto into the square.

Freeman, Francis, the two women and Leah ran the better part of two blocks until the sound was lost against the myriad noises that rose from a dying city. Winded, no one had words that could describe the fear that had not yet left them. All but the sarge, the only thing that scared him these days was old age.

Leah was the first to move as she heard Purplepaws plaintive meow from within the valise. Grazia set the valise down as she turned and searched the street for as far as she could see. *Where was that good-for-nothing fool? Where was Alphonso? For a moment she wondered if she would ever see him again; maybe God had blessed her?*

XXXII

It was a hot unforgiving wind. The air tasted of char, smoke, garbage, vinegar, roasted vegetables, scorched hair, burnt feathers from bedding, rotting fish, seaweed, paint, kerosene, and all matters of human enterprise quickly being rendered into ashes. The smoke rose from a dozen major fires across the city, each adding its weight to a huge plume above the skyline, which was black as coal with splashes of purple, rose, orange, brown. Dark and menacing, blotting out the sun.

A noticeable aftershock brought everyone on the streets around them back to panicked hysteria. After a moment or two, they settled back down to an amplified, slightly under control panic, as a dozen or more languages floated to their ears mostly lost within the dreadful din of the dying city. The sounds of the collapsing of buildings, the distant explosions man-made and not, became common place.

Overall, there wasn't a sense of panic amongst the people. After their initial panic they were steadfast and calm, neighbor helping neighbor, taking the hard lessons of the day with, as the British might say, *a stiff upper lip.*

As the soldiers spread throughout the city it became clear that they were there not to protect the people but to protect the city from the people. The people were not the problem—mostly—it was the soldiers. The army forts in the west had mostly closed, the Indian wars over. Many of the lower-rank soldiers who remained were rough and uneducated. This was not Sergeant Huckleberry Freeman's army, at least not anymore.

It was hard to conceive that one could be having a good time with everything that was going on around them. Alphonso was. For as long as he could remember his life had been one mundane routine. He was a maker and repairman of clocks, most of his days concentrated on tiny little wheels and gears. There had been little comradery among his fellow watchmakers. At home he had slowly grown into the role of a silent man—dull—bored—bringing little conversation to the kitchen table as Grazia found more ways to chastise most of what he might have to say or do.

After the earthquake everything had turned upside down. He suddenly had no job, nor had he told Grazia that he didn't. He had no home, and little hope for the future. For some inexplicable reason he now relished the devastation and chaos as it spread around him. He felt alive, virile, alive as a man for the first since—well—since he had been a young man. It had been a long time since he had confessed his sins at the parish—now—with a few embellished bragging rights he was a petty thief. And he didn't care what Grazia thought or said about it.

Katie, a woman perhaps ten years younger than he had caught his eye. He did not know he still had it in him. She was attractive, vibrant, funny, and from the first moment a pleasure to be with. It wasn't a sexual thing, at least he didn't think so. On the other hand, it had been a long time since he and Grazia had kept each other more than just warm beneath the sheets. That such thoughts might come to him added a sense of mystery and expectation—which wasn't a bad thing—not at all.

He could not remember ever meeting a woman like Katie. All that remained of her home, her boarding house, her soul source of income, was now nothing more than hot ashes and black smoke, but that did not seem to have phased her—at least not on the surface. She was a survivor, something Alphonso also admired.

She was cute, and when she laughed, it rang bells.

Morgan Piff was a survivor of a different sort. He had lived long and seen just about everything. There was little doubt in Alphonso's mind that the old man's brain was far less wrinkled than the rest of his body. He had things to say and was a talker with stories to tell, with an unspoken fear that he wouldn't live long enough to tell them all. To Alphonso's chagrin the old man wouldn't shut up. While his words were slow and carefully chosen, his voice, a foghorn, inviting, not warning, brought emphasis and humor to what he said. And damn, if that wasn't worth more than the price of a beer on a hot summer's day.

"This is the biggest quake* we've had here since…since…let's see now, oh yes, I think it was back in 68. It came in the early morning as I recall, just like this one. I was having breakfast at The Empire, a restaurant I liked on Sansome Street. The damage to Sansome Street was severe. The buildings between Washington street and Telegraph Hill suffered little, but south of Washington street, the damage in some places was severe, much like back on Sansome. I remember an importer who sold crockery, glassware, and stuff like that, whose store was at the corner of Sansome and Merchant streets. He sustained a loss of about $100, by breaking of stock which was thrown about. That was a lot of money back then.

Now, as I recall the building on the opposite corner, which was occupied by a grocery store and the Empire Restaurant on the ground floor, got the worst of it." He smacked his lips. "They had the best apple strudel; Viennese as I recall. The Empire was crowded with the usual folks. I was having my breakfast. The quake shook the dickens out of the place, and we all rushed out to the street as the windows of the restaurant were smashed to pieces. Mr. Blumenthal—Ed—the proprietor of the restaurant, and two other men—one of them a waiter—were severely injured, I got cut and still bear the scar right here near my right ear." He brought a finger up to the spot where the scar was now hidden by the wrinkles of age. "The restaurant never did re-open…I sure do miss that strudel."

"The city didn't catch fire back then, as she's burning now. I wasn't here the last time the old girl burned to the ground, but I've had my elbow bent many a time by the men who fought the fires."

✦ Known as the "great San Francisco earthquake" until 1906, one of California's most destructive earthquakes occurred on October 21, 1868, resulting from slip on the Hayward Fault. Heavy damage occurred in communities situated along the fault and in San Francisco and San Jose. Sadly, many of the engineering lessons learned from this earthquake and openly discussed at the time, such as the hazards of building on "made ground" reclaimed from the San Francisco Bay or the admonition to "build no more cornices," were long forgotten by the time of the 1906 quake.

"Let's see now, the big fire was back in the spring of 1851, sometime late morning, a fire, clearly the work of an incendiary, broke out in a frame house on Pacific Street near Powell, not far from this very spot. Strong summer sea-breezes fanned the flames, and the firefighter's fearless battles were of no avail against the fire's intense heat and speed. There was an article in the newspaper* the next day that said that ten blocks and portions of six others were destroyed, the city hall was consumed…" His tongue popped out with no words tied as he shifted thoughts. "Lost my thought there for a moment." He fell silent as his head and eyes shifted, taking note of the people and the urgencies of the moment as they wheeled him forward. Finally, he found his lost thought and continued. "Afterwards the city put water tanks on many of the roofs." He chuckled as he raised a wrinkled hand to point. "Of course, those tanks don't do much good when the buildings come down."

Alphonso knew the old man was old, but he had to ask, forgetting that Piff had already said that he wasn't.

---

*On December 23, 1848, the California Star and Californian ran an article indicating this would be the last issue. In a business arrangement with the firm of Gilbert, Kemble and Hubbard, a new paper, entitled ALTA CALIFORNIA, would be published at San Francisco, Upper California, the first issue of which would appear on Thursday, January 4, 1849. By 1849, the paper had come under the control of Robert Semple who changed its name to the Alta California. On January 22, the paper began daily publication, becoming the first daily newspaper in California. On July 4, 1849, Semple began printing the Daily Alta California on a new steam press, the first such press in the west. In 1863, Albert Evans became editor at the paper and continued in that capacity for several years. The newspaper continued publication until June 2, 1891.

"You were there?"

"No God-damn-it, I already said I wasn't. I didn't get here until fifty-five."

Alphonso tried to mentally guess his age.

"If you're asking, I was born in 1835. Now as I was saying, the city burned twice that year. The first time was in…"

Alphonso picked up a discarded birdcage.

"Mr. Paluso, what do you need that for?" Ms. McGillicutty asked.

"Please, Ms. McGillicutty, its Alphonso. Mr. Paluso was my father's name and I do not think that he would take it kindly if I used it being the disappointment that I proved to be." He completed the thought to himself then quickly changed the subject.

XXXIII

Following the sarge, constantly looking over their shoulders, Francis, Hattie, Grazia, and Leah quickly made their way to Washington Square. The events in Ports-mouth Square had quickly stripped away any thin threads of safety they might have felt.

"The white man wants to drive the yellow race to the abyss, to the bottomless pit from which it came, where their pestilence would trouble mankind no more." That is what Grazia told Leah, and Leah cried, because it was so unfair and mean-hearted. As a little girl of ten she knew that it was wrong, and more dangerous than the fires that bore down on them. After what they had experienced and seen she doubted that she would ever be able to think of people as she had before Portsmouth Square.

The closer they got to Washington Square the more regular soldiers there seemed to be. The square, surrounded by eloquent department stores, hotels, and restaurants, backed by Peter and Paul's Catholic Church on Filbert Street, was the commercial center of the city. Once there, soldiers blocked their way, and they were ordered to stay out of the park. The threatening bayonets and gruff words of the soldiers made it perfectly clear that the park—the largest portion of clear space—was for military personnel only. Civilians were told that they could camp out in front of the Catholic Cathedral if they chose to stay. Many did, as did many more around the edges of the park despite the bullying by the soldiers guarding it.

It was as if a tap had opened as more people flooded into the area.

The Park was lined with a decorative iron fence with small patches of grass between it and a sidewalk. Hatti claimed a small patch of green where they settled down to wait for Alphonso to find them. On the other side of the fence men rested, soldiers they presumed. All around them there was constant motion as people came and went, wagons arrived loaded with every sort of thing, soldiers on horseback barking orders at people who pressed in on the park which the army kept off limits.

A cacophony of sound and foreign voices made it impossible to rest. Grazia noted that people slumbered on every blade of grass not guarded by the soldiers. Rest seemed impossible. Never-the-less she closed her eyes letting all thoughts fade. Francis soon followed, as did

Hattie and Leah, the stresses of the day wearing on them in so many ways.

XXXIV

Alphonso and Katie took turns pushing Morgan Piff until they were turned back by armed troops a block from Portsmouth Square. They could see that there was something going on in the square which gave them pause to think about not going there. Portsmouth Square was rapidly becoming surrounded by the fires that raged out of control. It appeared that the soldiers were driving everyone east, back towards the waterfront; none would brook any disobedience or questions.

At first Alphonso was distraught as to where Grazia had gone—would he ever see her again—than he calmed as he told himself that she would be fine, that she…he let the thought that she might not be back linger for just a moment and for whatever reason it tasted sweet.

While turning the refugees away the soldiers had orders to stay near Portsmouth Square which allowed Katie and Alphonso to cut back north, then west again until they reached the already congested Washington Square.

The poster that Alphonso had seen proclaiming that marshal law had been declared was more than evident. Soldiers, all armed with rifles with long bayonets, guarded the square where civilians, perhaps prisoners, based on the way they were being treated, were digging large trenches in the park's green center. Horse soldiers roamed the streets making sure no one idled, or blocked traffic. There were more people in and around Washington Square than the soldiers would allow, and more streaming in. Many camped around the edges of this hurried construction—all carefully under the watchful eye of the soldiers on foot and horseback. Nowhere in sight were supplies of food, water, blankets, or anything to meet the basic needs of the people.

XXXV

Li Fengzhang knew better than to strike out on foot. He was Chinese, and despite his western apparel, he would be rounded up, arrested and herded with the rest of the surviving Chinese refugees to some unpleasant place and held there for God knows how long. The white business leaders of San Francisco had long wanted the valuable land beneath Chinatown, and once it burned it would be theirs for the taking.

Li, a businessman of high standing, was one of a very few Chinese who had an automobile. He hoped the soldiers would be too busy to notice his Asian features as he slowly meandered his vehicle through the debris littered and crowded narrow streets of Chinatown to his father's store.

His father, a proud man, would never let his life's work burn without a fight. As Li found his own way, his success becoming larger than his father's, a rift grew between them. Li, a proud man himself, hoped that he would not have to beg his father to leave behind everything he had built in order to save his honorable life.

XXXVI

Alphonso waved as he spotted Grazia, resting beneath a tree at the edge of the park.

Hattie waved back.

Upon his arrival he was not greeted with any concerns for his health or well-being. Grazia opened one eye, slightly. "At last, the great Alphonso Paluso returns," Grazia hissed, "and empty handed." She turned towards Hatti as if she assumed there would be natural support. "He went for water and returns empty handed…except for two more mouths to feed." She cast her hands about the air as if she were speaking to a congregation. "All of these people are hungry and thirsty, and there is nothing to be had. The army provides for itself with nothing for the people." Others nearby were now listening, murmurs rose as she continued to berate her husband, sympathy for the brow-beaten Italian rose as he shrunk beneath his wife's vindictive speech, their angst growing against the army who behaved as if they guarded the city from the people, and not the people from the devastating events that surrounded them.

Having emptied her larder of blame Grazia closed her eyes once again. Her energy spent, the pain in her chest was back as punishment for her harsh words. She determined that after she rested, she would rid herself of everyone but Leah. There would be more concern for the well-being of a little girl than an old woman. She pursed her mouth in a self-satisfied smirk thinking that she would keep Leah nearby. They were all useless, contributing nothing towards their survival. She did not like the way her husband looked at that boarding house woman. She snatched a quick glance at Leah—*the cat would have to go to.*

Alphonso smiled meekly as he stepped around Grazia giving the bird cage to Leah saying that it was for her kitten.

"Morgan Piff." The old man introduced himself.

Grazia ignored the introductions.

Katie had to bite her lip in order to not respond to Alphonso's wife's unbearable haranguing. What marital issues there might be between a husband and wife were private and it was cruel and unacceptable to brow-beat and deliberately humiliate her husband in such a public manner.

Leah's broad smile at the gift of the bird cage drew Katie's visceral dislike of Grazia to the refreshing innocence of a little girl's nurturing of a helpless kitten.

Hattie responded to the unusual deep oboist tone of the old man's voice; she had never heard anything quite like it. She was drawn to it as she had never been drawn to a man's voice before. If he were a younger man, she would be in trouble. He hadn't been a young man in a long time, and there was something safe about that.

It was Francis that caught the truth in part of what Grazia had said. The army was not protecting the people. They were protecting the city, the property of the rich and powerful from the covetous needs of a newly destitute population. The seditious zeal Francis harbored quickly overcame the pain in his injured hand as he began to sense a rebellion, a mutiny arisweing around them. While the dislike for the soldiers was real enough the people had more important things to worry about.

Sergeant Freeman thought about leaving his flock in the relative safety of Washington Square. What benefit were they to him? If anything, they jeopardized his own ability to fend for himself. He stood in the shadows, drawing as little attention to himself as possible. He did not need a mirror to know what he was. *He was an old crippled blackamore, last in line…hell, he was one of a kind. He had either outlived his troopers or they had moved on, and it might just be best for him to move along to. He would get no helping hand here.* As he took in the people and the events surrounding him it occurred to him that the fires were destroying the social, economic—and class structures that had defined San Francisco before this calamitous day had happened. When it was all over, when the fires had burned out, the ethnic neighborhoods would be gone. There would be no jobs for the laborers or the skilled craftsman. No jobs for domestic servants because the mansions of the rich will have burned alongside the shanties and boarding houses of the poor. The private clubs, expensive hotels, and lifestyles of the rich will have been brought down faster and mightier than what he had witnesses in the first stages of the *Ku-Klux-Klan* back home in Louisiana when he had been a boy.

Francis was beginning to see the same thing, only differently. Unfairness would not be vanquished. From what he witnessed at Portsmouth Square the Chinese, Historians generally classify the KKK as part of the post-Civil War insurgent violence related not only to the high number of veterans in the population, but also to their effort to control the dramatically changed social situation by using extrajudicial means to restore white supremacy. In 1866, Mississippi governor William L. Sharkey reported that disorder, lack of control, and lawlessness were widespread; in some states armed bands of Confederate soldiers roamed at will. The Klan used public violence against black people and their allies as intimidation. They burned houses and attacked and killed black people, leaving their bodies on the roads. While racism was a core belief of the Klan, Anti-Semitism was not. Many prominent southern Jews identified wholly with southern culture, resulting in examples of Jewish participation in the Klan.

Japanese, and other unwanted peoples would be driven from the ruins leaving the land to be acquired by the rich to become yet richer again.

In order to survive the unions would have to change—finally to fight the corrupt property owners, bankers, the bourgeoisie that got rich by keeping the common man down. He had seen the beginning fires of revolution in Russia. Perhaps now, the fires that burned around them would ignite that same revolution.

---

*Six Confederate veterans from Pulaski, Tennessee, created the original Ku Klux Klan on December 24, 1865, shortly after the Civil War, during the Reconstruction of the South. The group was known for a short time as the "Ku Klux Clan". The Ku Klux Klan was one of a number of secret, oath-bound organizations using violence, which included the Southern Cross in New Orleans (1865) and the Knights of the White Camelia (1867) in Louisiana.

The thought excited him, energized him. While still unsteady on his feet, he got up and began to walk around. *The people were hungry, tired, rendered helpless by soldiers with bayonets. Grazia had said it—people needed water—food as well as water. The army has both,* Francis thought as he began to plot a way to take it from them.

Katie almost fell backwards when she realized that the people she thought to be sleeping on the inside of the iron fence, were not in fact sleeping. They were dead. The army was digging a mass grave. A breathless shriek escaped from her throat as she placed her hand over her lips to quiet what she knew would be an earth-shaking cry of horror and alarm if she allowed it to come.

Alphonso quickly turned at the first sound of Katie's alarm. "What is it? Are you, alright?"

Before she could respond a wagon pulled up behind them. Alphonso intuitively knew what had upset the woman as soldiers wearing bandanas covering their mouths and noses unloaded and stacked bloody corpses onto those who had appeared a moment before to slumber. The bodies were Chinese, their remains the result of the desperate battle that had occurred at Portsmouth Square.

"You there," an officer on horseback rode up to the men unloading the wagon, "don't mix the Chink's with this lot." He pointed across the park. "There's a lye-pit over there. Just dump the heathen yellow bastards in." He shook his head at the row of dead white men. "These we'll try to identify. Lay them out, neat and proper in the trench, by and by, a priest will say some words over them."

The officer touched his fingers to his hat when he saw Hatti; then rode off. "Sergeant," he could be heard saying, "move these civilians back, they're too close to the grave sites."

XXXVII

At three o'clock in the afternoon the fires reached the out-skirts of Portsmouth Square. After the riot, the park remained under army supervision, mostly empty of civilians. A mass grave had been dug and filled with around fifty bodies before this effort was moved to Washington Square. The central police station and other government buildings were ordered to be abandoned as well as the Hall of Justice where the mayor was holding the initial meeting of the Committee of Fifty.

The fifty were to be prominent and influential citizens whose influence could be used, while the city still burned, to provide care and shelter for the refugees, and to find the colossal resources necessary to begin rebuilding the city. The committee did not entirely have community service as its vested interest.

Mayor Schmitz and all the City Supervisors controlled and had their hands into just about everything the city of San Francisco needed to function. Utility rates were fixed, you couldn't get a phone without a special permit. Public transportation was hamstrung because both railroads who wanted to put in more street cars and trolleys were tied up in court because they couldn't get their permits approved. Building permits were mostly dead upon arrival at city hall, unless large and often discrete fees were paid. A working man couldn't join a union, and that includes the Longshoremen's, Carpenters, Plumbers, Butchers, and Music Unions, unless he was willing to pay a fee which many couldn't afford. Schmitz was the President of the Musician's Union before entering politics as the chosen candidate for a powerful Lawyer—Abe Ruef. Mostly Schmitz was nothing more than a rubber stamp lining his own pockets if he did what Ruef said.

The first meeting of the Committee of Fifty was cut short due to the danger of approaching fires. As was the second meeting… the fire proving to be in charge.

XXXVIII

As far as Grazia was concerned the space they shared on the grass wasn't big enough for the four of them. She would make room for her husband of course, but where that would come from would be at the sacrifice of the others. There was no room for Ms. McGillicutty, nor an old man in a wheelchair. "I'm sorry Mr. Piff, but it is obvious to me that you are of an advanced age where without proper medical attention you are not likely to live much longer. Pardon, my frankness, but as you can see…" she gestured with one hand towards the dead and the soldiers not far away, "there is none to be had here."

"Don't bother yourself with me," Alphonso fumed, "We'll find space elsewhere. Katie, shall we! Morgan, your call.

So far Francis had not spoken much, nor did he waste any words here as he quietly followed. Grazia had become insufferable, and this was as good an opportunity as any to put a distance between them. Today was about surviving and for the moment that is exactly what he planned to do. Survive, and he had a better chance with anyone other than Grazia.

Hatti looked a little bit baffled at the turn of events. She gave Leah a reassuring smile as she rose and held out her hand. Picking up the birdcage she and Hatti followed leaving Grazia behind. After a few steps Leah turned and with sad eyes said, "You're a mean unhappy old woman."

Grazia cold stare followed them.

Leah said nothing more, she had said enough.

—

Morgan Piff chose a spot near the Church of St. Peter and Paul where a wooden wall blocked the afternoon breeze. The church was not large. A few redwood boards came loose. There were cracks, and more than a few shattered stained-glass windows, otherwise the church had withstood the quake well. Alphonso did notice that the bell tower looked as if it might come down at any time. When, not if, it came down it would be on the far side of the church, so they held tight to their little green oasis. It was a bit larger than the spot they had just left and pleasantly located in the shade with the church blocking much of the wind; with the wind came the smoke and fire. There were no soldiers leaning over your shoulders, nor dead bodies as your immediate neighbors. Two priests stood at the front door to welcome those who might enter to give thanks for their blessings, to seek sustenance for their souls, and to gently turn away those who wanted to camp out in God's house.

There was no water, and what little food they had was in the valise. Grazia had the valise. Alphonso thought about going back for it, finally deciding that his wife of many years could have it. He had nothing else to give her. They were Catholic so there would be no divorce and as far as he was concerned, they would never live under the same roof again. He was done and felt no guilt in walking away.

Francis stood, surveying everything around them, as the others settled in for hopefully the rest of the night. Tomorrow they would see what the fires had left and decide what to do from then. Hopefully, it wouldn't be long until the army would bring in some blankets and food. There were so many hungry people, and the night would bring cold, living near the ocean had its plusses and minuses.

From the edge of an ally across the street, still close enough to see, the sarge studied the young Hungarian for a moment, watching his face, his eyes. He could see that the younger man was thinking. Whether this was good or bad, he didn't know. He did not want the young man to go, they needed his youth, his strength. While Francis had not won any awards for manliness when it came to suffering his wound the sarge suspected that he could take care of himself. He was a young man full of ideas, but ideas did not feed you when chaos ruled the day.

Huckleberry Freeman shrugged his old shoulders. It was a longways to Brownsville, Texas where he had heard a few of his old troopers had settled in. Texas was a former confederate state with god-awful heat, prejudice to spare, and Jim Crow laws. It did not exactly sound like a trip worth making. Cautiously he crossed the street towards the shadows cast by the catholic church. *This is as good a place as any,* he thought as he stepped up quietly besides young Hungarian. "What are you thinking my young friend? How is your hand?"

"Water." Francis replied as an intriguing glint came to his eyes.

Alphonso also noticed that glint, and having just discovered his own, he found an abettor—a rapscallion—that crossed the difference between their years. "Thirsty, are you?" Alphonso scratched his chin as he looked beyond the question he had asked.

'We're all thirsty," the young reactionary answered, assessing the older man for trust and confidence. "I'd like to find enough water for all of us to take a drink with enough left over to mix with a little dog-shit and rub it in the soldier's faces." He hesitated as he realized that he just might have insulted the sergeant.

"I'd be careful there, son. Looking at those stacks of corpses you might want to be mindful that these soldiers am serious. I'll help you find the water…but we'll want to be keeping it a secret from the soldiers or they'll confiscate it all for themselves."

Alphonso gave a knowing glance to the church. "Perhaps God will lend us a hand."

Being an atheist Francis DeGeorgie was tempted to argue the point. With the size of the task, his useless hand that screamed with pain whenever anything touched it, a reminder of his limitations, he wouldn't risk their relationship with an argument over religion—at least not now.

The three men made a devil's bargain. Finding the water, and making it their own might very well bring them up against the soldiers whether they liked it or not. The Marshal Law Edit gave the soldier's lethal persuasion. Huckleberry Freeman knew this was no fool's game; never-the-less, a game worth playing.

Morgan had found another man's ear to bend in a one-way

conversation and for the moment content to stay where he was. Being run up and down the streets of a devastated city in a wheelchair was far from being a grand adventure. One of the advantages of being near the church he suspected was that they would not turn down an old man in a wheelchair from the use of their facilities. Looking around there wasn't a privy to been seen for what he guessed might be eight hundred or more people. The army was digging graves, not latrines, which they would regret before days end.

Katie and Hatti busied themselves with girl talk, Leah napped, while Sergeant Freeman, Alphonso and Francis bid them farewell with promises for their safe return with gifts for all.

XXXVIV

Li Fengzhuang's heart felt broken. Half of Chinatown was fully ablaze, soon not one structure would be left standing leaving easy pickings for the wealthy white men who coveted the land. The painful truth was that if left to them there would be no Chinatown, no Chinese people in all of San Francisco, an effort begun with the 1992 Chinese Exclusion Act. He could tell by the fires that his garment factory had already succumbed to the flames. Soon his father's lucrative business would be the same as his, ashes and char.

His father, Li Hanzhuang was in a tizzy, spinning in an indecisive whirlwind. His long white whiskers and bifocals a blur. He wanted to save everything, and no matter how hard Fenhzhuang argued his father's stubborn streak remained as unrelenting as the Great wall of China. The room was caught in the eerie colors and flickering of the nearing firestorm as the flames reflected in the windows. The retched stench of hot ash was everywhere as the air grew hot; smoke tickled their throats causing both men to cough as they began to struggle to breath. Li Fenhzhuang made the decision for his father as he loaded eight twenty-five-pound bags of dried tea into his car.

Blazing cinders danced around him as Fengzhuang yelled to his father that time had run out—it was time to go.

His father remained in his shop pulling and packing items he thought that he could not leave behind. In frustration Fangzhuang ran into the shop, passing his father until he reached the rear of the shop out of sight of his father's eye, there he struck a match lighting a box of straw packing material. The straw burst into flame much faster than he expected—spreading as if he had poured kerosene on it. He rushed back to his father, grabbed him by the shoulders, locking his eyes on the old man's smoke strained desperate eyes. "It is time, look the fire has taken hold. We must leave now!" He urged as he could see the red and orange glow of the growing flames in his father's spectacles.

In that instant he saw fear carve its mark across his father's face. The old man dropped a porcelain statue as he slowly spun around finally seeing the massive fire through the windows, his breath caught as the smoke from the spreading fire within his store would have brought him to his knees had it not been for his son's firm grasp. He nodded vigorously to Fangzhuang that—Yes—he had lost the battle and it was time to go.

XXXIX

Conrad Wolff was a large flushed-faced penguin shaped man who seemingly hides his naturally short legs beneath his ponderous central girth. His head, while large, is long and unnaturally narrow—not fat—his forehead being his predominant feature. His nose, perpetually red, narrow and beak-like brings focus to his grand smile and curious owl-like eyes. When standing, he leans on a cane, at barely five feet five, three hundred pounds, with a posture, he appears as if he will topple over at any moment. He wears a well- tailored gray suit, the coat impossible to button, is well kept. A dark blue, white spotted bow tie tops a tent-like white shirt spotted with the pea soup he had had before closing the door to Wolff's *Antiquarian Bookstore and More* for what will be the last time.

Despite his weight, and unusual looks, Conrad is man in his mid-forties still flush with life, unabashed humor, and a natural curiosity for all the mysteries that life has to offer. While it is true that most people laugh when they first lay eyes on Conrad, he will return their laughter in such a way as to turn ridicule into a profound respect for the brilliant mind that alters one's opinion to that of a mighty eagle rather than that of a waddling penguin. He did have one vice, known to a few, but often forgiven, even by the archbishop. Conrad Wolff dearly loved a good game of cards, gambling, often losing more than most thought he could afford. It was not the winning or losing of money that interested him, it was playing the game with the right people who understood the skills of the game, and the collecting of favors.

He carries with him that one may think at first glance to be a physician's bag which is filled to bursting with his best medicine for whatever might plague the human species—books. It also contains a framed hand-drawn cartoon that had appeared in the San Francisco Chronicle the year before.

The cartoon had been drawn by a frequent customer of the shop showing the penguin-shaped proprietor sitting awkwardly on a stool telling stories to an attentive flock of books, pages open, and taking in his every word. Morgan Piff has a keen eye for character, as did Conrad Wolff. As their worlds were being torn asunder, each to immensely enjoy each other's company.

There was nothing noble about the wounds. One look at Grazia told him that she would be more of a hindrance than a Nurse Gibson. "Show this to the old woman," he told Francis as he sat the bag by his side.

It did not take long for Katie and Hatti's girl talk to be put aside as they were drawn into the two men's conversation. As was everyone within earshot, and what followed was the sound of laughter as rich as the ebb and flow and as pleasant as the babbling of a fresh spring brook.

XL

Alphonso knew his way around the financial district, not that he had ever had a bank account or any financial dealing there. If not for the watches which he repaired and delivered he might have been as much a stranger Huckleberry Freeman. The old buffalo soldier had never dared cross that line where wealthy white men dwelled. Francis, who had never been in this part of the city insisted on taking the lead, setting a pace that his shorter companion had trouble keeping up with. Twice Alphonso's directions were ignored as the Hungarian guided them mostly in circles, mostly to avoid army check points. The sergeant more concerned about someone—anyone—objecting to him being there.

Out of breath, Alphonso called a temporary halt to their quest. "Stop, my young friend, and allow this old man to catch his breath." Hands on his knees he wheezed than slowly straightened himself out. "We left the others with no plan between the three of us other than we need water. We have passed restaurants, bars, and several small grocery stores inquiring with none about whether or not they have any water." He raised his hands as if to question the sheer insanity of continuing without a plan in mind.

The street they were on was severely damaged, what businesses there had been either inaccessible or had already been looted. They could clearly hear the roar and crackle of the fires barely two blocks away.

"Stop. Enough is enough," the sarge said. This is a rich man's neighborhood. If anyone sees me poking my black nose where it doesn't belong their going to shoot and not bother to ask any questions. "If the soldiers see us coming out of any of these ruins with anything but our empty hands we will be shot." Moping his forehead with a dirty rag he turned his eyes back in the direction of the Presidio. "I was thinking that…"

"Yes…yes, this I know, but if we don't try all we will return with is our empty hands. Francis glanced frantically around them searching for something, anything. Look, there is a fine restaurant just over there. I can see from here that there are or were decanters of water on each table. They can't all be broken. The front of the building is gone, no one is there. You and Mr. Paluso keep watch while I go in and collect as many as I can find. Then back to Washington Square. What do you say? Yes." The hesitation in his voice was evident.

"And over there…" The sarge pointed towards the entryway to a bank that somehow remained intact where four soldiers stood guard over the bank and the neighborhood. The three men's gestures in the middle of the street were being noticed.

"There are many people, thirsty refugees, who will look upon us with jealous eyes and greedy gullets when we march back here with just enough water for our small lot. No, my friend, we must bring back enough water for all -at least a small sip for each man, woman, and child." Beseeched the young Hungarian activist.

"But how?" *This guy is exasperating,* Alphonso thought.

"Come, we had best move before those soldiers want to know what the hell we are doing here." This time the sarge made it sound as if it were an order. They turned around, away from the soldiers, then turned right at the first intersection. More soldiers could be seen both ahead and behind, turning east again at the next corner, from there the fire could be seen as it consumed buildings five and six stories tall.

"But how," Alphonso queried again?

Francis hadn't a clue.

The sarge nodded towards an alley hidden behind a wall of rubble from a collapsed office building. There stood an abandoned fire department pump wagon. A hose connecting it to a fire hydrant, the underground plumbing shattered leaving most every hydrant in the city useless.

"We are going to commandeer a fire truck," he announced smugly.

It just might work, Alphonso thought. "But how," he said, more a statement than a question.

"The wagon is too heavy. How are we going to move it?" Francis answered as he peered back from the alley towards the last place, they had seen any soldiers. There were soldiers, but none seemed interested in them. He then pushed against the wagon to test its weight. The large wooden cistern built into the wagon could hold 500 gallons. He did a quick calculation;

he had always excelled in math back in his school days. *Four thousand one hundred and seventy-six pounds plus the weight of the wagon,* he thought, the realization slacking his confidence. A sharp flush of pain in his burned hand sucking it dry as he fell silent, his look of defeat obvious.

The sarge knew that look having seen it on one too many new recruit's faces. He tested the wagon which felt and sounded as if it were full to the brim. The pump wagon was horse-drawn—there was no way they were going to be able to move it without some horses.

A lone fireman stepped out of an open doorway where he had been relieving himself. "You there," he demanded," what are you doing there?"

"Stealing your fine wagon," Alphonso said, his charm a distraction to the truth.

"If you can harness it to your strong shoulders and pull it up the hill you can have it. It's of no further use to me."

It didn't take but a moments conversation for the three men to determine that the fireman meant what he had said. Francis wanted the wagon but lacked the means to take it. The fireman had come back for tools, the fire department officially abandoned it when it was found that there were no hydrants for the pump wagon to draw water from. "I meant what I said", the fireman said. "The army confiscated the horses. If you can find a dozen stout men to wheel it out of here, you can have it…but I'll caution you that the army most likely will shoot you for trying."

The men pondered their options, few that there were.

"Can you give us twenty minutes. Your presence will be of value should the army nose around asking too many questions. I'll be back with all the help we'll need."

The fireman nodded knowing that trying to stop the fires was a feudal effort. A few more minutes wouldn't make a big difference.

Alphonso took off at a run towards Washington Square. He slowed to a fast walk before reaching the end of the block. Finally making it back to Washington Square winded, sweat-soaked, with a painful stitch in his side.

Katie greeted him with concern in her eyes with a hand on his. "Alphonso, are you, all right?" He looked ashen, his normal paler white-washed by his pushing himself too hard.

"I'll be…I'll…I just need to sit for a moment."

He did, with nothing more than labored breathing coming from him for a short silent eternity.

Leah looked anxiously back and forth from one adult to another. "No water? Where is Mr. Francis?"

"Hush child, allow Alphonso to catch his breath." Katie's words were soft and kindly spoken.

Morgan Piff and Conrad Wolff stopped their conversation interested in Alphonso's response. Conrad cupped a hand to his ear to hear better. As Alphonso began to speak, he stepped closer as Alphonso's voice was lowered to little better than a whisper so curious neighbors couldn't overhear.

"We found a horse-drawn water-wagon which the fire department has abandoned because all of the fire hydrants are broken. There are no horses. The good news is that it operates on a hand-pump. There may be as much as two or three hundred gallons remaining in it. If we can raise enough volunteers, we might tote it here." He paused to catch his breath again.

A horse soldier rode close by, stopping for a moment, to near for comfort.

"If the soldiers see us, they are more likely to shoot," Alphonso continued. Katie dabbed at his forehead with a dry cloth, wishing she a wet one to cool his brow. "As soon as the army finds out about the water, they will confiscate it for themselves." Alphonso's shoulders briefly rose up and down as he looked at the faces of his extended family.

Everyone remained silent, there being no question that the challenge was both large and difficult.

The answer came from the least likely amongst them—Hatti. "The church…"

"But of course, the Mother Church…" Conrad said, his voice carrying both enthusiasm and curiosity. "If the church were to retrieve the wagon most likely the army wouldn't interfere." He looked admiringly at Hatti, a look she was not used to. "Brilliant!"

"It can't be that easy?" Alphonso said.

"Come with me, and please don't drag your feet, we haven't a moment to waste." Adolphus declared as he placed his cane in front of him as he waddled off towards the steps to St. Peter and Paul's. "The Archbishop and I are old friends." Time to call in a favor or two.

Alphonso was steadily finding that age and lack of sleep along with the strenuous drama of the day were taking their toll; Conrad's lumbering gait easy compared to his recent trek with Francis.

—

The fireman looked at his watch saying that he wished them well, but he was needed back on the fire-line—though the San Francisco Fire Department was far behind in a losing battle.

Francis paced nervously as he fretted that their miracle wagon would never leave the alley. The fire had crossed into the next block, the army abandoning what soon would burn, the efforts of the San Francisco Fire Department's finest fighting a hopeless battle on the eastern side of what was becoming a firestorm that would soon envelope the entire financial district.

Shouting from the far end of the connecting alley Alphonso could barely be heard. "Sorry we took so long; we've been trying to find an easier way to get the wagon to the church."

"Church?" Francis wasn't sure what a church had to do with moving the wagon. The thought of the church becoming involved rankled his indignation. He did not believe in God, religion under any…however,…suddenly the church became elevated in his eyes. *You sly old dog,* Francis thought as he falsely greeted a catholic priest, several Salesian Brothers, two deacons, three lay ministers and a hand full of broad- shouldered church members willing to lend a hand. Try as they might they did not have enough brawn to move the wagon and its valuable water back to where it was needed at Washington Square. Francis tried to hide his smirk as he observed that they brought with them so many church customs and regalia he thought that if they mounted a proper throne on top the Pope himself would be pleased for the ride. He had to remind himself that these were superstition based, obedient, blind to a myth Catholics, not the *Wobblies,* the unskilled workers, *The International Workers of the World* made efforts to organize. His oratory skills had little effect here against the commanding presence of these men of the cloth. He tried, his voice falling just as short as the Catholics whose faith could not move the wagon one inch. On one hand, he could imagine himself being carried on the shoulders of the workers, a hero bringing life-saving water. On the other hand, he could just as easy see himself slinking out of town with nothing more than his injured hand and pride to show for his efforts.

The sarge had a different perspective. He saw himself standing alone as the good catholic eyes reacted with surprise at his presence. In the pecking order of their prejudices how far above the Chinese did they place him. In San Francisco there had not been much of an attempt to keep black folks in their place, away from good catholic white folks, because the Chinese were always nipping at their dark sides. And frankly, there just hadn't been that many black folks who had wanted to settle here. He had seen that look before and more than once had had to stand tall. Straightening his shoulders, he gestured towards Francis, who had now climbed atop the water wagon.

Regardless of his race Sergeant Freeman, in his sergeant's uniform, represented authority, and Francis despised authority, in particular the military and police. The almighty church was the authority here and he begrudgingly had to admit to himself that he would have to bend his revolutionary fervor to the winds that prevailed. He leaned down to hear what the black crusty old sergeant had to say.

"The fire will incinerate everything from here to the waterfront before you can move this dad-blasted wagon. There is too much rubble in the streets and no reasonable route open. If the fire department can't move it what the hell do you think you are going to be able to do?"

Francis looked around. *The sarge was right, they were not going nowhere, no-how, no way.*

Alphonso, hands on his hips, sweat on his brow, sucking in breath having run most of the way, looked at the sarge and nodded. "What now?"

"As long as you have these helping hands, I need to move this fire hose to somewhere where it might be useful." The fireman said frustrated at the delay.

Pushing his short legs, the best he could, Conrad Wolff finally caught up just in time to hear the sarge discretely take command. Next to him stood Father Gerhard Martin, a Salesian

Brother* who frequently visited Wolf's bookstore.

"Good to see that you are well my friend."

"Time will tell," answered Conrad as he continued to listen to the retired black sergeant.

"The books, I hope that God has blessed and protected…"

Conrad waved a finger to shush the priest as he tried to make sense of what was being said.

Father Martin took no offense and listened as well.

To his own surprise, Sergeant Freeman realized that he had a small but interested audience that seemed to be agreeing with what he had to say. "So, you see, trying to move the wagon is a damned waste of time; the fire is right over there." He pointed. "What needs to be done is to move the water, not the wagon, but as you can see there is not enough hose to reach

---

*The Salesians of Don Bosco (SDB), formally known as the Society of Saint Francis de Sales (Latin: Societas Sancti Francisci Salesii), is a religious congregation men in the Catholic Church founded in the late 19th century by Italian priest Saint John Bosco to help poor children during the Industrial Revolution and named after Saint Frances de Sales 17th-century bishop of Geneva.

The Salesians' charter describes the society's mission as "the Christian perfection of its associates obtained by the exercise of spiritual and corporal works of charity towards the young, especially the poor, and the education of boys to the priesthood". Its associated women's institute is the Salesian Sisters of Don Bosco while the lay movement is the Association of Salesian Cooperators. Their western headquarters is in San Francisco and their church is the Church of St. Peter and Paul's.

from here to Washington Square where the water is needed." He scanned the crowd for any uniforms knowing that the United States Army would not appreciate an old Buffalo Soldier speaking against their purpose in the field. "The water must be made available to the people, not for the private use of the soldiers who for the moment seem more interested in protecting buildings than lives."

A murmuring wave of agreement drew more members of the clergy and volunteers to the old soldier's pulpit.

"We can spread out and find more hose, someone shouted."

The fireman stepped next to Sergeant Freeman. "What hose there is in being used by the fire department to protect the financial district. The water mains are broken through-out the city rendering the hoses useless until the navy brings in some fireboats from Mare Island."

"Then we'll go to the financial district and borrow the hose needed." The same voice.

The crowd began to turn.

"There is no way in hell, sorry Father, they will let you have it." The fireman argued, seeing that it might already be too late to prevent the well-intended crowd from marching towards the financial district on what he knew was most likely a useless mission.

Father Martin stepped forward. "There is another way."

Conrad Wolff rapped his cane against the side of the water-wagon to gain everyone's attention. His voice, a bit too high to carry well.

"Listen to the man" Francis shouted.

The crowd stopped, giving their full attention to Father Martin.

They couldn't move the wagon to where the water was needed. The hose was not long enough to reach Washington Square, nor could they acquire any additional hose, at least in a reasonable amount of time. What hose they had could reach Greenwich Street which was the next street over and uphill from the church.

The Salesian Brothers led by Brother Martin returned to the church to find as many empty barrels as they could that were stored in and near the church. Enough volunteers were to be found to roll the empty barrels up to Greenwich where the fireman along with the rest of the volunteers were able to lay the hose. The first two barrels rolled and shattered; their weight too great to manage on the hill. Finally, sarge found enough rope to tether the barrels to allow four men to safely restrain the water-laden barrels as they were rolled to the back of the church where Brother Martin had opened a door to secure them inside. There were seventeen full barrels, not a great amount but rationed it would last through the day if the army did not confiscate them.

Proud of their accomplishment Father Martin uncapped one of the barrels prepared to offer a ladle of cool refreshment to the parched throats of those who had labored and sweated to bring the water into the sanctuary of the church.

Father Martin spit it out, almost swearing inside the sacred walls. With the smoke and the urgency of the moment no one had noticed that the water had smelled differently. The wagon had been filled with sea water that had been pumped from the bay. The wagon had but four pouches filled with drinkable water.

No one noticed that the sarge had disappeared.

XLI

Alphonso and Francis had worked at the top of the hill never entering the basement of the church. When the last barrel was drained from the water-wagon they returned to the camp with grins as wide as two schoolboys who had just purloined a fresh apple pie from a windowsill, with them they brought four plump leather water pouches that the firemen had loaded aboard the wagon for their own use. All were thirsty taking deep draws from the pouches as they were passed around.

Having satisfied her own needs Leah tried to give her kitten some water but the skinny cat would have nothing to do with it. The kitten barely off her mother's milk didn't know water. Leah dipped her finger into some water touching it to the kitten's mouth—the kitten found it wet, touching its tiny tongue to the wetness but nothing encouraged it to drink. "Hatti, Purplepaws won't drink. What am I to do?" Leah beseeched her newfound friend, who was close to Leah's mother's age had she lived.

Hatti was beginning to see herself in the role of an older sister. She had never had a cat or a pet of any kind—except for two lovebirds she had kept in a bird cage when she had been fourteen. They had died of neglect. She felt Leah's concern and turned her eyes to Katie hoping the older woman would have an answer before Leah burst into tears.

"Fear not, little one, I have heard of your plight and have brought you some milk for your wee whiskered friend." The voice that came from behind them had a rich Scottish accent each word wrapped with warmth and a taste of his Scottish homeland. He introduced himself as Graham, a waiter from the Ristorante Fior d'Italiano which was a stone's throw from St. Peters and Paul Church. Like the church the ristorante had survived the earthquake with little damage except to windows, crockery, and glassware. Of course, The Fior d'Italiano, was not open. With a broad smile the waiter poured some milk into a small porcelain bowl which he pulled from an apron pocket. The small container of milk he placed on the ground next to Leah. He then smiled, bowed graciously to the ladies as he then turned towards the stairs leading up to the main doors of the St. Peter and Paul's Church where a Priest smiled, giving a small wave back.

—

At first Grazia, having been evicted by the soldiers from her small patch of grass next to the park at Washington Square, was somewhat bewildered. Her husband had abandoned her. *Abandoned? Why?* She beseeched God not so quietly in her mind. *I'm an old woman with nothing more than an old house dress and a valise with God knows what in it.* She stopped, an all-knowing expression coming to her face, as if with the next thought God might find her an accomplice. *The valise, it's stolen!* She looked around, expecting a squad of soldiers to suddenly surround her with gleaming bayonets while someone pointed at her shouting "thief—thief!"

She set it down and started to walk away.

"Excuse me, Ma'am," a policeman, his uniform scorched and soiled, a gauze bandage wrapped around his left hand and wrist, stepped in front of her. His presence sent an ice-cold shiver straight through the marrow of her bones.

He held out the valise. "I wouldn't be leaving this anywhere unattended; odds are it won't be there when you return, Ma'am."

You must be mistaken, that isn't mine. Is what she wanted to say. "Oh, ah, thank you. I'll be more careful."

She said, taking the valise, looking as guilty as if she had just stolen it from the officer. Four soldiers appeared, seemingly headed in her direction. She froze in fear, the stress so great it caused her to flatulate—loud and aromatic.

Revolted, the officer bid her good day.

Mortified, Grazia turned towards the last spot she had seen her husband and the others. Certain that dozens of people were all staring at her she hiked her dress and marched to where Alphonso stood drinking from a leather water pouch.

The soldiers passed by without a glance in her direction. They did pause for just a moment as they observed Alphonso and his coterie drinking from the leather water pouches; they too were thirsty. The sight of the water reminding them of how dry their own throats were. A private whispered "That ain't right. I say we confiscate them as stolen goods."

Another answered back. "Not here—the church—the priests

are watching." He tried to wet his chapped lips with his tongue as they continued their patrol around and behind the church building.

XLII

The sun set on what obviously was a catastrophic disaster for the city of San Francisco. The fires were out of control devastating whole blocks at a time, the fire department helpless in their paths. It seemed as if the entire population were on the move, most hopeless, carrying with them what little they could rescue before the fire's wrath. In many cases people were more afraid of the military than the monstrous firestorm that consumed everything they had accumulated in life. The plume of obsidian smoke that hung over them was darker than black braided coal with ominous tendrils of orange, crimson, white, hellish red, flickers of white, and a blue that only comes from a fire so hot the devil himself will turn away. Skeletons of steel stood as defeated guardians wilting before this mighty storm—the flames being sucked up the steep hills. The cable car tracks had melted away as had the vision that only twelve hours before had blessed this once beautiful city by the bay. This was the end of the first day and no one knew how long the fires would burn; their fear, until nothing is left.

Where to go? Four hundred thousand people were all asking the same question. *Where to go?* Many made for the ferry boats that would take them across to Oakland and other cities across the bay that had been damaged by the quake but not afire. Fort Mason and the Presidio drew throngs of refugees, as did the great expanse of Golden Gate Park. Throughout the city there were pockets of people, some surrounded by flame. They were scared, in shock, tired, hungry, thirsty, in some cases shivering as they watched the flames dance, its fury mirrored in the broiling smoke that stole not just the stars but the night from the sky.

The refugees were destitute with little to no help available from the city, the army, or amongst themselves.

"It's going to be a long night," observed Adolphus, a long night indeed. There is a night breeze. It blows hot. You can see the smoke as it snakes around and over Russian Hill. It should keep the fires away at least until morning when the wind can be as flighty as a fifteen-year-old girl." He smiled at ten-year old Leah. "Which isn't always a bad thing."

Morgan Piff continued the thought. "You are suggesting that we should stay put—stay here for the time being?"

"Until the momentum of events tells us otherwise." Adolphus answered back. "There is some shelter provided by the church. Its walls provide a barrier between us and the rest of our fellow citizens; at least that's something." The wall reflected the towering flames that burned not that far away. They all eyed the mass of people crowded onto the street and sidewalks around them. The Park, empty now, except for the soldiers who had orders to keep the people away from its comfort and open space.

No one except Alphonso took note of Grazia's unwelcomed rejoining of their little group.

"I agree, we should stay here, at least until morning." Katie said. "We have water, but nothing to eat."

Grazia almost smiled, there was still a small amount of food in the valise. *She had something they needed, perhaps that would be her leverage when and if the opportunity arose.*

With a few nods it was agreed. They would stay.

XLIII

Marooned in the Barbary Coast, Dimitri Paleologos, a ship's carpenter by trade, had been enjoying his extended layover in Frisco until he had been rudely awakened by the quake which had literally thrown him off his lumpy floor mattress. The flophouse occupying the third floor above a barbary saloon, the second a crib for prostitution of the lowest sort. The room was small, the bathroom shared with four other rooms on the same floor, the bedding minimal with mattresses or mats on the floor, or canvas sheets stretched between two horizontal beams creating a series of hammock like beds. The hammocks preferred by those who came early or strong enough to throw the current occupant out.

The buildings rock and roll woke the other nineteen wayward souls who had paid their ten cents for a bed. Dimitri's thump caused those in the whorehouse on the floor below to think the building was coming down on their beds. Hangover, or not, he barely had time to pull on his boots before an aftershock brought part of the ceiling down around them.

He breakfasted on a wedge of cheese wrapped in old newspaper he had in a pocket then spent the morning hanging around bars and saloons; those whose walls and roofs still stood, which stayed open until the army arrived. By then the fires had emptied the streets of all but the most alcohol numbed. He hadn't drunk that much—so he thought—as much as he had entertained. That was until the fires became dangerous and he realized that the whole city was in trouble.

He had thought about staying in America, the land of opportunity. So far, he hadn't seen much more than the city's waterfront and the squaller of the Barbary. He could read and write, but mostly in Greek. Was there opportunity here, for him?

By late afternoon he found himself at Washington Square where there were many refugees, mostly German, Irish, and Italian all seemingly content to bunch like sheep waiting for someone to herd them elsewhere. That was fine by him, from where he stood nowhere seemed much safer than right where he stood now. He found a place where he would not be stepped on to take a nap where there was some soft grass next to a church's wall.

He woke, cobwebs cluttering his mind, hungry, and thirsty, eyeing a leather water pouch that lay not three feet from his head. He started to reach for it until a woman's shoe lightly crunched down on his fingers which he quickly withdrew.

Katie looked down on the portending water thief who looked more like a beached hairy walrus than a human being. His blue eyes blinked up at her as if that alone would suffice as an apology.

Katie took a second look at this ne'er-do-well. San Francisco had always had its share of castaways, men who pass through life without a contribution, vision blurred through the murky glass of a whiskey bottle, fouling the very air around them. This one had that look and the smell, but there was something she saw in his unusual blue eyes—robin's eggs marred with thin bloodshot spider-web red veins. Deep within she could see that this man had a soul…that intrigued her despite the hairy smelly beast he was. His eyes seemed to twinkle at her slight smile as she turned back to the group's conversation.

That they should stay at Washington Square seemed to be the consensus. She found no fault in that. Wondering in search for a place to plop their weary bones seemed to be an exercise in futility. Her eyes went from each member of the gathering to another as she sought to determine the value of each. What were their strengths and weaknesses? Why had God or luck brought them together? How had this odd group of individuals come together in the first place? If her lot was to be cast together with them, she needed to know more. Her eyes explored Washington Square studying the hundreds of refugees, knowing that they all had one thing in common—after the fires had burned its last there was going to be very few resources for so many in need of so much.

She brought her thoughts back: *first to Alphonso, realizing that in less than a day's time she was developing an affection for the man. He had a good mind, was willing to take a risk, and appeared to be a man who would do almost anything to provide for those around him. Grazia, his wife—a divider—and mean-spirited at that. Morton Piff was a man everyone liked, never-the-less, because of his age and infirmities, a burden on the group. Mr. Andrews, full of wisdom and mirth, would struggle with most physical tasks, however he appeared to be well-connected and might prove to be their most valuable resource. Francis DeGeorgie, their anarchist, chaser of windmills, champion of the people even if it meant sacrificing the individual. Loyal to the cause which is his excuse for not being loyal to anyone else. A selfish, would-be saint. He did get us the water; on the other hand, she had been told it had been the old negro soldier who had done that. Then there's Hatti, beautiful Hatti whose smile can move mountains or bring men to war. She has the unusual ability to manipulate powerful men. Yes, she can definitely contribute. She will also attract predators, dangerous to her for their evil desires and to the rest of us because we're in the way. Little Leah, ten years of age and as innocent as her little kitten. A wonderful burden on the group's survival and just like Morton Piff someone the group will have to provide for. As for herself,* Katie thought, *I guess that I am the mother hen. All in all, our little group's chances for survival aren't very aspiring.*

She hid her smile behind her chagrin.

She closed her eyes and let out a sigh. *What we need is a strong man.* When she opened them, she saw Alphonso, small in frame and long in courage, Morgan in his wheelchair, and the wise and comical penguin shaped Adolphus. Francis who studied his wounded hand paying little attention to the decisions they were trying to make. Like it or not, these were her newly adopted family. She looked around one last time for the old buffalo soldier who was not to be found.

"For how long," Hatti asked? "Staying here, I mean." It had not dawned on her until now that there was no warm room with a hot bath and room service waiting. She looked at her dress which now showed some of the stress from their first day. She had not another, and the thought of what she might look like in a week, or a month, which shook her to the core. "We are all going to be camping out for some time, I fear. Are we to move from place to place, follow the masses, be forced by the army into some place we don't want to be, or stay here?"

"The young woman has a valid point," Adolphus pondered aloud with an edge to authority. "I pray that God, in His infinite wisdom, will spare His church, leaving it a sanctuary in what will soon be a great a terrible wasteland. If we go elsewhere more than likely we will become wards of the army." He shook his head in such a way that caused everyone else to do the same. "If we choose to stay in this spot," he tapped his walking stick for emphasis, "near the very doors to the Mother Church, I think we will fair far better."

Everyone but Francis agreed.

XLIV

Sergeant Freeman could neither stay nor go; San Francisco was not his home. It was a place where he waited for time to pass, for old bones to grow brittle, for memories to fade, to die. There had been times when he had wished that he had gone the way of a soldier's death. This morning, as the foul smells of human waste wafted around him offending his sense of the world, he had wondered if it was time to just lay down next to the graves of his old buffalo soldiers and simply fade away. Now he did not know what he wanted; this day had not turned out even slightly what he had expected it to be. The city of San Francisco was dying all around him, but he was alive—old and tired—but damned if he did not now want to see what would be left; to see, at the end of the day, if there was any hope left.

San Francisco did not want his old black ass. And with that he agreed, he did not want to be here. He had nowhere else to go but why should he. He had risen from slavery, fought to civilize the west, and labored to protect the majestic beauty of its new amazing national parks. With these things he could hold his head high with no shame on his shoulders or on his soul for being brought into this world different from the white men that somehow managed to rule the earth.

He looked back at Washington Square where he could still see his new friends; friends, well they did not spit in his face as others had. He chuckled to himself, deep down where he could feel it lighten his load, ease his heart, and helped him feel a day or two younger. "Why the hell not?" He muttered to himself as he squared his shoulders, looked about him to see if anyone cared, and crossed the street.

XLV

The decision made; Conrad smiled broadly. "Have I mentioned that the Archbishop and I are old friends?" His smile suggested that their privileged relationship might benefit them while they encamped on church grounds.

"I have a suggestion," a heavily accented voice said from behind them." The walrus sat up and was grooming his beard of crumbs and bits and pieces of nature's debris with his fingers as he addressed whom he thought must be to their newly anointed leader. The oddly shaped man's appearance amused him greatly.

Conrad wasn't sure if they should allow this raggedy stranger to meddle in their affairs.

Francis was the one who opened their door a crack. "And who are you, sir?"

"No one important, just a ship's carpenter shipwrecked just like you."

"Well, what is it you have to say?" Conrad changed his tone just enough to let the carpenter know that despite his looks or smell, he was intrigued.

"If you plan on staying here tonight, perhaps a day or two, you will need to build yourselves a shelter." He looked up testing the hot wind with a dirty finger he wetted with his tongue. The demon fire might have other plans.

"Why? Where and how are we to build a shelter?" Alphonso queried. It was a legitimate question.

"As we speak more people are crowding into this space. There is already not enough room." He shrugged his shoulders, "As long as the fires burn it will only get worse. "By building a shelter we will mark our territory. That, and if built of the right materials it might protect us from the hot ashes that now fall around us. Ahhh, if it were only snow." He mused as he reached out and caught a feather of ash which disintegrated with his touch.

The sarge, who had quietly rejoined the group heard the word us that the carpenter had used. For the moment he kept silent.

Conrad immediately saw the wisdom in building a shelter. Not just to protect them from the elements, but also to mark their territory—especially since they had a prime spot. They had the sturdy wall of the church on their backside which connected to the two sets of stairs that led into the church. The sheer numbers of the refugees already pushed against them. A young couple with a baby sat dead-center in the corner which meant adding more dependent souls to their troupe or evicting them—of which they had no right, and if they tried that they very well might be evicted themselves.

Without further comment, and to Morgan Piff's surprise, Conrad spun Piff's wheelchair around wheeling it to a spot so close to the young couple he practically ran them over.

No invitation offered or needed, the Walrus got up and lumbered over to where Conrad stood and sat next to the wheelchair, his bulk blocking any remaining view the young couple had. The mere presence of the large Greek seaman and the constant jabbering of the old man was all it took for the young couple to seek more pleasant surroundings.

The Walrus's blue eyes gleamed with the success his few words and brought him. He patted the ground between them. "This is where we need to build our shelter."

Katie giggled aloud at the Walrus's degree of self-awareness. *Beneath all that dirt and wild hair lurks a sharp mind,* she thought as she offered him a drink from the leather water pouch.

"How are we to build a shelter?" Grazia asked. These were the first words she had spoken since rejoining the group. She spat out the question as if daring anyone to defy her. "We have no tools, and nothing to build with. I doubt the Mother Church would appreciate anyone marking its pristine walls with nails and tar paper."

"Hush woman, if you haven't anything positive to contribute than keep your mouth shut." Alphonso snapped.

Grazia, who had never been spoken to by her husband in this manner clamped her mouth shut for fear that lightening might strike her if she didn't.

Katie' s respect for Alphonso shot up another degree.

There was no doubt in Francis's mind that the group was committing to an extended stay if the changing winds did not change their plans. Without contributing his thoughts, he wondered off, in search of windmills or a secret mission of his own making.

"I see," puzzled Conrad as he slowly paced off the distance to where Grazia sat. "A little larger would be nice, but as the lady said we have our limitations." He touched a finger to his chin as he thought for a moment as he spoke. He turned back to Walrus. "I hope you won't take me for being rude young man, you are aware that you are in dire need of a hot bath, a bar of lye soap, and some grooming. That being said," he turned to each member of their family with a mischievous glint to his eyes, suggesting they would all be needing the same soon. "I dare say that we could all use a bit of grooming as it may be some time before much else becomes available. He turned his attention back to the walrus. "Allow me to introduce myself, I am Conrad Wolff, currently an unemployed haberdasher of books and such. And you, Sir?"

"Dimitri Paleologos, former senior ship's carpenter, for the Puget Sound Navigation Company. I keep leaky ships afloat. I've been at sea for seven months. I thought it time to test my sea-legs out on steady land. I'm afraid my ship has sailed without me taking the wages I'm due with the tide."

"Your English is good, though your accent does offer a small challenge. Are you an educated man, able to read and write?"

"I am. Why, do you know Greek? Where I come from, we often speak in Cappadocian. Do you know Cappadocian?"

"No." With that he turned the conversation back to the others. "Katie, Hattie, Morgan, Alphonso, judging on the size of the man he may very well eat as much as the lot of us all together, but I'll wager his skills may prove to be as valuable as gold.

Everyone nodded.

"Will you join us Mr. Paleologos?" Katie asked.

"Delighted, lovely lady," the big Greek answered. "Please call me Dimitri. When someone asks for Mr. Paleologos, I look around for my papa—may God bless his soul."

—

Francis De Georgie was absent for the vote to adopt Dimitri. He doubted the fires would leave the park unscathed. The Financial District, Chinatown, and parts of Little Italy all burned visibly nearby. He wandered the square taking in the sights and sounds, the trepidations of the refugees and the soldiers alike. The Park was filled with little room to spare as more refugees squeezed in each wanting their little space where they could wait out the night, for the soldiers to order them to safer grounds wherever that might be.

He stopped for a moment and eavesdropped on two soldiers talking about the fires approaching Nob Hill. Nob Hill held many of the grandiose mansions of the robber barons of the gold rush era. The thought of those mansions burning, the mighty bourgeoise left as homeless as a street sweeper excited his interest—almost to the point he wished he had a match that he could take to the mansions to start the revolution. The soldier's greatest fear was that once the fires crowned on Nob Hill, the unpredictable shifting wind might bring the firestorm back towards Washington Square, then they would be trapped with fire on three sides with a tricky evacuation route to the bay.

No one knew how many refugees the park could hold. Francis estimated a thousand, perhaps more. The soldiers expected orders to close the park to any additional refugees at any moment. Those that were there had no food other than what they had personally brought. No water. So far, the church had made no real attempt to distribute the water he, Alphonso, and the black sergeant had found. No blankets, though the fires kept the night air strangely warm. No latrines or sanitary facilities. Francis had seen what had happened when a hundred thousand protesting workers had no place to go other than the streets of St. Petersburg, Russia. When there was no wood for cooking fires or to build shelters. He knew that once they found the materials and began to build others would want to do the same.

Francis eased over for a chat when he saw the waiter who had brought Leah's kitten her milk standing with two other waiters in front of the Ristorante Fior d'Italiano. "I doubt there will be any looting, there are too many soldiers with trigger fingers about." He said to the one he recognized. "I want to thank you for the milk you brought for the little girl's kitten."

"One of the brothers asked if we had some to spare, who am I to turn down a request from the church?"

Francis had to bite his tongue not to lash out about how religion had kept the masses impoverished and uneducated around the world.

"Just some broken windows," the waiter answered, "the damage doesn't look too bad, but the truth is that the floor in the kitchen has dropped a full foot, the kitchen itself will take a long time to repair. The glassware and china are a total loss."

A tall thin waiter with pronounced dark black ink blots beneath his eyes joined the conversation. "It's the damn soldiers, they'll shoot yah if you reach for a crumb a damned seagull dropped, but damned if they won't take what they want without a care for who it might belong to.

These here blue suits haven't been fed since they first arrived this morning. If the army don't take care of their own soon, sure as this city's ah burning, the soldiers will be coming here looking."

"If you can't stop them, then why are you here?" Francis asked.

"That's a good question, son. I'll have to ponder on that." The tall waiter took a long-stemmed pipe out of an apron pocket. He then set his gaze out over the bowl, never lighting it. "Yes, Sir, something to ponder on."

"What happens when the fires reach here," Francis asked? "I mean, the people—there are so many—where do we go from here?"

"That depends upon the wind. If the fires come at us from the west or south, we'll have no choice but to flee to the waterfront and hope we have time to get to Fort Mason." The first waiter said as his eyes searched the reflections beneath the broiling smoke that denied the sky."

"Swim," the tall waiter said with his teeth clinched tightly on the pipe stem. "There ain't no way we can get this many people, moms, and kids, all the way to Mason. Those that can swim, they're the ones who might have a chance."

An explosion fueled a fiery display that rose hundreds of feet above the financial district.

"Those that can't, well…" Putting his pipe back in his pocket he took one last look at the restaurant. "Hell, and damnations, I've done my pondering, and have decided to take my leave and make my way towards Golden Gate Park. You coming, Jack?" The thin man took a tobacco pouch out of the same pocket pulling a pinch before he saw that he had already put his pipe away. Putting the pinch of tobacco back in the pouch he put it away then pulled his pipe back out. "Of all the cock-eyed, lame-brained fools…"

Jack didn't quite make out what the man said and just looked at him curiously.

That was the first time Francis had heard the waiter's name—Jack."

After a moment Jack answered. "No, you go ahead. I might join you later. There's no view from the park, and I don't want to miss the show. Take some of this morning's bread with you." He then turned to Francis. "Care to take some bread back for your people? I'll wrap you up some in a flour sack."

XLVI

The fires in the Financial District seemed to grow exponentially. The fire, hungry for fuel, engulfed whole buildings, as the flames roared skyward, the heat creating its own vortex—the hot wind blowing ash, smoke, and sparks west. As glowing embers and lung-choking smoke reached Washington Square the people began to stir like cattle before an approaching thunderstorm.

The winds blew in opposite directions. Since the first break of dawn, the earthquake, the fires consumed incredible acreage. What was once the Financial District, the hotels, shopping, and theater districts, Chinatown all burned. From just west of East Street, to Powell, north to Washington Street; and south of Market from the Ferry Building to as far south as Townsend Street, onwards to Twelfth Street on the west, the Civic Center from Eddy Street and Golden Gate Avenue west as far out as Octavia Street to south of Market.

A miracle, and several navy ships, saved most of the wharves allowing for access to the ferries, otherwise the firestorm would have taken more human lives.

A new wave of refugees surged into the park taking those there to move with them. Military control of the center of the fenced Square gave way as the mass of refugees grew beyond their control. You could sense their fear of a rout from the approaching firestorm that seemed much closer than it was. They had no orders. Only people not on the move were the dead.

Grazia rose to her feet afraid of being trampled as a sea of feet threatened. The scrape…scrape…scrapping sound of hundreds of trucks, odd pieces of luggage, and personal belongings mixed with the sound of voices babbling in various tongues, soldiers shouting, the roar of the firestorm itself became a cacophony that pressing on the eardrums testing the nerves of people who had already been through so much.

Francis forced his way through the throng until he reached the church's steps where he found Alphonso, Conrad, and the sarge in a heated discussion with the hairy walrus who had been slumbering nearby when he had taken leave. The space they had endeavored to save had quickly shrunk down to a space barely sufficient for two let alone the nine their family had grown to. To his surprise he learned that their debate was not about fleeing before the storm, but how to build a proper shelter.

The hierarchy of the church came out to the front steps to observe from the human tragedy and the dramatic fires that threatened what the earthquake had not brought down. St. Peter and Paul's Church itself was in danger and there was nothing they could do to stop what God willed. Prayers were spoken as they debated what seemed inevitable—abandoning the building that contained the holy church while saving what holy relics they could with the resources they had on hand.

"Father Yorke, might I have a word with you," asked

Conrad Wolff as he quick-stepped his penguin-like stride up the steps to where the priests had gathered.

"Ahhh, my dear Conrad, it is so good to see. I've been wanting to ask your opinion on an article I'm thinking of writing for *The Leader*. Perhaps another day when there are not so many other pressing matters."

"We'll save that conversation for a rainy day to be shared over a delightful brandy, a cigar, and a game of cards perhaps." Conrad chuckled.

"Pray God to grant us a gully-washer this day." They both looked up at the broiling smoke cloud that the Prince of Darkness had painted to blot out heaven.

"Are you thinking of leaving, Father?"

"That we are—as it appears, we might have no choice."

"That would be a shame. While the city may burn, I don't think God has it in mind to raise this grand building."

---

*Father Peter Christopher Yorke (15 August 1864 in Galway, Ireland–4 April 1925 in San Francisco, California) was an Irish-American Catholic priest and a noted Irish Republican and Labor activist in San Francisco. He was the youngest child of Gregory Yorke, a sea-captain, and his wife Brigid, née Kelly. He was pastor of St. Peter's in 1914. In San Francisco, he became the editor of The Monitor, the official newspaper of the Archdiocese of San Francisco. In 1901, he supported the workers in a Teamsters strike. In 1902, he founded and edited a local newspaper called The Leader.

"Oh?"

"I'm thinking that the winds will shift and this church and the public square in front will be spared—a sanctuary surrounded by a desert of gray ash and ruins. Hundreds will seek sanctuary here for weeks if not months to come. The heart-heavy question that remains will be who will provide for them?"

One after another the priests fell silent as they listened to Conrad Wolff's contention that all would not be lost while the firestorm roared to prove him wrong. The man's eloquent speech just right for the bully pulpit.

"Father, I have a proposition for you. As sure as the sun will rise tomorrow the park across the way, the grounds surrounding this beautiful edifice, will be filled with the faithful. The fires will have passed us by. It is not clear what the Army, or the city fathers will be capable of providing with the entire populace of this once great city left homeless with deep grumblings in their bellies. To the point, sir, we propose that the area of grass tucked next to the right side of the steps be set aside for providing sustenance for the masses as much as the church can provide. For the immediate future it should be roped off until a reasonable shelter can be built. My friends, my new extended family and I will stay on to serve these meager offerings to those in need."

Father Yorke turned to the Priests around him soliciting agreement. "As your first offerings are, shall we say—silver-tongued—your words have merit. How would you propose to build this shelter?"

Conrad hadn't thought that far ahead. After a moment of silence Francis spoke up as if he were the architect of their plan. "We intend to bring the water wagon, which we left up the hill, and bring it down and park it just to the right of the first step near where I am standing." He walked halfway up the steps to be heard easier."

The sarge had learned a few things about logistics during his years in the army and knew that the water wagon was not going to get anywhere near the church unless it was dismantled. Being that he was black, speaking up meant taking a risk, but there were too many women and children around that were going to be needing some help.

With the grace of an over-weight sow, Dimitri rose and stood next to Sergeant Freeman. Freeman spoke. "This here young fella has got the idea half-right. There needs to be a shelter built." He tapped on the wooden railing to the stairs with his cane, "Right here. We don't have the time to take that wagon apart, that and it won't provide enough material. A better idea is for the ship's carpenter to dismantle these steps to the church which will open enough space to build a small field kitchen. The wood salvaged from the steps can be used to build what will be needed."

It's a good start, thought Father Yorke. *He's right, if the church is still here in the morning there will be people in need. How we will meet that challenge only God knows.*

"You will do this?" He asked.

"I will," asserted Dimitri.

"It is said that our Lord Jesus Christ was a carpenter,"

Father Yorke said as he smiled down on this motley crew who had just convinced the priests to trust in God to save his church.

"Is not this the carpenter—a *tekton*, the son of Mary and brother of James and Judas and Simon? Mark 6:3." Conrad added.

"Then get to it. What help will you need?" Asked Father Conolly, Pastor to St. Peter and Paul's Church.

"And a fishing pole." Said another.

The tall Hungarian was clearly uncomfortable in his idea being voted down. His further discomfort was in partnering with the church. The young man, who was naturally pale, appeared anemic, tired, and obviously in pain from the still bleeding wound to his hand. Father Yorke suspected that his presence would be missed long before dawn.

"Father could we us the same men who helped us move the water wagon earlier." Alphonso asked.

"Father Yorke, who had not been present at the time turned the matter over to Father Michael Conolly. Yorke had no authority at St. Peter and Paul's other than the respect of his brother priests. That he had served as secretary to Archbishop Patrick W. Riordan lent him unspoken authority.

Yorke had started his day as the fire swept the South-of-Market district earlier in the morning, St. Mary's Hospital, at First and Bryant streets, was evacuated by the Sacramento

River steamer *Modoc* which took the patients across the bay to Oakland where those patients ultimately ended up at St. Anthony's his Parish church. Yorke had taken the ferry to San Francisco earlier in the afternoon to see for himself the threat to the church and to the Archdiocese itself. Now he needed to return to his own Parish.

Yorke took leave of the church taking a moment to share a few words with Conrad Wolff, who he had become friends with when he had been the Secretary to the Archbishop. "It's a sad day my friend. Your books, have you been able to save any of them?"

"Just a few. My suitcase is small, and I couldn't bear the weight. I suspect that all are ashes by now."

"Please come and see me when this is all over. The archbishop will be needing your expertise in helping to resurrect the Archdiocese's library."

"I would like that very much."

"Your carpenter—while he is truly one of God's creatures, he appears to have just crawled out of a foul shanghai tunnel beneath the Barbary. Can he be trusted?"

"I haven't known the man for an hour yet—time will tell. That and a good bath and a haircut will allow us to see more of his true character. For the moment," Conrad said, "his redolent reminiscent of a whaling ship's bilge, keeps us all an arms distance away."

Francis felt his anger rise as his sense of self-worth shrunk. He had opened the door but left with no role—no leadership position. He couldn't very well rally the masses against building a field kitchen. Nor did he want to attract the army's attention, he was a wanted man after-all. To his own surprise he turned to Conrad and the sarge. "A few minutes ago, I met one of the waiters at the restaurant on the far side of the park. He was the one who brought the little girl's kitten the milk. I'm sure that if asked we could borrow all of the pots and pans needed."

"That they will," Father Conolly practically promised. "I will go with you, lad." He nodded to the brothers gathered nearby. "We'll borrow what tables and chairs we can since they're being so generous."

"I'll pray for all of you, Padre Yorke said, and ask one of the Sisters to prepare a small bath from what water can be spared and some clean clothes for our carpenter here.

"The priests, do they always talk this way?" Francis asked Conrad.

"It's all the theater of the church, my boy…all theater. Mr. Paleologos, shall we begin?"

"Dimitri, please." The big Greek said with a pleasant smile that could almost be seen beneath his shaggy facial hairs.

"I have a pair of scissors here in this sewing kit. Their dull as a well-worn hammer, but I'll manage to carve some of that hair away." Grazia offered. She looked as if she relished the challenge. "Now you set right down here on that step, and we'll get to it."

The only one not laughing was Dimitri as she set to work, the scissors snapping and clipping more than cutting the hair away from his head and face.

"I'll see to the bath," said a nun who had been standing just within the door.

"And I'll pray for you, my son," Father Conolly said with humor etched to his words as he re-entered his church to organize the labor needed.

XLVI

Abe Ruef sat across from Mayor Schmitz, his suit pressed, bow tie perfectly aligned, mustache trimmed, face clean shaven, seeming unruffled, considering the state of the city.

A snifter of expensive brandy sat between them. There was but one glass. Ruef was the brains and the power behind a potent organized crime syndicate that ran the city. There were other men in the room, each listening to Ruef, few adding any thoughts of their own. They were the first to assemble, the committee chairs of the emergency committee to save San Francisco. The fires that devastated the city only seemed to feed Ruef's power and his influence over them.

Ruef sipped at his brandy, intently observing each man, as the mayor laid out Ruef's plan to salvage what would be left of the city. A committee of fifty men was to be formed…A committee of fifty men, Ruef looked over the list, most of whom he knew, many who were on his payroll, or could be if he used what he knew about each one, and he knew most of their transgressions. These men held the future, the destiny of San Francisco in their hands. Since when have fifty men, especially those who are wealthy and influential, agreed about anything that did not line their pockets. There were five who he would prefer to have nothing to do with. He could hardly stand to be in the same room with James Phelan, the former mayor of the city. Fifty outstanding and concerned citizens. It would look good to the press and to Washington from whose coffers huge dollars would be needed. If he controlled the committee chairs, it would be a win for him.

"Who authorized the dynamiting of Chinatown?" Ruef asked. He was now asking as the self-appointed chair for the committee to decide the future of Chinatown and its valuable real estate assets. He thought that the dynamiting that had spread the fires in Chinatown had been done by three police officers who were seasoned in doing his dirty work under the cover of a uniform and a badge. This time it had cost him twelve hundred dollars. Expensive, yes, but worth every penny. Ruef had been assured that his plan had worked, the policemen fleeing town all the richer for their trickery, while the incompetent use of black powder by the fire department and army finished the job.

Schmitz shifted uneasily in his chair. He suspected that the man across from him was responsible for the burning of Chinatown, but those words would never cross his lips. "I'm told the army," Schmitz answered. "General Funston informed me, that they lacked the authority and suggested it was set by members of our own police department. They also suggested it was the fire department. Fire Chief Sullivan is critically injured and could not have given the order. I doubt anyone in his command did so, the explosions were poorly placed, spreading the fires rather than hindering them."

"I've heard rumors that it was the Chinese themselves." Ruef added. "They have a long history with explosives, who is to say that the ignorant heathens didn't blow themselves up."

The mayor sat up. "Yes sir, that makes more sense than

anything else I've heard so far. Why if that were to be true, and the good people of San Francisco were to find out that the Chinese had started the fires, they would lynch every one of the slant-eyed devils from what few surviving light poles we have in the city."

"Yes, that would be most unfortunate," Ruef chuckled, "and I might add, could have considerable influence regarding Washington's decision on how much emergency money they might be disposed to send my way—our way."

Schmitz thought about that. "I see what you mean…" He held one hand out, finger gesturing, as if he were about to make a point."

Abe Ruef knew that Schmitz was posturing to save face. The other men in the room knew the same, that it was Ruef who would make the call, and the mayor would only rubber stamp it. "At first I wasn't so sure about your martial law decree, but now that it is in place, might I suggest that you issue orders to the army, and all relevant legal authorities, that the Chinese are to be arrested—no, I don't mean arrested…I mean taken into protective custody and escorted out of the city for their own safety and welfare."

Ruef paused for a moment, the room thick with smoke, either from tobacco smoke or the fires rapidly approaching outside.

The meeting was interrupted as an aide burst into the room announcing that the fires were now dangerously close, and everyone needed to evacuate once again.

XLVIII

Some of the tables and large cooking pots had been brought over from the restaurant across the square and dumped between the two wooden steps when Dimitri stepped out into the smoky night air. At first, no one recognized him. He was still as large as a walrus, albeit a domesticated one—his once hairy head shaven to a sheen, his body smartly wrapped in crimson choir robe, belted with a white cotton belt. Only his old soiled boots remained to tell the story of the filthy seaman that had only a short time ago disappeared through the church's portal.

Katie recognized him by the mirthful twinkle in his eyes.

With or without his hair Conrad Wolff instantly recognized him by his size and by the saw and the potato sack of tools the church had lent him.

Hatti was a woman who was used to being around weighty men, many of her gentlemen sponsors were corpulent from greed, pride, and easy living. Here was a man whose weight added to his character. She couldn't help but giggle—just a little—at the thought that the church and Grazia had magically tuned him into a Benedictine Monk.

Katie made note of that giggle.

"Mr. Peluso, I can use a good right hand if you're able?"

Dimitri said, eager to start.

"I know little of carpentry. Will the unskilled left hand of a novice craftsman do?"

"Let us begin then. More than one novice with steady hands, and willing eyes, has become a Four-square Mason.*

Truth was that Alphonso was exhausted—his attention spans short, missing what Dimitri had said about Freemasonry.

Conrad Wolff hadn't, he was a good catholic and had no stomach for an enemy of the church to be this close to its sanctuary.

Grazia, who had stayed behind for a moment of confession, returned taking a seat on the grass next to Leah, without saying a word.

Careful not to look directly at his wife, Alphonso could tell that she was proud of her grooming of the big Greek—although too vain to ever admit to such a thing.

---

*The Catholic Church first prohibited Catholics from membership in Masonic organizations and other secret societies in 1738. Since then, at least eleven popes have made pronouncements about the incompatibility of Catholic doctrines and Freemasonry. From 1738 until 1983, Catholics who publicly associated with, or publicly supported, Masonic organizations were censured with automatic excommunication. Since 1983, the prohibition on membership exists in a different form. Although there was some confusion about membership following the 1965 Second Vatican Council (Vatican II), the Church continues to prohibit membership in Freemasonry because it concluded that Masonic principles and rituals are irreconcilable with Catholic doctrines.

Their little piece of the park had been roped off with white braided rope provided by the church. Several soldiers watched from across the street smoking while talking about the absurdity of the encampment. Scuttlebutt had it that within the hour they would get orders to abandon the park forcibly removing all civilians from in front of the fires path.

The mass of humanity had already left Washington Square afraid of the fire storm that towered menacingly nearby. Its heat beating down like a merciless sun burning a hole in what should have been the cool dark of night.

Passing refugees gawked at the industrious monk busily dismantling one of the steps leading up to the church doors. Many wondered where the firemen were at, having seen few along their sad trek from their burning homes. More than a few inquired about water, few had even a drop, others unwilling to share. So far, the church had made no provisions to distribute the water now tucked away in its basement. The church had a long history of protecting its secrets, that the barrels were filled with undrinkable sea water, would remain unspoken as were many sins locked within the confessional.

Morgan Piff's blissful old man's snore matched the wraspzzz… wraspzzz…wraspzzz of Dimitri's saw as he meticulously dismantled the steps carefully saving each board and nail. The sarge and Alphonso sorting and stacking them nearby.

Despite the noise and the oncoming threat of the fires Katie, Leah, and Hatti joined Piff in a dreamless exhausted sleep.

Likewise, exhausted, Conrad Wolff sat, his back against the

church's wall and watched Alphonso—lifelong catholic—conspire with the devil. His heart was pained with the knowledge—guilt—of allowing an enemy of the church, a Mason, to be laboring under the shadow of, if not the direct auspice and protection of the Mother Church. He knew in his heart that he had been responsible. Of course, part of the blame had to be shared with Francis DeGeorgie. That gave him no comfort knowing that Francis had no faith and was, if anything, antagonistic to the Church. He looked around wondering where the miscreant was.

Twenty minutes passed as Dimitri found Alphonso's helping hands far from helpful causing the craftsman to spend twice the amount of time had he been working alone. Part of the stairwell had buckled when Alphonso had unknowingly pulled the nails that had held a support beam in place. Attempting to correct his mistake he ended his short apprenticeship with a painful wrap with a hammer to his thumb splitting the nail. Holding his throbbing thumb, with tears in his eyes, he retreated sliding down to the ground next to Conrad Wolff. He wanted to close his eyes, to let sleep envelope him, but the throbbing of his thumb argued sternly against it.

The sarge offered to help Dimitri who just continued to work, saying while biting down on a nail, "all in good time. For the time being just keep all that kitchen equipment out of my way."

Grazia rested cautiously, sensitive to the threats around her, strangers, soldiers with guns, fires, crumbling buildings, aftershocks, and a Mason so dangerously nearby. She looked on with one eye half-open, with no sympathy for her foolish husband. She had been watching Conrad Wolff with interest wondering what he was going to do about this Free Mason encamped on the church's doorstep. Conrad was a man of influence, she had little, but if he were not going to do something about it, she would.

If Conrad were married then surely the voice in his head would be that of his wife nagging him about the Freemason in their midst, along with little insignificant things. He turned to Alphonso. "Your wife is strongly opinionated; how do you manage her?" He paused as if considering what further he might say carefully.

"Manage? Hah! You can't manage a woman. Why do you ask?"

"Oh, nothing really," Conrad said. "That must hurt?" Meaning his thumb.

"Not as bad as Francis's hand, I'm thinking. Speaking of Francis, I don't see him about."

"He disappeared shortly after volunteering the Greek's labor."

Alphonso grimaced as his heartbeat like a kettle drum, the pain in his thumb matching it beat for beat. "Dimitri is a skilled craftsman. We're lucky to have him."

"He is also skilled in treachery and deceit. We must be judicious in what we allow him to do."

"What do you mean?"

"He's a Mason and being so an enemy of the church."

Alphonso looked puzzled. "I have never heard of this."

"The case for the Catholic Church's condemnation of Freemasonry is open and clear. By its very nature as formulated in its philosophical statements and as lived in its historical experience, Masonry violates the First and Second Commandments of God. It worships not the One True God of revelation—Father, Son and Holy Spirit—but a false god, symbolically transcendent but immanent: the *'god'* called *'Reason.'* And it invokes without adequate cause the Name of the One True God. After such a case as this, to cite the secrecies of initiation and the further secrecies of machination called *conspiracy* is not only anti-climactic, but also beside the point. To conclude: we Catholics should now see the Masons more clearly for what they essentially are. They are the heirs, unwitting or otherwise is irrelevant, of a religion which purports to be the one religion of the one *God*—and therefore the enemy, intrinsically and implacably so, of Catholicism."

"Dimitri hasn't said a word about this Freemasonry. If it is free, then wouldn't that mean that one is free to choose the way one worships? I am Catholic, and I do not feel threatened by this man. There are some who worship in tongues. If I shake hands with one, does that mean

I will begin to speak or pray with words foreign to the Catholic church? I don't think so. I have worked beside Dimitri. He tried to teach me how to hold a hammer—a lesson poorly learned I might add. I say let him play his trade on our behalf until such time as he tries to convert us from our faith. If he does this then speak to a priest about it and pray for his salvation." Alphonso was not used to speaking openly about religion.

While uncomfortable, he was beginning to know Conrad Wolff as a man of great intelligence and reason.

The voices in Conrad's head dimmed to a distant whisper. *Alphonso is right, the man has done us no harm. Leave it alone for the time being.* Reason and the late hour won the argument for the time being.

Reason is not something Grazia was known for. She had watched Conrad's face soften as he talked with her husband. As far as she was concerned the penguin-shaped man was too fat and lazy—too cowardly—to protect her church from the Mason. As if stung by a bee she bolted to her feet and stormed past Dimitri into the church where she would gather the priests to drive away the heretic. She smiled smugly to herself. For better than half a day her husband had turned against her, no one listened or respected her words. Well, now she would show them.

XLIX

A series of explosions walloped the night, mighty Zeus getting his two cents in, startling everyone. A brilliant flash of light followed as a mansion of the south slope of Russian Hill collapsed in on itself. It was dynamited in hope of creating a firebreak against the onslaught of flame. The mansion had been made of redwood which did not burn as easily or fast as many of the surrounding structures. Unfortunately, the first two explosions blew the furniture, the contents of the house, up and out before the final blasts brought down the redwood structure. This spread the fire faster and farther than anything else.

Everyone stopped and stared—there was no question now that Russian Hill would soon become fully engulfed. The light breeze that had held smoke close to the ground changed to turbulent gusts as the fires on Nob hill drew strength from the one on Russian Hill each feeding on the other soon to combine the two fires into one massive firestorm.

Washington Square was no longer safe.

A Captain in the United States Army followed by four soldiers on foot quick-stepped up the steps to St. Peter and Paul's Church with orders for the church to be abandoned, Washington Square was to be evacuated immediately.

"You there, climb down from there," a soldier shouted at Dimitri. His next order was meant for everyone on the inside of the white rope barrier. "Get up, gather what you have and be prepared to move out immediately. Well, don't just sit there… Git!" His last word was accented by a strong wrap with the base of his rifle on what was left of the steps.

From where Morgan Piff sat in his wheelchair it looked as if the fires were now burning on three sides—what was happening behind the church he had no idea. The roar of the flames emphasized that in the blink of an eye events had gone from grim to perilous. The fear showing on the soldier's faces echoed by their shouts and orders gave the civilians no sense of confidence that the army had any inkling of what they were doing.

"People needing assistance report to the north side of the church." A soldier yelled as he ran south.

"Single woman and the elderly are to meet at the eastern end of the park."

"Families with children…"

"The elderly and those in need of assistance are to report to the west side…"

A bugle blew calling all the soldiers to the army's command headquarters at the center of Washington Square.

The air grew hot, the smoke acrid and thick as burning ash blew about.

Shaking his head with disappointment Dimitri spat the nail out, threw his hammer into a large soup pot, and raised his large, calloused hands in frustration. "Now, what?"

Katie dusted off her house dress as she went to get Morgan. Leah woke, rubbing sleepy eyes, not sure where she was or what was going on. Hatti reassured Leah while making sure the kitten was locked and secure. Alphonso and Conrad Wolff awkwardly got to their feet each expressing their opinion on where they should go.

Sergeant Freeman retrieved the hammer suggesting that they should take all the tools that could be comfortably carried.

The priest, a lone sentinel against a bad day and a worse night, was startled by Grazia's intrusion at such a late hour. Except for the light of candles, the church was dark and claustrophobic, the high darkened ceiling seemingly a barrier to heaven. It was silent apart from the whisperings of a few of the faithful asking for forgiveness and guidance on this fateful day.

"Father, there is a heretic…" Grazia's voice not meant to be a shout echoed causing heads to turn.

The priest quickly pressed a finger to his lips "Quiet my child…."

Grazia's attempt to expose Dimitri was interrupted before she could say another word by an army captain whose dominant voice chased her echo throughout the church as if it were a braying hound in hunt of a timid fox. "Father, the fires are out of control. If we don't leave now there may very well be no way out. The church is to be evacuated immediately."

Less than half of the priests and staff were awake. The evacuation order now left to be delivered from mouth to ear as the priests who had heard the captain's orders went throughout the church rousing those who remained blissfully ignorant of the chaos outside.

Grazia stood with a silent rage. She would not be silenced. A Mason…a heretic was at the very doors to God's House. The devil might demand his due, and she was here to deny the devil just that. She saw Father Conolly. "Father, I have the most urgent news."

The Priest had dealt with over-excited self-righteous women before. "Please, my child, whisper this news in my ear so as not to frighten others.

She did.

He just looked at her and shook his head, "The good Lord in his wisdom has left us with more important issues this day. This will be our secret for the time being." Nothing more needed to be said.

Grazia's faith was shaken at that moment, doubt not in God but in the holy catholic church. Who could she turn to for comfort and forgiveness against her many sins? Was she wrong? Her faith, her strength, had been shattered in that moment. Her acerbity left her in the church alone, rejected by her husband, those who reached out their friendship she had rejected, and her own sense of self-worth. She sat in a pew, leaned forward into her hands, wanting to cry. There were no tears. She tried to pray finding no words. There was only an empty silence deep within that swallowed her soul. She had never known an emptiness so great finding that she had no emotions strong enough for her to withstand the void. The only thing she felt was a heavy pain in her chest as her breath caught. She slumped quietly onto the hard-wooden pew. All she heard were voices as the darkness seemed to flow taking her away…away.

Things happened fast after that.

"Where are you going," Alphonso asked Dimitri as the Greek started to mount the remaining stairs.

"To return these," he answered as he held out the bag of tools the church had lent him.

"I don't think the church will miss a few tools," Alphonso said. "Perhaps later when the ashes have cooled, and it is time to rebuild."

Dimitri looked first up the steps towards the open doors to the church. "Hmmm, tools are expensive. I'll keep them in protective custody…for the time being."

"North, south, left, right, which way do we go?" Morgan asked Katie.

"It appears that the soldiers may be leaving without us." Dimitri said from his slightly higher vantage point.

Priests began to gather at the entryway to the church as the captain and his small squad of soldiers left in double-time to join the troops who were now marching in columns of two out of Washington Square heading north on Stockton Street.

Small groups of refugees watched helplessly as the soldiers left the behind. They had followed the soldier's orders and gone to their assigned departure points. Now the only thing coming for them was a ferocious firestorm and all exit points seemed to lead towards Hell.

The soldiers were out of sight. The swirling smoke like a myopic fog, created optical illusions in the real but threatening world they found themselves in. Breathing became difficult. The flames seemed closer, brighter, and hotter than they were. Tiny fires sparked throughout Washington Square and the roof tops around. The priests discussed among themselves returning to the sanctuary of the church to pray and trust in God that the Devil and all his minions would not dare trespass on Holy ground.

The level head and courage needed came from Morgan Piff as he looked up from his wheelchair to Katie saying "If you don't get this contraption moving, I'm going to get up and walk. The soldiers are breaking trail, showing us the way. If we sit here and jaw about it then we get what's coming to us. Me, I don't plan on finishing my days a crispy critter."

Father Conolly overheard the old man's words nodding his approval. There was no time to rescue anything left in the church other than their own lives.

Morgan reached out for Katie's hand for help in getting out

of the chair. "Father,' the old man said, "if I were you, I'd send a few of your priests to get some of that water you've got stove away in your basement. Bring it out the back door, which will be quicker." While he paused to allow his thoughts to catch up with him his tongue peeked out like that old coo-coo clock again. "Then you might give a holler at the rest of them folks—meaning the people waiting around the square for the soldiers to return to tell them what to do—to dust off their walking shoes, pack up their doubts and in…insecure… insecurities and follow this old bag of bones the hell—the heck—out of here. Let's go Katie, you watch out for my chair, I may be needing it after a while."

Hattie supported Morgan's elbow as he took his first slow steps forward.

Leah set purple paws in his birdcage on the wheelchair as she and Katie followed along. Conrad Wolff gathered up his small suitcase of books taking his place next to Morgan his cane keeping side with the old man's steps. Alphonso and Dimitri, alone with three of the priests, hurried about Washington Square gathering those who would listen.

"Anyone got a damn piccolo? I feel like that fellow in the story…the Pied Piper," Morgan said.

"I believe he used the flute," Conrad injected. According to legend it all happened on St. Paul and Peter's Day." He glanced back at the now vacant church, its doors wide open. "Appropriate, wouldn't you say?"

"Conrad, has anyone ever told you that there are times you've just got to keep your trap shut."

"Everyone, please, it's time to go." One of the brothers motioned for the last of the faithful to follow him as he blew out a nearby candle. Once his fearful flock had left the church, he closed the door behind him leaving Grazia truly alone.

L

It wasn't his dislike for the church that caused Francis DeGeorgie to take leave of the group. He liked Alphonso and Hatti but didn't care much for the rest, personal relationships had never been his strong point. Washington Square had too many authority figures with the police and military around. He had noted that with the flood of refugees passing through there were more and more police. There was a warrant for his arrest for assault on a police officer after the longshoreman's strike in Oakland. Though he doubted that he would spend any time in jail, if arrested he most likely would be taken down a deserted alley and beaten within an inch of his life. What he wanted to do was get out of town, go down to Los Angeles, or up to Seattle. There the *Wobblies* were becoming more active, and men like him were needed. Taking the bread, he had been given at the restaurant and his water bag he decided to test his luck by backtracking through neighborhoods that had already burned and work his way inland towards Daly City and San Jose. It was going to be a large walk, but nothing compared to his escape from Russia. No goodbyes or last words of encouragement. He did hesitate, just for a moment, as he briefly glanced back experiencing unspoken regret.

LI

"Sorry, Sergeant, you can't go with them."

"Sergeant Freeman, ignoring the blond-haired, pale-skinned corporal on horseback, kept on walking; neither looking up or looking back. His stride slow and labored, aching feet and tired bones the remnants of a long day.

"I said, 'Sergeant, that is far enough.'" The corporal's expression now vaguely irritated, taking a little pleasure in ordering the black sergeant where he could or could not go. It had not yet registered with him that there were no buffalo soldiers stationed at the Presidio Garrison.

"It's all right corporal," one of the brothers who had helped move the water interceded, "he's with us and has labored well."

The corporal took off his hat changing his voice to a less threatening tone. "Father, I don't give a damn…ahhh, I meant to say…. I've got my orders and the captain has said that there ain't no room in the park for chinks, they've got to go to a special camp back behind the Presidio. As for the sergeant, well we're only looking for trouble if we allow a darky to camp with good Christian white folks."

"God's skin is black, brown, red, white, and even yellow. Every man's the same in the good Lord's sight. Where we camp, so will the sergeant." The brother placed himself between the soldier and the old sergeant.

"I'm sorry, but I have my orders, and this old buffalo soldier ain't going…

"That will be all, Corporal," an officer ordered, "keep this column of refugees moving—the fire isn't waiting for no one—that includes the sergeant."

Sergeant Freeman nodded in appreciation guessing that the officer had been raised here in the west with northern inclinations.

"Thank you, Lieutenant," the cleric responded. "Shall we sergeant? It's still a long walk to Golden Gate Park."

Freeman hadn't intended on going to the park, there wasn't a place for him there, odd man out. Never-the-less, it appeared that was where he was bound.

LII

Li Fengzhang stood out like a sore thumb. His 1905 Pierce Great Arrow Touring Car was a rich man's car, a rich white man's car. There were only three of its kind in all of San Francisco because it was a rich man's car no one thought it could belong to a China man. Hiding in plain sight is sometimes the best place not to be seen.

He and his father escaped the devastation of Chinatown with their lives and a few bags of tea leaves. The military waved him by without noticing the color of his skin—or thought him to be a servant racing to his master's aid. The Pierce Arrow was just powerful enough to take them up Filbert Street as the fires first started chasing up Nob Hill. Negotiating the rubble and damaged streets was difficult but easier than trying to climb its steep hills on foot. He had to be careful, for if stopped by the police he had no papers on him that proved the car was his. They were shooting looters who were white men, would a Chinaman dressed in western apparel fare any better? Once across Van Ness Avenue there were few fires, the military concentrated downtown. Their biggest risk in passing the thousands of refugees on foot was if someone took it personally seeing a rich man's car being driven by a chink.

"Where are we going," his father asked in Chinese. It had been a long time since the old man had been outside of their ethnic ghetto, everything outside seeming strange and forbidding.

He hadn't thought that far. Just getting out of Chinatown with their lives and not being beaten or arrested had been enough of a challenge for the moment. There were few options—the military had orders to round up all the Chinese, for their own safety, and keep them under guard at the Presidio. There would be other camps all of which he wanted to avoid. The wealthy men who ran San Francisco coveted the valuable land beneath Chinatown and this was their chance to rid the city once and for all Orientals—Chinese and Japanese as well.

When he had been a boy in China there had been a missionary family that had come from California. When they learned that he was bound for San Francisco to be with his father they sent a letter in his care to a member of their Mission—Pricilla Ann Cody—who was now an elderly dowager who lived out of the avenues south of Golden Gate Park. She was English, a nurse and, had lived in Shanghai in the early 1880's where her husband served with the American legation. She was widowed, with no children of her own. Now she lived somewhat reclusively with a Japanese housekeeper, spending most of her days gardening or doing oil paintings of China and Japan the way she remembered them. She had a kind spot in her heart for the Chinese, especially those who were educated and Christian. Li Fengzhang had developed a long-term friendship with the old woman spending many afternoons over the years discussing China over tea in her garden.

While he enjoyed his conversations with her, he did not like talking about China. Fengzhang was Chinese, but he did not consider himself to be a Chinaman. He considered himself to be an American, though he would never be allowed to become a citizen. His place in society was held by a few tattered shoestrings because of wealth; otherwise, he was not accepted within the Chinese Community nor any community outside that. There was little if anything left of his business', property, or wealth. Any Chinese found living in what remained of Chinatown would be driven out of Chinatown by well-paid vigilantes. He had seen it happen before and knew that it could happen again. His father had old friends in Mendocino. But once there, how would he ever return? His life and destiny had roots here in San Francisco. What money he had was invested with the Russian Chinese Bank,* if the bank did not exist—what then?

He noted that his car was low on gas. With a wry chuckle he answered his father; "We are going to Shanghai," he answered. The bank represented Russian interests in China, one of its largest branches was in Shanghai.

"No...no. Too far. I am too old. I have no desire to try to start over again, enough is enough."

He looked at his father knowing that he would now be taking care of him; but how, where?

---

* 1904-1906: The largest bank in China. A branch bank was established February 1904 in San Francisco, the only one in the United States, which was destroyed by the April 1906 earthquake.

LIII

As they followed the soldiers away from Washington Square their numbers grew as refugees trickled in from the financial district, Little Italy, and Barbary Coast. Joining the trek were single men—rowdy, intoxicated, and willing to take advantage of the defenseless. The way they looked at Hatti drew concern from the entire troop—especially Hatti who knew why they were looking at her the way they were. If the caravan stayed close together, they were relatively safe. Unfortunately, the hour was late, many had not slept in twenty-four hours or more, eaten little, and despite their self-imposed stoicism suffered shock from the extreme events that had brought them together. Those that fell behind or stopped to rest, who looked like they might have a coin or a babble worth taking soon fell victim; the soldiers too far ahead to do any good.

As they approached the first hill Morgan once again claimed his wheelchair. The birdcage and mewing kitten he held in his lap, the steepness of the hill too daunting for the exhausted little girl. Here and there they passed a steamer trunk; its contents too burdensome to drag up the incline. Next to one lay the shards of someone's fine china, the thieves were more interested in jewelry and silverware was more easily pawned. The thieves not realizing that what was left of the pawn shops was charcoal, any silver and gold melted and lost in the gray ash.

Dimitri pushed the wheelchair, his strength and brawn speeding their steps as it did those following behind. Hattie, Leah, and Katie stayed close to their big Greek guardian as brazen men lurked nearby using the disability of the hill to help isolate their victims.

It was Conrad Wolff and Alphonso who struggled the most on the incline. At the top of the hill, they had a choice to either follow the soldiers to whatever waited for them at the army camp at the Presidio, to head down towards the waterfront and back towards the wharfs in the Barbary Coast, some burning, others soon would be. It was decided to go towards Golden Gate Park where they had heard the largest refugee camps would be set up. The soldiers were leading the long column of homeless refugees to the Presidio, where what supplies the army had been sure to run short almost immediately.

For the time being there would be a shortage of almost all necessities which the army would strictly ration. The only surplus would be space which there was plenty of in Golden Gate Park.

"When my time comes, I'd like to be buried at the cemetery at the Presidio," the sarge noted with a certain reverence to his voice. "It's only fitting and proper that I should join other black soldiers buried there. But I will tell you this, the white soldiers today are not the same men I once rode beside. Don't get me wrong, the troops were not mixed but we were also all part of this man's army. When things got rough, whether it be Indians or a forest fire napping at your ass, we were of one mind, black and white alike. But as soon as things simmered down, we rode separate paths and ate apart. Now I can see things from a different perspective, and I can tell you this, it's as plain as I can see that my hand is black that some of these soldiers are uneducated lazy riffraff without unit pride or any sense of decency. If you choose to go to the Presidio, you go right ahead. Me, I'm headed to Golden Gate Park. Where I go from there on ain't for me to say now. I may not have an old worn-out horse blanket, but at least the grass I can lay my head on won't be army issue."

Alphonso did not show his surprise at how the sarge felt; however, he had learned to trust the sergeant's instincts.

Dimitri was no longer looking for a ticket as a ship's carpenter. Life at sea was hard, the crew likely to rob you blind first chance they got, and the food was lousy. With the fire's devastation of San Francisco, he was beginning to see opportunity. He had himself a good set of tools and able hands. Originally a stone mason he had become a carpenter preferring to work with wood rather than stone.

---

*After the earthquake shook San Francisco in 1906, Golden Gate Park became a site of refuge for many who found themselves without shelter. The undeveloped Outside Lands became a prime location to house these masses of people, and "earthquake shacks" popped up all throughout the area. Of the 26 official homeless encampments in the Golden Gate Park region, 21 were under the control of the United States Army. The United States Army was able to house 20,000 people in military style encampments, and 16,000 of the 20,000 refugees were living at the Presidio. Within the Presidio were four major encampments including a camp exclusively for Chinese immigrants. Despite being simple lodgings the army organized 3,000 tents into a geometric grid complete with streets and addresses. "The Army constructed a virtual town with large residential barracks [with temporary] tented housing, latrines and bathhouses, laundries, and other services."

He had no idea how many thousands of buildings would have burned before it was all over, but he had no doubt that someone would want to rebuild them. With the tools the church had given him he would be one step ahead of the game. If he went to the army base, they would likely confiscate them. He felt inside the bags he was carrying to make sure they were still there. With these he could scrape out a living, buy food, and in time put a cover over his head. He looked at the women and the children in the long line of refugees and gave the sarge his answer. "This Park, it is a nice place? If so, I say we go there."

Though tired, things were cheerful for a while in a pleasant bustling way. They had left the slow meandering army style column, the expressionless faces of those who just took one step after another, too tired to care, ghosts soon forgotten. They were making their own way—away from the Presidio towards the green and sea breeze promised at Golden Gate Park. Hatti and Katie were the only ones who had ever been there, neither by the route they were taking.

"Will this day ever end?" Katie let out a dramatic sigh.

"Wouldn't that be the irony; we've died and gone to hell, and no one thought to tell us." Hatti tried to adjust and dust some of the grime and ash off her evening dress. In the dark shadows provided by the surrounding trees it was useless, her once elegant dress beyond hope.

"How far do you think it is, the park I mean? It can't be that far, can it?" Katie hated to be the pessimist, but exhaustion was creeping in on her.

The shadows provided by the high cover of the eucalyptus trees added an unsettled feeling as he nervously glanced from side to side. Spooky. The shadows shifted with an unnatural hot wind, while Dimitri's bulk blocked what little view they had of the road ahead. Beneath the rustling of leaves the fires lurked. They nervously glanced from side to side as they drew near wary of their imagined creatures of the night.

"Have you ever been to 'The Chutes'? Hatti asked, idle prattle needed.

"Oh, I've seen it and marveled at the audacity of such a thing." Katie answered. "I couldn't imagine paying 10 cents for one ride. Of course, that was when it was located out on Haight Street near Cole. She remembered the way it had been. Surrounded by pastures and grazing cows, the Haight was a sleepy village far from the debauchery of the Barbary Coast and downtown hustle. Then one day an eccentric showman and a railroad attorney decided to build a giant attraction that became a brief, global phenomenon. *Shooting the Chutes* meant boarding an elevator up a skeletal 60-foot structure, climbing into a flat-bottomed boat with other passengers and racing it down 300 feet of rollers at 60 mph into the man-made lake below, where the vessel would fly into the air and skip several times, splashing crowds and exhilarating riders. The idea of traveling 10 times faster than any automobile could drive for 10 cents proved irresistible especially to the rich.

Leah stepped closer to listen. She had never heard of an amusement park being here in the city, not that her grandma would have taken her. After her parents had died and her grandma had taken her in, there was always a shortage of money; not one penny to be wasted. She had seen a picture in a magazine and oh how so wanted to go someday.

Hatti had ridden it several times, always with a gentleman patron with much more than a dime in his pockets. Careening at the end of the ride into a lake at "a mile a minute" always brought a flush to her cheeks and that smile no one seemed able to resist. Her favorite had been the flying swing. One trip to the zoo had been enough, it stunk. She wondered how it ever could have survived and if she would ever be able to ride it again.* So much had changed in one day. She took Leah's hand. "Sergeant, are we going to walk all the way out to the park this evening? Leah's pretty tired."

"I don't think it's a good idea to find where the camps are being set up in the dark. The wrong kind of people are apt to be about. We'll find a place for the night soon.

---

*The Fulton Chutes survived the April 18, 1906, earthquake in good condition as it was well-removed from the damage and fires happening on the east side of town. The Chutes closed during the relief efforts, but reopened on Sunday, May 20, 1906. A return to normal entertainment after a month of clean-up, rescue and resettlement in refugee camps resulted in heavy streetcar traffic to the Chutes. The Chutes also struck a deal for the Orpheum Theater to move its calendar of events to the Chutes Theater. The Orpheum would continue to operate out of the Chutes Theater through January 20, 1907. As one of few places of merriment available after the earthquake, the Fulton Chutes did well. Thousands of people were now living nearby in Golden Gate Park, Park Presidio, and other smaller parks in refugee camps. However, a "new" downtown area in the Fillmore district got built up in the wake of the earthquake, which included another smaller amusement park called the Coney Island Amusement Park. As the refugee camps ended, and the Fillmore District rose, attendance at the Fulton Chutes began to wane.

LIV

It was dark, they were weary, the night enveloped euca-lyptus trees thinning then mostly disappearing as Presidio Boulevard crossed Geary. The night sky raged with roiling plumes of dense black smoke underscored with flickering colors that did not belong. Just below a hill's low horizon, the city hidden, flames roared, their tongues tasting those very clouds. The reflections cast an unnerving spectacle as ghostly flames seemed to rise from the graves around Lone Mountain.

Lone Mountain, a cemetery surrounded by cemeteries. The Masonic, Calvary, Odd Fellows, and Lone Mountain cemeteries were now mostly abandoned. The hundreds of thousands of graves since abandoned. The hundreds of thousands of graves dug there since the first settlers had made Yerba Buena their home were slowly being moved away from the advancing needs of the living. The plan to move the dead to a place called Colma, away from the city, out on the peninsula was costly and time consuming, more a promise then reality. The thought that they had died and gone to hell crossed their minds again as they stood aghast at the specter of the vast boneyards ahead of them.

Leah's grip tightened, she pulled closer, as she began to cry, not even trying to hide that she was frightened with the visions she could not understand.

Morgan Piff knew the place well. Lone Mountain had once been the chief burial place of San Francisco. He had arrived in San Francisco in 1855, the first grave dug on June 1, 1854. Before that, the pioneers had been buried at the Yerba Buena Cemetery, where the city center was now. The investors thought that Lone Mountain would be big enough to manage the dead for the next half a century. They were wrong. Twenty miles of avenues were laid out through the grounds, but many of them had not been used now for years and were overgrow with bushes and weeds. The cemeteries were a place of stark contrasts. There was a Chinese vault in which they deposited their corpses until there were enough to be shipped back to China. The Protestant Orphan Asylum, several lodges of Odd Fellows, and the Firemen, each had their own respective lots in which their dead were buried. There were a few graves unmarked and lost to time. Most of the potter's graves were over at the City Cemetery near the city's outside lands.

Morgan sat there in his chair gazing up the grave marketed hill towards the horizon blazing just beyond. He wasn't long for the grave himself and wondered where that might be. In San Francisco cemeteries were cold, lonely fickle places one day there and another day gone. The city kept growing, needing the land, the graves moved. Most were being moved to a place called Colma wherever that might be. He suspected that might be where he would be taken; sooner rather than later.

There was a dark shadow on the crest of the ridge, refugees like themselves, who could not resist a closer look as the—as the Chinese might say—earth dragon spit fire as it gorged itself.

As Alphonso and Dimitri made their way to the crest of the

hill the rest sat, thinking they had not one ounce of energy left, to walk that last unsurmountable mile to the promised land. The ghost fires that danced on the graves seemed to laugh as they shimmied, beckoning them to another promised land.

No one noticed when Hatti slowly walked down the hill and disappeared behind the dark shadow of an old mausoleum where she thought she had seen an old piano. She had—an ornate hand-painted baby grand piano that someone had carted, what must have been a prized possession, out of the burning city, away from the wealthy mansions on Russian Hill, to the edge of this dilapidated graveyard, where its wheels finally gave way.

Hatti sat on a gravestone testing the keys. An F Sharp and an E Flat, little vixens of sound, floated at first anxiously then playfully inviting the giggling ghost flames that shimmied amongst the gravestones to come hither.

Eighty-seven of its eighty-eight keys remained, otherwise the Baby Grand was remarkably in tune.

Leah wiped her tears with a dirty hand as she looked around for where the singing was coming from.

She recognized Hatti's voice, and with no thought as to why, she began pushing Mr. Piff's wheelchair towards where she thought Hatti to be while Purplepaws meowed in its basket as if to urge her on.

"Well, I'll be gal-darned, and I thought I had done seen just about everything there was to see…and hear," Morgan Piff said as his eyes took in the flickering grave fairies.

The last dance was over, the music had ceased,
And the dancers were leaving the hall,
A few men were saying their last goodbyes,
To the beautiful belle of the ball,
Alone by the window a youth sadly stands,
His heart she had stolen away,
And just as he gazed on her beautiful face,
He was startled to hear someone say,

Kattie, who knew the song, joined in the chorus and stepped beside the piano as Hatti's fingers danced across the ivories, flames seemingly running like laughing spirits, merrily away.

"She lives in a mansion of aching hearts,
She's one of a restless throng,
The diamonds that glitter around her throat,
they speak both of sorrow and song;
The smile on her face is only a mask,
And many the tear that starts,
For sadder it seems, when of mother she dreams,
In the mansion of aching hearts.
Alone by the fireside, a man sadly looks,
At a picture that hangs on the wall,

Morgan Piff slowly fetched an old harmonica out of his shirt pocket and tried to play along.

"My picture I send, I have loved you, but only in vain,
Oh try to forget that we ever have met,"
Then he thinks with a heart full of pain. . .

As the chorus was sung again the people scattered about the graveyard made their way, a few singing along.

> *"She lives in a mansion of aching hearts,*
> *She's one of a restless throng,*
> *The diamonds that glitter around her throat,*
> *they speak both of sorrow and song..."*
> *They both speak of song and sorrow.*[*]

As the last note faded a sea breeze pushed the night fog, the smoke plumb, and the reflections away. The flickering grave fairies lay down to sleep as did the exhausted human refugees. Her head resting on Katie's lap the last sound Leah heard as she closed her eyes was little Purplepaws as she settled into her basket for the night.

---

[*] The Mansion of Aching Hearts 1902

Words by Arthur J. Lamb; Music by Harry Von Tilzer.; New York: Harry Von Tilzer

Part Two

The Tent Camps

LV

Waking on a weed covered hillside in an old cemetery is something that none of them will ever forget. The rising sun looked more like a moldy orange as smoke snaked through the trees and wrapped around the stone-cold graves that surrounded them. The air was sultry, more reminiscent of an August day in Louisiana than a mid-April morning beneath the fog-belt in San Francisco. No one wanted to start the day, but they were rattled by a mild aftershock reminding them that their jitter-bugged reality was still very much in charge.

The water they needed had to be judicially rationed not knowing when they would find or be allotted more. If only it would be as easy as knocking on a neighbor's door for help. While there were homes in the outside lands surrounding Golden Gate Park, they were few in number spread out among the windswept sand dunes. What water there was brought up mainly by wells that had been most likely damaged by the earthquake.

"Young lady," Morgan Piff asked Leah from where he had slept upright in his wheelchair, "would you be kind enough to pass me that magic pebble over-yonder by that gravestone?" He pointed towards a cracked gravestone that was leaning halfway over its neighbor's grave.

Leah read the tombstone aloud as she picked up the marble sized stone the old man had asked for. She looked back as the old man wiped his spectacles. "There's no date like on all the others, how come?"

Piff read the gravestone the best he could. "I guess it don't matter much. See there, carved into the top of the..."

> *REST IN PEACE*
> *COUSIN ZAKARIA*
> *WE ALL KNEW*
> *YOU DIDN'T DO IT*

"...stone—that there is a hangman's noose."

"Oh." Looking sad, Leah brought him the stone. "Magic pebble?"

"That's what my pappy told me back when I was a boy.

The old man said as he plopped the stone into his dry mouth. "You find yourself a magic pebble and you won't be thirsty no more."

The sarge brought what was left in his waterbag over to Leah. "An old Indian shaman told me the same thing back on the plains of Nebraska. I doubt that there are too many magic stones around here. Don't drink too much, it's got to last the lot of us for some time." He nodded to Alphonso, his nod showing the vacant spot where three water bags had been the night before. The sarge looked discernibly about the graveyard where there were now plenty of people but none that he could see had their waterbags. "Well, I guess we should be moving out, there is nothing much keeping us here."

Dimitri walked over to the piano. "I sure do wish we could take it with us. Miss Hatti played it real pretty." In trying to move it one of the legs broke off, its thump reverberating among the stones surrounding it.

A gaggle of boys, who had been playing cowboys and Indians just up the hill came whooping and hollering to see what all the ruckus was about.

Conrad Wolff clapped his hands. "You boys get away from there," he barked, his high-pitched voice more comical then authoritative.

"Let them be, Mr. Wolff, they can't do much harm." Katie counted the boys, nine in all, perhaps five to eight years of age, most on the younger side. She couldn't see any parents about. On a normal day she would have just let them play but when one of the bigger boys began to thrash the keyboard with a dead branch that he had found beneath a nearby white oak tree she changed her mind.

It sounded like the piano was on the losing end of the stick. *Boys will be boys,* she thought, *but not today.*

"Where to from here," Conrad asked anyone and everyone willing to listen.

"Anywhere but here, this place gives me the willies. Alphonso took Katie's hand as they slowly began to walk down a path out of the graveyard, towards the more open fields of the great park.

Surprised by Alphonso' intimate gesture Katie slowly glanced at his whiskered face, smiled, then looked back to see that Mr. Piff was being taken care of.

With Piff's wheelchair in hand, Purplepaws in her basket on his lap, Leah walked along side, they gladly left the cemetery. But not before Hatti marched determinedly towards the baby grand, grabbed the stick from the little boy's hand, and walloped him good across his butt. The boy ran screaming up the hill towards where a trail of smoke from a campfire stirred. Each of the boys ran screaming up the hill, over and through the tombstones, as if their fannies had been spanked too.

—

Smoke snaked across their path while the distant roar of the gargantuan fires behind them left them no doubt that their future lay ahead; there was no turning back.

Dimitri cradled his tools with anticipation of putting them to work. Working with his hands, making something beautiful and useful was his life's work. The only thing he had liked as a ship's carpenter had been a chance to see parts of the world he had never seen in his small corner of Greece. The isolation, food, stench, boredom, and stupidity of his shipmates had driven him to drink. And drink he had, almost to the point that he had lost his interest in being a craftsman. That was all changing now, he did not know what was lying ahead but most certainly it was opportunity.

Conrad Wolff was sad, if not a little lost, perhaps befuddled. His life had always been on a singular path—his love of knowledge, of books. His vice a simple game of cards. He had never been a handsome man; women had always shied away from him; whether it was his looks or superior intelligence he did not know. For romance he depended on the classics, he had read most, some more than once: Wuthering Heights. Don Quixote. Pride and Prejudice, and Great Expectations. His favorite, one of the treasured books in his bag was *'The Hunchback of Notre Dame':*

> *'In the vaulted Gothic towers of Notre-Dame lives Quasimodo, the hunchbacked bell ringer. Mocked and shunned for his appearance, he is pitied only by Esmerelda, a beautiful gypsy dancer to whom he becomes completely devoted.'*

He was devoted to the written word, taking great pleasure in the touch of their leather bindings. His was a world devoted to thought, to see what most men cannot begin to understand. That was one of the reasons he had chosen to be suckled by the Holy Mother Catholic Church, for if one knew the way, theirs was not a world lit by a single candle, though that light was denied to most of God's simple creatures. To discuss, to explore, the many philosophies of the world with a Jesuit Brother, to Conrad Wolff that was erotic. The many books that now crackled, their pages curling in the flames of the devastation that grew behind him brought tears to his eyes. Now there was nothing to do but put one foot in front of the other as he recalled some of the many passages that crossed his mind. Oscar Wilde, a ghost often through is mind. *"The only difference between the saint and the sinner is that every saint has a past, and every sinner has a future."*

Hatti Poirier was not ashamed of her past; she had had one

damn fine time. She was an acknowledged well-paid sinner but perhaps the time had come to sin no more. Sure, she could earn a remarkable living doing what she had done so well but the world was changing, and she was beginning to think that in order to survive, things were going to have to be different. She took a long-caring look at Leah and smiled. Yes, things needed to be different.

Leah saw Hatti's smile and wondered what she was thinking about.

Alphonso had not thought of Grazia since she had stormed into the church at Washington Square. He did not think about her now. That she was gone from his life was what mattered, and he felt like living again. He lightly squeezed Katie's hand as they walked towards their future. She squeezed back. Life had changed and Alphonso could smell and taste his late spring with vigorous curiosity.

Katie had always been a positive person, even after the death of her husband she had always found a way to go about her day with a smile and a kind word to everyone about her. Only her heart did not smile. She had put her passion into the simple daily routine of running her boarding house. She had not allowed for a single dust bunny or cobweb to put a blot on her day. None of that mattered now. Her life, the boarding house, it was all gone now and the thought of starting out on a new adventure no matter how difficult brought a song to her heart. She glanced around her, seeing everything, as she returned the gentle squeeze Alphonso had given her hand.

LVI

Francis had walked all night, finding the shadows, the chaos and confusion that was all around him somewhat comforting. He barely felt the pain in his hand as he put his mind, his waning energy, into getting as far away from what had been San Francisco as he could. His paranoia of being arrested and paying the price for his zealous political ways was real. He had not worried about it much until after he had barely escaped from the bottle warehouse. In St. Petersburg he had been one of the many, the army of the unemployed, risking all for…for what? His revolutionary fervor left him when he had come face to face with the thought of what an ass he had been, thinking of his own self-importance as the world burned around him and his new friends simply needed water. Now he was running away, to where, for what? Where was he going, not the destination he had in mind—as far away from here as possible?

He had no purpose.

He stopped, dead in his tracks. He was exhausted. The pain returned to his hand, sharp, and throbbing.

The sun had come up without him realizing it. His eyes, red, tearing, and blurry slowly took in his surroundings.

He was lost, or perhaps he had died, and somehow wound up

in paradise. He was leaning against the rail of a footbridge that crossed a quiet brook. It was a forested area, man-made, not a place in the wild. He turned where he stood and watched the water flow sweetly beneath him.

Damn he was thirsty.

A moment later he found himself kneeling, scooping water with his good hand, time after time, tasting the nectar of the gods.

"SCREEEEE SCREEEEEE, AIYEEEEEE!"

Startled by the loud abrasive scream, he turned, slipped, and fell backwards into the stream. His hand stung like hell as he broke out in tear-flooded laughter. In the center of the bridge stood a large bird; a peacock he thought. He had seen pictures but had never seen one in real life. Its colorful feathers fluttered, vibrated in fact, as the bird cocked its head looking at him, its eyes never blinking. The peacock gathered its tails to turn away, its dark glowing eyes, violet fringed with golden amber, seemed to study him.

It took a moment for Francis to stop laughing. Finally, when his laughter settled down to a few deep throated gasps, as he watched the birds run away, a hand reached down to help him from the stream. It was a woman's hand.

LVII

Li Fengzhang knocked politely and waited.

Chiune Suematsu answered the door, then bowed in formal welcome to Fengzhang. Suematsu, dressed in a black housecoat and matching pants, with carefully manicured snow-white hair, was older than Li Fengzhang's father. He had been Pricilla Cody's Japanese housekeeper, caretaker, and gardener since her return from China. While he had reason's deep within his family's past for not being particularly fond of the Chinese, he shared Fengzhang's bitter experience with western prejudice. Forgiveness and understanding was a Christian value Pricilla had helped him embrace. "Mister Li, you are most welcome. It has been too long since you have graced Mrs. Cody's parlor."

The Chinese businessman returned the customary bow.

Suematsu slowly straightened his eyes noting the Pierce Arrow parked just outside the carefully maintained not yet in season rose garden. "I see that you are not alone."

"Yes, Li Henzheng, my honorable father is with me today. Chinatown, where we both had business interests, has been lost to the fires." Li Fengehang noted that the house had suffered minor visible damage other than a few bricks fallen from a chimney and a broken window frame. I hope that things have been less eventful for Mrs. Cody?"

"Chiune, who is it." The elderly dowager called from somewhere in the house. She had a lilting, beautiful voice, still remarkable for her age.

"It is Mr. Li, and he has brought his father with him."

"Please, show them in, then get us some tea please. For you too, Chiune. I am sure they have had a most remarkable day."

They had and hoped to never repeat one like it again. The polite tea-chat did not last long as both father and son were exhausted as was Mrs. Cody. Suematsu made up comfortable mats on the floor of an enclosed gazebo at the back of the house; it not being proper for a China man to sleep in a white woman's house. Before excusing themselves, Li Fengzhang asked a favor. He needed a few days to track down monies that were rightfully his from a bank that had been lost in the earthquake and fires.

Li Fengzhang's father slept in his chair as he promised Pricilla Ann Cody that he would return within the week to collect his elderly parent from her care. She looked at Chiune who nodded that he would be most respectful with Li Hanzhang's care.

The truth being that Li Fengzhang did not know if he would be able to recover his money and any hope for their future—or if he would return himself. As western as he tried to be, he was Chinese, and thus his destiny was not entirely in his own hands.

LVIII

They did not have to walk very far into the park which spread out over a thousand acres. They could have walked all the way to the Pacific Ocean if they had wanted to. When a sea breeze kicked in, no longer tasting of smoke and char, they stopped and took in their surroundings. There was no camp, no shelters of any kind, no soldiers to make promises that in time everything would be all right. There were some small groups of refugees which seemed to grow with each blink of an eye—that was not a plus.

"Just over there," pointed out Morgan Piff, "is Lloyd Lake. It ain't much but it just might be the best spot around these parts to plant our bums—pardon me ladies—to wait and see what's next.

There was nothing remarkable to mark the clay-lined edge of the lake they thought they had claimed for their own.

Folly!

Initially there were two curious mallards to great them and delight Leah. As more and more refugees seemed to migrate to their space gulls and pigeons soon swooped, demanding alms, of which under the circumstances none were to be had. What had begun as a respectful if not cloistered few, soon became a boisterous, space demanding throng, few with resources, each demanding what was not to be had from each other.

Hatti had never wanted to sew; the last time she had tried she had been a child. The result had been an embarrassment, one she had had to wear. When the other children had stopped laughing, she promised herself that she would never sew again; and she hadn't. Now, as she sat in the park, feeling tired, hungry, her dress having taken a beating, she looked at herself and whispered to Katie—"Do you sew?"

"Yes." She did not have to guess why Hatti had asked. San Franciscans dressed for all and everyday occasions. It wasn't uncommon to see people dressed in what people in other cities might call evening wear for just a walk around the block or to an early lunch. Men's formal daywear consisted mostly of cutaway morning coats, high-buttoned waistcoat, and creased fly-front trousers worn with a high-collared shirt, top hat, and gloves. Women's blouses and dresses were full in front and puffed into a "pigeon breast" shape that looked over the narrow waist, which sloped from back to front and was often accented with a sash or belt. Necklines were supported by high boned collars. A housewife of modest income might have but one or two dresses which were carefully maintained and cared for. The trains, which reached the ground and often a little longer, were difficult to maintain. Many of the refugees that soon filled the shorelines of Lloyd Lake were dressed this way, few brought any additional clothing; there hadn't been time.

Hatti always dressed well, striving to never be embarrassed again. She had good taste and purposely dressed to set a fashion statement. Secretly, she wished for one of her gentlemen friends to take her away from this nightmare. They could spend the day, First, she would bathe—lots of bubbles, in the tub as well as the glass. Then have a new dress, several of them, delivered by I. Magnin.* They knew her size and what she liked. She thought that they should dine at the Tadich Grill. She might have their Petrale Sole Meuniere, a steak a little too heavy. The thought made her mouth water. She sighed, unaware that it was aloud, her reality, now a bitter pill to take.

She brushed at a soiled spot on her dress, which only made it worse. "Oh nothing, just thinking aloud, that's all."

She couldn't ask Katie, a woman she had only known a few hours to mend her dress, if it could be mended. She took in all of the women who she now shared the park with promising herself that as soon as she could find the time, place, and a pair of scissors she would make the adjustments necessary for what might be a long unwanted vacation in the tent camps not even built yet.

Dimitri's presence proved to be a blessing in disguise as the crowd squeezed their space tighter as each hour past. All he had to do was make his huge presence known with an unsettling glare and suddenly the far side of the lake suddenly became more attractive by those who crowded in too close.

Can a child be a hooligan at eight years of age; at six or nine? That was the question Conrad Wolff asked himself as a pack of screaming kids thundered through the camp. The obnoxious screech of the gulls overhead could not compete with their racket.

Hatti's words were less kind.

Morgan Piff laughed aloud pounding his cane against the grass as they stormed through oblivious to anyone or anything about them—until one wide boy, too big for his knickers, grabbed hold of Piff's wheelchair, spun it several times around before pushing it towards the edge of the lake. Piff, unable to raise his arm high enough to wallop the brat with his cane stopped laughing as he swore "leave me be, you god-damned hooligan." A dozen wild-eyed squawking snot-nosed brats appeared treating the old man as if his chair were a maypole, before Dimitri grabbed the biggest, and first offender, tossing him into the lake.

Red-faced and sputtering, Conrad Wolff appeared more menaced, dazed, and vulnerable than Morgan Piff.

The crowd around them appeared momentarily stunned by what they had just witnessed; none willing to own any of the miscreant youth.

"Yowie, what a ride!" Piff cackled, "was that a passel of wild pigs or what?" He started to stammer, then pushed it aside. After a moment of questionable silence, he cocked his head just enough to look meaningful and said to Conrad, "Is it too early in the day for a drink?"

"It is for me," Conrad answered with a slightly pious tone to his voice.

Alphonso rolled his eyes, his expression sympathetic.

"Katie, look in there," he said, pointing at the bag that had so far managed to not have been left behind or stolen somewhere along the way. Inside she found the last measure of brandy, left forgotten, not neglected.

Katie took the small bottle to the old man, clicking a thumbnail against it as she pulled the cork.

"It seems that for you, the bell tolls."

Morgan Piff's eyes crinkled upwards around the edges as he smiled. Taking a sip, he wiped his lips with the front of his dirty, age-wrinkled hand, looked at Leah and sang part of the traditional Swedish *Maypole* song:

> *'Små grisarna, små grisarna är lustiga att se.*
> *Små grisarna, små grisarna är lustiga att se.*
> *Båd öron, båd öron, och svansar hava de.*
> *Båd öron, båd öron, och svansar hava de.*
> *Å nöff nöff, å nöff, å nöff nöff nöff. . .'*

Morgan Piff did not speak Swedish, but he did know the lyrics. Seeing that Leah wanted to sing along he sang them again, this time in English.

> *'The little pigs, the little pigs are funny to observe.*
> *The little pigs, the little pigs are funny to observe.*
> *Both ears, both ears and tails do they possess.*

---

*I. Magnin was founded in 1876 by Mary Ann Cohen Magnin, who named the store after her husband Isaac. While the store first sold lotions and high-end infant wear, it expanded to include bridal wear and fashions imported from Paris. The 1906 earthquake and fire destroyed the original Market Street location built in 1877; rebuilding occurred at 50 Grant Avenue in 1912.

Both ears, both ears and tails do they possess.
Oh, oink oink oink, oh oink oink oink,
Oh, oink oink oink oink oink
Oh, oink oink oink, oh oink oink oink,
oh, oink oink oink oink oink.'

He slapped his knee and laughed, "You see, I knew it was a herd of wild piggies that had paid us a visit." With a broad, almost toothless smile, he finished the brandy.

The rest of the day remained uneventful unless you count the flood of refugees as being interesting. Mostly they were annoying and smelly. They smelled of sweat, smoke, and stress. The stress raised the unpleasant odors emanating from hundreds of bodies to be something that was difficult to get used to; of course, theirs wasn't much better. Hatti recognized *Detaille,* a perfume that had become popular in the last year. Personally, *Detaille,* a Chypre Floral fragrance, she found to be too strong for her own liking. The lingering ammonia smell of lye soap marked those who had a chance to bathe before being evicted by the earthquake and fires. Add this to the other obnoxious smells in a crowded space which tended to upset one's senses. Smoke from the fires, stale tobacco, and accumulating trash soon brought on a lack of appreciation for one's neighbors.

No one could count the number of children about, the raised voices caused by their loud behaviors, and parents yelling at them to behave, which they could do no better than the multitude of gulls squawking above.

There were no bathroom facilities, and certainly no privacy. Some men and children relieved themselves in the lake.

Stronger odors strangling the air around clumps of bushes, which was also the only place for women to go.

If there had been food available, there was little interest, except for the cries coming from hungry babies.

Sometime in the early afternoon two soldiers on horseback strolled through the encampment, promising that blankets, water, and food would be arriving shortly.

A thousand questions asked, few answers given. "All I know, ma'am, is that the army is doing the best it can. No one knows how bad it is, or what's left—everything is still burning.*"

"Bring me a wagonload of canvas and I'll make tents for as long as the canvas lasts" Dimitri both begged and promised.

---

*During the memorable 18th and 19th every hotel and bank, every large store and nearly every storeroom and wareroom in the city had been destroyed, three hundred thousand people were homeless, and thousands more were left without the means of livelihood. The rations, tents, and blankets on hand at the army posts adjacent to the city were dealt out to the sufferers with no account of the responsibility involved; and within two days, relief supplies from neighboring states and cities and army supplies from various army posts had begun to arrive and were being distributed under the supervision of the Presidio depot commissary.

LIX

Francis was more than pleasantly surprised when he saw that his helping hand belonged to a gorgeous young woman. She had locks of sable-black hair that surged over her shoulders. His heart nearly stopped when she gazed at him with eyes like two plasma-blue gems slumbering in milky pools which were a-smolder with passion for life which gleamed with an unearthly quality above her concave cheekbones, and they shone with the faraway look of a star gazer. Her sliver-of-moon eyebrows were burglar-black and stole his soul. A cherubic smile framed bewitching unicorn white teeth.

"Don't worry, Quinn is all bluster," she said with a dulcet voice as sweet as a meadowlark. "He's really quite friendly."

"Quinn?" Francis looked around to see who she was with as she helped him out of the stream.

"The peacock who startled you. His name is Quinn.

He is quite eccentric and thinks he owns the place. If there were any pea-hens left he would be insufferable."

He did not know what to say. He had walked all night, not knowing where he was going, had gotten lost several times, until arriving here only to be startled witless by an oversized bird. "Peacock?" He had never seen one before.

The next moment Quinn raced excitedly back to where they stood. Francis quickly stepped back.

"You are skittish, aren't you?" She said as she took a handful of grain from a pocket. Quinn quickly pecking it from her hand, causing no harm. That was when she noticed Francis' injured palm. "Oh, you're injured." Taking his hand in hers she turned it, inspecting the wound. "Painful?" Her voice empathetic.

Francis grimaced slightly, all the time keeping an eye on the animated bird, which kept an equal eye on him.

The woman playfully scolded the peacock as it finished the grain and strutted off. "Antoinette," she said, introducing herself as she looked up at him with a *femme fatal*e smile.

"Ahhh, Francis. I am Francis DeGeorgie."

She helped him dry off with the aid of a small canvas bag she had been carrying.

The peacock no longer a threat in his mind, Francis took a moment to take in his surroundings. He was inside some kind of park with gravel paths that followed a stream bed. The sound of running water indicated a larger water source nearby. The trees and shrubbery, and a rose garden not yet in bloom. "Where are we?" He asked as she took a piece of cloth in which to wrap his hand. "I spent most of yesterday keeping just ahead of the fires in the city. Are we still in San Francisco? Is anything left?" He noted the lack of people around. "Where is everyone?" He suddenly felt a little woozy, having not eaten in quite some time.

She noted his pallor, sitting him down on a nearby bench. "Here, this will help," she said as she handed him a small yellow apple from her bag.

"We are at the very edge of the city in what was once called the Glen Park Zoo. It was quite something in its day with close to two hundred animals, five lakes, rides, music, and even balloon acts with aeronauts. It was closed to the public about five years ago. Since then, it has been fenced off to the public. Most of the animals are gone now, except for a few the birds and monkeys. That is what I do, I take care of the aviary and the monkeys. We used to have eighty monkeys but only thirty are still in their habitats. A few have escaped and gone wild, they will not hurt you unless you threaten them though. I was just going in to feed them when I heard Quinn say hello." Antoinette talked fast; her smile beamed when she spoke of the animals under her care.

Francis' eyes immediately searched the trees.

"Don't worry, silly, they're more afraid of you then you are of them." As if on cue a small monkey no more than five inches tall dropped out of a treetop, skittered up Antonetta's leg, then into the bag with a happy squeak. A moment later it emerged with a dark blue plum and retreated quickly back up into the tree's canopy.

Francis could not help but laugh. "What was that?" He asked while framing his eyes with a hand to track it as it disappeared.

Antoinette blew a kiss up towards where the tiny primate had disappeared. "That was Nina. She is a marmoset. She knows when I am coming and that the plum is just for her. She lives up there somewhere with her family—five at last count—but I can never be sure. She is an escape artist, so tiny and clever that she is impossible to keep in a cage." She placed a second plum on a nearby tree branch. "We can't allow too many of them to run wild, their gum chewers and will bite into tree branches to get the sweet gum inside. You can imagine the problems they would cause if they ever got into someone's garden or fruit orchard." She looked at his hand. "Your pallor is looking a little better. Come with me and I'll fix you some boiled eggs and a banana or two.

Francis hadn't seen the tall fence that was hidden discreetly behind the trees and was surprised to see inside what a small but tidy zoo had once been. He had been to a zoo in Budapest when he had been a boy and could almost imagine a lion pacing back and forth in what was marked as 'Lion Country.' There was no lion, most of the cages empty in what must had been once a grand place. Weeds, held captive, now the lonely guardians of the past.

LX

Li Fengzhang parked his car then followed a path to the top of Noe Peak, one of two twin peaks overlooking the city. The peaks form a divide for the summer coastal fog pushed in from the Pacific Ocean. Their west-facing slopes often getting fog and brisk winds, while the east-facing slopes receive more sun and warmth. With a wall of fog retreating in the west he had the hellish vision of the city burning for its second day below him and to the east.

There were explosions where the army was attempting to create a firebreak by clearing the fire's path of fuel. He guessed that as he watched they were dynamiting somewhere near 12th or 14th Streets near Mission. He had seen how useless that had been in Chinatown where the dynamiting had only spread the flames. Although there were few buildings on or near Twin Peaks he wondered if the flames would catch in the cow pastures and burn all the way to the sand dunes or the Pacific Ocean itself.

He knew that Chinatown was gone but the scorched earth that marked where it had been the day before unnerved him. San Francisco's Chinatown had held the largest Chinese population outside of China itself. Where would they go? There were a few small communities of Chinese across the bay in Oakland, Sacramento, and the Sierra Nevada's. The Chinese in Mendocino seemed to have integrated with some level of tolerance. But there were so many, if they were not allowed to rebuild in San Francisco, where? Would they be all be evicted and sent back to China.

He would not.

He stood, frozen in place, frozen in time, as he watched San Francisco burn. Options, what were his options? He did not know.

LXI

On the morning of the quake Liam Tige Malarkey was prepping for his regular customers at *Golden Gate Johnnycakes* a small ham and egg café he worked at off Deloris Street. He reached for the pint of rye whiskey next to the stove. It was half empty, he looked at the clock. Just short of half an hour until he needed to have breakfast ready.

The floor rocked, the ceiling dropped, and ham, eggs, and biscuit mix were all over the floor. One looks out the broken windows and he knew that this morning breakfast had just been cancelled. He reached for the whiskey which was no longer there.

Liam Malarkey did not like to make decisions. He did not like change or anything that interrupted his day which was usually a blur of whiskey, baking, bacon, and scrambled eggs; don't ask him to do them any other way, although the menu said, *'Eggs Your Way.'* He knew that it had been an earthquake, a damn big one, and swore at his bad luck. His rye whiskey was now seeping through the floorboards and like it or not he was going to have to face the first light of day. He preferred working alone at night when there were no people wanting to discuss nonsense that made no matter to him.

One look outside told him what he needed to know.

He borrowed his boss' horse and dray wagon, which was already loaded with the old wood and coal burning stove, that had been replaced the day before by a new gas stove. Weary of a gas leak, he loaded the wagon as quick as he could with some utensils, a large iron frying pan, three Dutch Ovens, a coffee pot along with a few pounds of coffee, and three slabs of bacon. He had just loaded forty pounds of flour when the earth rocked a second time, the old café leaned ominously out over the street. Very much aware of the risk, he ran back in, down rickety stairs to a storage room where he hefted onto his shoulders a small keg of rye whiskey. Securing it in the wagon, he did not have to be kicked twice to know that it was time to get his fat ass out of Dodge.

Liam did not have a fat ass, he did have a large baker's belly riding on spindly legs, his backside being without much form at all. At fifty-two he otherwise remained fit, able to throw forty-pound flour sacks around as if they were rag dolls. His most remarkable feature a reddish-brown horseshoe mustache with a splash of grey on what was otherwise a mostly hairless face and head.

He was not a talker and did not cotton to folks who were. Long years of working alone in a small kitchen and early morning baker's hours had left him content with his own company.

The second jolt brought a heavy smell of gas to the air as he abandoned the café swearing beneath his mustache that he wished he had time to bring this or that. Passing the loading dock behind Yancy's Corner Grocery he loaded up three barrels of water and a small keg of coal oil leaving Yancy sputtering with raised fists as he rode off a moment before the café exploded with a deep thump then a roar as the gas line for the new stove exploded. Liam knew that within a few hours the grocery and everything else in the neighborhood would be charred to ash.

Liam covered his load with a blanket he nabbed from a backyard laundry line and moved from place to place the best he could as he was chased by the fires. Several people tried to hitch a ride along the way, but he would have nothing to do with them. If he let someone on board, they would just jaw his ears off, and he would have to throw them off anyways. As the crow flies, it wasn't that far to the Presidio—but with the fires burning all around, soldiers telling you where you could and could not go, debris blocking one street after another, there was no easy way to get there.

Try as he might, there was neither the time or a place to stop and pop the keg; the longer the day the more he needed a drink. By the time he got to the Presidio he was bone tired. It had been a long day and he had gotten up at his usual baker's hour of three in the morning. He wanted to sleep, his eyes hound-dog tired but he sat up throughout the night, eyes wide open, fretting that someone might ask if the wagon was rightfully his. Carefully glancing around to see which noisy people might be looking his way, he popped the keg, filling his cup to the brim, drinking half of it down in a belly-warming, eye-watering slurp.

He had no doubt that given the way things were going the army would confiscate the wagon leaving him with nothing more than a useless receipt for goods sequestered for the common good. At four in the morning, with only a few soldiers about, mostly around the Chinese camp, he clicked his tongue for the horse to start down the road and quietly as he could found his way to Golden Gate Park. He had not eaten since the night before last and decided that what he most needed was a strong cup of black coffee. Hitching the horse to a tree by the side of the road he collected what wood he could find while never letting the wagon out of sight.

The problem with coffee, he thought, *is trying to make it when you have not had any.* The coffee made, he sipped at it, as he leaned up against a rear wheel of the wagon and fell asleep. His had been a long day and any dreams were evasive. With the taste of bad coffee in his mouth, he spat, then poured himself a second cup of the black tar-like, bad-ass elixir, adding a generous inch of rye whiskey. The sun had come up, the smoke in the air was not from campfires but smelled of ash, char, and lost dreams. A crow cackled from a tree branch just above. He threw the remnants of the coffee at it. *Tar and feathers, just what I need.* There were people about, *damn them all for being a pain in my ass. God save their souls if they so much as breath in my direction.* He was in a foul mood, and he owned it. While he did not much like talking with people, he did on occasion address his own mood when his whim tickled his fancy. "Nemo,[*] your dumb son-of-a-bitch, what the hell have you gotten me into now?"

He stood, pitched the rest of the coffee from the pot, stretched, and thought about where he ought to be going. They came from all directions at the same time; children yelling and screaming. He turned; his glare mean enough to scare the children right

---

[*] Nemo, meaning nobody.

back into their wombs. The oath he was about to utter slowly changed into a lower gut chuckle as he saw one of the kids spin an old man in a wheelchair round and round practically pushing him into a lake. The fat kid tormenting an old man was an unkind moment, that should not have seemed humorous but for some reason it did. "Now ain't that a caution," he heard Nemo laugh within. He guessed that he just needed some comic relief—an outlet. Though, those who knew him never thought he had much of a sense of humor. What really had caught his attention was the lake, small without much of a shoreline.

After all his years of toiling in a small kitchen, he suddenly felt like he was back in big sky country. The Yellowstone Valley, the prettiest place he had ever seen, especially before there were too many people. He had made his way West working as a cook on steamboats and the advancing railroad. Montana had been raw, wild country back then, home to a few trappers, Indians, and the cavalry who chased each other around a lot. It wasn't until after the power of the Sioux was broken that the white man felt safe in the Yellowstone Valley. He had arrived late in the season and stayed on at the station at Carlton for what proved to be a hard winter. He stayed through one more freeze-your-nuts-off winter and finally had enough, so he pushed on west finally arriving in the biggest city this side of the Mississippi.

San Francisco had been the unlikeliest place for him to put down roots but his small world within the four walls of a kitchen kept him away from the madness of the masses, baking and rye whiskey his partners in life.

The little lake before him reminded him of better days and the thought crossed his mind that maybe it was time for him to go back to Montana. He rolled himself a cigarette, laid back on a small knoll, looked at the lake, and remembered the good days when there had been plenty of space. The morning pleasant, Nemo slumbered. A light breeze moved the smoke around, the sky gray above the blue waters of the lake beneath.

A grumble in his stomach disturbed his momentary peace of mind as he thought about biscuits. He was hungry and thought about baking a pan or two. His stomach grumbled, please. His mind told him that would be a foolish thing, opening up Pandora's box or worse. The aroma of fresh baked bread would drive people nuts, especially folks who had not eaten in a day or two. The kids would be snatching biscuits right and left. None of these poor devils would lend him a hand, if he needed one, which he didn't. Next thing they would be demanding that he fry up some bacon—then where would he be. Best he be moving on, out into the dunes until he saw no one about. His mouth watered as he thought of biscuits with honey and fried bacon. "'Yes, sir-ee, that's just what I'm going to do," he uttered aloud, having made up his mind.

"What's that you said?"

"Whatever it was, it wasn't meant for you." Liam rose and chewed on his last word as if he had a pissed-off scorpion in his mouth. Leaning on a cane next to the small knoll he saw an old Nigga who looked as old as Mississippi mud, had one good eye, and wasn't much good for nothing anymore. But there was something about the way he held his head, the way he spoke. This old boy was not intimidated and could stand with confidence in front of a white man. Hell, even some of the old buffalo soldiers had kept their eyes to the ground. Niggas were okay by him, if they knew their place. Chinese he wouldn't give the time of day to, nor would any other right-thinking white man. Indians, now there one had to be careful. Indians were at least a step above a chink, but you had to be careful or the next thing you know you might be missing a hair piece. He touched his own baldpate thinking that it had been some time since he had to worry about that. *Never-the-less, a Nigga had just addressed him as if he were an equal.* That was when the scorpion bit him. *The Nigga is old and crippled, he doesn't mean no harm—just let it be.* He heard Nemo say as he turned away.

Sergeant Freeman wasn't about to let it go. He had seen that look before, in both white and black men. *This here white man was hiding something, and a pint of good sipping whiskey against a hole in a donut, it had to do with whatever was on that wagon. Now if I were smart, I'd just leave him be and let the army sort it out. But the man is wearing an apron and men don't wear aprons unless they work in a kitchen, behind a bar, or a butcher shop. What does he have on that wagon?* Freeman braced himself guessing that the man was strong enough to knock him off his feet with one punch. "Going to do what?" He asked again.

"It ain't got nothing to do with you, old man, go about your own business" Liam said as he toe-kicked some dirt onto the last smoking embers of the fire.

"Hmmm-ummm, you sure are one pissed-off white man. I'll tell you what, you tell me what I've done to upset you so, besides me being black, and I'll do it again." This time the sergeant smiled.

Liam looked up, admiring the old nigga's grit, almost smiling. "I don't have the energy to pretend to like you this morning, so skat."

"It's okay if you don't like me, not everyone has good taste. I figure I might be coming up in the world. This morning I was driving a shit-wagon, and now I'm talking to you." He switched his cane to the other hand. "Do what," he asked again?

Liam Malarkey answered with a short barking laugh. Scratching his chin, he answered, "damned if I can remember. Oh, yeah, now I recall. I was thinking about getting out of this ashcan and heading off to Montana. I spent some time there a few years back. All, in all, not a bad place, sure gotta be better than what we got left here. I had just made up my mind to get out of Frisco before another god-damned quake finishes everything, leaving nothing fit to feed the wharf rats." He gave a grim chuckle then abruptly shut up.

"I had some troopers who transferred in from Montana. That was back in 1896. General Pershing led a unit of the 10th Cavalry on a mission to round up Cree Indians over the space of 600 miles and deport them to Canada. It was hard riding but pretty country, or so I was told. I was riding herd on a troop of buffalo soldiers up Alaska way at the time." He tapped his leg with his cane for effect. "Now I guess that I'm too damn old to ever get up that way."

Liam gave the old black soldier a *'does it look as if I care'* nod. What the old man had said gave him pause to think. *I am not old, yet, nor am I as young and fit as I once was.* He patted his protruding stomach. *Maybe Montana is not in the cards.*

The old soldier turned and just looked up the road at nothing in particular.

For some reason Liam felt compelled to stay a few more minutes and talk with the man. Talk, that was something he did not indulge in very often. Choosing to talk with a black man, now that was something else altogether. He reached into the back of the wagon and pulled out the keg of coal oil, splashing a few drops where a spark still burned. Tossing some dead wood on the fire he gathered up the coffee pot. "Coffee." It wasn't a question; it was an offer.

"I haven't a cup." Freeman answered. "Thank you, anyways. I just as well be getting on down the road." He knew better than to ask to use a white man's cup, who would just as soon throw it away after a black man touched it, let alone drank from it. And it seemed to him that good cups might be hard to come by for some time to come.

"Where you headed?" The man asked as he pulled a blue dented coffee cup from the wagon then holding it up for him to take. "You're wearing the uniform, but I take it that you have been cashiered out. Here, take it and keep it," meaning the coffee cup. "I've got more."

"Thank yeah, kindly." He took the cup, wiping the inside out with a handkerchief he pulled from a pocket; the handkerchief more soiled than the inside of the coffee cup had been. After a silent pause as he considered the empty coffee cup and the meaning of its gift. "Sergeant Freeman." No hand extended, his eyes still locked on the white man, he took an extra step. "As you might have guessed I was a buffalo solder. A thirty-year man, but they cashiered me out due to infirmities a few months short."

Coffee was poured, this time a decent cup.

"I knew that you were a tough old bird." He eyed two men passing by least they might have other intentions.

"I'm Tige Malarkey. You can just call me Malarkey, you're already thinking that I'm full of it, so let's just drop any pretenses. Yesterday morning, I was serving my time in a small neighborhood café, baking bread and frying up bacon and eggs."

Sergeant Freeman sipped his coffee. "Until yesterday morning I was passing time driving a shit-wagon to help make ends meet. Whew, this here coffee tastes about as bad as that old wagon stunk."

"Glad you like it."

Their conversation paused as they sipped at the coffee.

"Like I said, you're a tough old bird." Malarkey shook the coffee pot to see how much was left hen held it out to the sergeant.

Freeman politely waved it off; not that he didn't want more. "Thanks anyway. Like I said, I've got to be moving on down the road."

"You only got yourself for company?" *Now that is a dumb-ass question,* Malarkey thought to himself, *what the hell do I care.* That fact was that for some reason unknown to him he was taking a liking to the old buffalo solder. He did not wait for an answer. "I don't know you from any other nigga in the field, but you strike me as a trustworthy old goat with tough leather on your hide. Montana is a long way from here, a little company might not do me any harm. You got anywhere else you got to be?" Nemo gave him a quick shot to his temple. *Take it back you damned fool before the nigga takes you up on it,* he chastised himself.

Freeman sipped his coffee looking up over the cup and through the steam, his eyes locked on the old baker. Neither said a word, letting their silence seal a bond neither wanted, nor could explain.

"Well, don't trip on any shadows," Malarkey broke their silent appraisal of each other.

"Well Sir, I guess that I'll be buying a heap of troubles if I rode off to someplace in Montana with you. The bumping and the bruising of a long wagon ride would just about finish me off." He shook his head as if he had a powerful case of the miseries. "So, I'd be damned if I went." He looked down the long winding road that wound through the park, his feet not moving an inch.

"What's down that road you keep looking at?"

"I guess that's a fair question. You told me what you are planning on doing, so I don't see any problem in telling you what is down that road." A smile crossed his face, he's eyes showing the way to good memories. "I don't rightly know. Yesterday, I was the Command Sergeant of a shit-wagon. Not much to be proud of there, but it was what it was, and the best the good Lord felt fit to give me. If I have any kin left, I don't rightly know where they might be. Most of my friends are buried and waiting for me up at the soldier's cemetery over there at the Presidio. This morning I barely had a damned shit-wagon to call my own, but somewhere over the hours I had acquired friends, closest thing I ever had to a family since I was a boy and still a slave." He paused briefly to see what expression might cross the white man's face. "I decided to move on because I did not want to cause them no trouble. I don't I don't want to become a burden for them, or anyone else, folks got enough of their own troubles."

"And down that road?"

"My pappy once told me to never stop looking down that road. One never knows what possibilities might be coming your way. Just keep looking, one never knows…"

Liam Malarkey watched as the old man slowly turned and walked back the way he had come, his gait slow, his head held high. Without further debate, the thought of going back to Montana was no longer on the short list of options in his mind. Pouring the coffee once again on the fire he untied the horse, climbed up on the wagon, and followed the old soldier. "Get on up here, Mr. Freeman, I'm looking for some possibilities too. Montana and me parted ways some time ago for all the right reasons. I have trapped beaver, dug for gold, and worked for the railroad in Montana, but I never found any real possibilities. No need to go back. I think I'll just go down this here road same as you, not necessarily knowing where we're going, just keeping an eye out for one of those opportunities that might come our way. It gives a fella cause to ponder. Opportunities you say. Opportunities." The last word he pronounced slowly and from the top as if he could taste the sweetness as he might the sugar topping from a fresh baked hot-cross bun.

"Lordy, what a curious day." Huckleberry Freeman said as he accepted a hand up onto the wagon." As the horse moved forward Freeman stole a glance back at the cloth covering the back of the wagon.

"As long as we're on first name basis, at least for the time being, you might as well have a have a looksee."

"All in good time," Huckleberry Freeman said, "all in good time. He needed a moment to digest being on a first name basis with a white man; that had been a long time coming, and not something he had thought he would live long enough to see.

"Now I know why you have everything covered up," Freeman said after he looked. "That stove just might come in handy sooner, or later."

"Long as the army doesn't take it."

Freeman pinched the sleeve to his uniform. "Now why would this man's army go and do something like that?" He smiled as he tucked the sheet back over the stove and kitchen goods.

"Come to think of it I'm a free man now. No army to tell when to get up, where to go, when to shit. I will admit that there was a time or two when I did enjoy ordering those young bucks to do the same."

"Being a nigga in the army must have been a tough road to hoe." Malarkey said as he tried to ponder what it must have been like. He could not.

"Do me a favor since we're supposed to be partners of some kind now. My first name is Huckleberry, not nigga. Huckleberry is a lot more friendly."

"I think I can manage that, Huck."

"You ever have a nickname?" Huckleberry asked.

Liam looked thoughtful for a moment as he wondered how he should answer that. "Risky", he finally said. "I was once called Risky for the way I used to play cards back when I worked for the railroad."

"You win?"

"Nary, a hand."

"Malarkey it is then."

There was a half-breath of silence followed by a thunderclap of laughter. For the next hour or so the two men jawed and spun yards neither knowing when the truth might be told; more importantly, what was spun was a most unusual friendship.

LXII

Someone once said that change is a process. Then again, there are times that it can be an intense monsoon. This must be one of those times. Their lives had been upended by a powerful earthquake followed by a whirling storm of destruction and fires. They were brought together as strangers, naked with not much more than the clothes on their backs. They had lost their homes, their places in society, and at least for the moment—hope. No sir, Conrad Wolff thought, there is no doubt that what we have here is a full-blown monsoon.

Three days and nights they had been in the park and as each day and night had come, and passed, he wondered whether or not they were doing the right thing—were they in the right place, and if so, why? Should they pack up and leave? Pack what? Go where?

Wolff was a man who never missed a meal and liked his personal comforts. He was an educated man never meant to waste his time or mind with riffraff. He did not think of them as riffraff, they just were not his kind of people.

Alphonso's bag, now empty of anything to eat or drink, seemed of little importance, except to Alphonso who guarded it with his life.

The army had set up field kitchens which served meager

portions of soup and bread; none were nearby. They could move to the larger camp where the field kitchens were, where it was crowded, dusty, to none of their likings, and there was no shade. So, they took turns going to the field kitchens and endured the long hours of waiting. Discouragement was added to their exhaustion as the long lines of refugees looking for something to eat seemed to be never ending. Flies were plentiful, swarming in growing numbers as the sanitary conditions in the camp continued to decline. There were no tents, shelters, latrines, or available troops to dig them. While everyone complained that they had nothing, garbage sprouted like unwanted weeds was becoming increasingly of a problem.

Conrad Wolff liked Francis DeGeorgie, even though he had a dangerous mind. DeGeorgie despised the bourgeoisie. Admittedly, there were places where the distribution of wealth and property could be improved, but that was of little concern to Wolff who saw himself as a member of the intelligentsia. Just as the Catholic Church took care of its treasures so should the minds and the needs of the intelligentsia should be closely guarded. The young revolutionary frightened Wolff and liking him made it all that more difficult.

Francis DeGeorgie had left without saying a word during their first night in the park. Whether he had been arrested, or not, could only be guessed at. His youth and vigor were dearly missed, his glumness was not. His radical ideas still crossed their minds.

They all liked Sergeant Freeman. He had arrived as a black man; they ignored what he could not. They had all tried to stop him from leaving, each telling him in their own way that it was okay that he was black, that he was welcome anyway. He had thanked them, then they had parted ways, the old sergeant knowing that he would not be welcomed by the good Christian white folks that would fill the refugee camps yet to come. In a city that once had over six hundred thousand people there were fewer than a couple hundred Black people, with no black community to speak of. He did not leave to find and be with his own kind, he did not have a clue where to start. Going south, that was not about to happen. He was not a man to chase *'the could have beens'* or for that matter bitter memories. He left because he did not belong, that was the long and short of it.

LXIII

On the shores of the lake there must have been a thousand people, all juggling the same problems. Just before dusk, on their first night by the lake, two women came to their campfire. For one reason or another the two women asked to join them. When asked why, the older of the two, Maude Perkins, said that it was Leah's kitten. "Anyone who can love an animal that ugly is all right in my book." However, her next comment got on Leah's bad side. "If it were me, I'd have downed it in an old potato sack. It is not so much that it's ugly as sin, with that hairless wrinkled forehead, and those glow-in-the-dark eyes, and purple stained paws. It is the expression on its face. There is a demon in there waiting to come out. It might just be a kitten now, but one day it will grow up. Even now I can guess what it must be thinking…plotting, 'Tonight I'll gouge your eyes out and rip out your throat as you sleep. The beast has the evil eye and will bring you nothing but misfortune.'" She crossed herself more as a gypsy than a Christian. Her mean-spirited comments sent Leah into tears.

Later, Efah, the younger woman, shy, and soft-spoken confided with Hatti that it was because all the men in their group were old. Efah was young, eighteen, and frightened by the way some of the hard-scrabble men they had come across looked at her with hungry eyes.

Hatti understood but held her tongue, thinking the young

woman to be spindly, if not ill-favored. On the other hand, the older woman reminded Hatti of the dower, strict, unapproving German housekeeper for a former paramour of hers.

Later that night, while they slept, the two uninvited women smuggled into the campsite thirteen boys. How they managed to do this is a mystery unto itself. When the sun rose the pack of boys untangled themselves from where they had slept, and laid siege to the camp and everything within running distance that would have made Genghis Khan proud. They were rambunctious, rowdy, and as misbehaved as a pack of stray dogs in a chicken coop.

When jarred awake, Mr. Piff got a full dose of Maude's own evil eye, when he took a long hard look at the children, sniffed the air, as he batted at a bevy of flies. His experience of almost being dumped in the lake the prior day gave him no sense of joy with their arrival.

Conrad Wolff took a stronger disliking to the howling hooligans. "One thing that I have learned in my years is to speak direct and don't hem-haw about the point. Call a spade a spade, a jack a jack. I can tell you this, the one thing that is not wanted right now is an unruly brat. God must have a sense of humor this morning which is not much appreciated by yours truly. He looked up towards the heavens and winked. As I speak, they seem to be multiplying." He looked hard at both women who were doing nothing to reign in their tribe. "They are a gang of street Arabs, who know nothing of manners and civilized ways, and I suspect a whole lot about thievery and hell-raising shenanigans. These Bedouin waifs need a good Christian education, a guiding hand with a firm belt."

Maude's eyes flared as she choked back what she intended to say in defense of the children just as they were interrupted by two of the boys who ran whooping and hollering, jumped over the morning fire scattering sparks, spilling a small cup of prized water dowsing the green wood which added more smoke into the morning air.

Alphonso nodded in agreement as he stretched, then checked his bag to see if it had been violated by thieves during the night. Katie looked on both sides sympathetically, and in hope that something to eat might have been overlooked.

Dimitri, who had left the old stove as is, had been foraging for wood, dropped what little he had been able to find at Maude's feet. He was a man who commanded his own space and quick to flare when crowded. "On board a ship behavior like this would call for at least ten lashes." His menacing look far more potent than hers as they locked scowls. "That is the last of the wood. There are a thousand people about and not enough kindling for ten. The water that was spilt was our last drop. There is water in the lake for boiling and to wash with, but I would not drink a drop of it considering what has been going into the lake the last few hours." He nodded towards where a group of men could be seen relieving themselves shamelessly at the edge of the lake. "*Mágissa,* old witch, you are a bad omen and bring nothing with you but bad luck; that we do not need. You are not welcome here. Go! Take these, how do you say it, Mr. Wolff…street Arabs out of here. You are not welcome."

"Well, I never…" Maude fumed.

"You can say that again," Hatti retorted.

The old woman's expression remained belligerent; her face turned from shocked to ashen.

Katie fought back an urge to add her own voice as a trio of the boys finished off what was left of the fire with their game of cowboys and Indians, leaving no prisoners.

Leah was visibly shaken. Since the loss of her parents her life had been protected from the harsh realities of the world outside of grandma's house. She had been raised with a vivid imagination that had slowly moved from the nightmares that were a result of her parent's deaths to pleasant dreams and imaginary stories based on books she had read and stories her grandma had told. The rowdiness of the boys, the woman's mean comments regarding her kitten, adults arguing, threatening each other, and their sudden bleak seemingly hopeless situation, caused her to unleash a waterfall of tears. This deflated Maude's fluster as the group's attention shifted from her unreasonable outrage to Leah's tears as Hatti and Katie brought her under their soothing embrace.

Leah's dam needed to break, as even Mr. Piff rolled to her side.

Dimitri, Alphonso, and Conrad met in council, each suggesting, more often demanding, one course of action or another. Alphonso was not one to throw his weight around, he was getting on in years and in truth a novice when it came to standing up as a man for one's rights; his history with Grazia was not something easily left behind. Dimitri, while a gentle giant, had often had to use his physical presence and charisma to knock heads with drunkards, sailors, longshoreman, and men of ill-repute. Throwing a punch or crushing an opponent with an intense bear hug were not of much value now, although he was sorely tempted to give the she-devil a good drubbing.

Conrad Wolff knew that what they needed most was to find food, shelter, and a course of action that would remove them from the maddening crowd. It would take some time to rebuild what all had been lost within the course of a couple of days. The smoke, and the influx of refugees from the firestorms that were ravaging San Francisco brought their hearts and hopes towards still darker times; not better. He was not emotionally equipped for such a challenge, becoming sullen and introspective as he sought his own course.

No one noticed as Maude and Efah rounded up the boys to play a new round of cowboys and Indians, to be played out as they retreated towards the refugee camps at the Presidio. As Maude and the boys disappeared around a bend in the road Efah stopped and looked back.

She was torn between her sense of duty to the boys, who in truth she found unbearable, and her dislike of the firm self-righteous matron that oversaw them all. Efah had aged out of the orphanage that Maude ran as if it were an insane asylum. A year and a half working alongside Maude had been as useless as trying to stop a stampede with a raised handkerchief. She turned, following the hard-bitten matron a few more steps, before turning back, finding hesitancy a crippling weakness in her knees, until finally she steeled herself to return to the campsite asking for sanctuary from the women gathered around the still weeping Leah. Katie was the first to welcome Efah understanding that while older she was still very much a child as Leah was.

The ache in Conrad's ponderous gut was all the protest he needed. He had not heard a valid argument or remedy to the dark clouds that surrounded them from either Alphonso or Dimitri. As his eyes searched around them, he saw more of the same, hungry people, without resource, abandoned by civilization to an unknown fate that he was not about to endure. They reeked of their experiences, and he knew that he smelled as wretched as they did. It would not be long until their stink overwhelmed the god-awful sewage they left behind. As Alphonso and Dimitri continued to argue about things of which they had no control, reasonable and unknown, he made up his mind and walked away. His only thought was that God would never allow St. Dominic's Church to be sacrificed to the fires of hell that had already taken so much. Believing that it still stood, he sought to find his good friend the archbishop, who surely would see to his care. He looked forward to a friendly game of chess, as they sipped brandy and discussed the literature of the world, this hurricane of change passing them by. Time to collect a favor or two.

LXIX

The Committee of Fifty far exceeded that number as the fires were brought under control and the immense task of taking care of the displaced populace became a stark reality. They met in small groups to wrestle with the problems and to decide who would oversee what. Good citizens all, men of experience, wealth, and influence, sifted through the ashes of a city now laid to waste. There were a few who calculated and connived to line their own pockets. These rogues included Mayor Eugene Schmitz and the Board of Supervisors, all minions of the infamous lawyer Abe Ruef.

The unions still held a strong sway over most civic actions within the city of San Francisco. Telephone, Railroad, water, Electric, and the multiple labor unions paid graft through Mayor Schmitz, much of it lining Ruef's pockets.

It would take at least two weeks for the core thoroughfares of the city to be cleared of thirty-foot piles of debris. It would take as long to get the refugee tent camps, sanitation and flood services in the various parks up and running. The fires had laid waste to San Francisco and what was needed to rebuild had to be brought in by the army and by railroad.

Those who sought to line their own pockets because of this epic disaster only had to look down the road for opportunities; Abe Ruef was at the front of the line.

If things went as he planned there would be another gold rush, this time for the land that San Francisco was built upon. The biggest prize would be the land where Chinatown had once stood. He looked around the room, at these men of power and influence, seeing that there was no one to get in his way.

L

Francis DeGeorgie put aside his politics for the moment content to just be himself, and to fall inescapably in love with Antoinette. He did not speak nor share much of his own past intent on discovering the multitudes of secrets and talents hidden openly behind Antoinette's laughter and twinkling eyes. She seemed to have an instinctive if not mystical connection with the remaining animals as they truly sought her attention and treats. His concealment of his past was quiet, when asked he wound turn the questions around to her—the why this and that, her favorite colors in the rainbow, music, books, dreams, and childhood memories; never once revealing his own.

It was not long until she became a bit peeved at his reluctance to speak of himself but her growing desire to touch and be touched by him weighed more. Her feminine instincts told her that in time he would open up to her. It was his hesitation to return the intimacy she desired that caused her concern. What was he hiding, was it so dreadful, something so awful that one day soon he would vanish leaving her with a sense that he had only been a dream?

It was on the fifth day when they were tending to the birds kept in the aviary at the castle° that he ran his fingers through her hair, said her name softly as he touched her checks raising her lips just enough to kiss them. Their embrace was at first hesitant. She was surprised at her own hesitancy before she pulled herself in closer, their kiss lingering. She had never kissed a boy this way; the way it excited her. She opened her eyes, finding his, not wanting their embrace to ever end. She giggled just loud enough for him to hear as she felt their kiss begin to fade.

"Antoinette, I've been looking for you." The voice belonged to Lazlo Zolton, an Assistant Supervisor in charge of the Glen Park Properties for Crocker Company Real Estate. Lazlo was Antonette's immediate supervisor, who she mistrusted on several levels. He was an odd-looking man, tall and reedy, with sharp square shoulders, topped with a long neck and elongated head. His eyebrows were thin if not invisible, with a dark mustache shorter on the right side than the left. His hair, laid back with grease, hidden by a bowler hat. His blinked rapidly as if his eyelids were having a fit.

Antoinette pulled away from Francis as if her life depended on it. "We…we're in here."

Lazlo peered through the open cage door to a room that was no longer used other than wild pigeons who thought nothing of leaving their mess for Antoinette to frequently clean up after. "Ahhh, there you are," Lazlo could not disguise his surprise at finding her in the room with another man. While married, he had not hidden his desire to have a dalliance with her, that

---

* A Moorish-style castle was once perched on the east side of the sweeping ravine at the foot of San Francisco's Glen Park neighborhood.. Morro Castle was built in the late 1890s along with a tea house, a children's playground, and an aviary by the developer Archibald S. Baldwin of Baldwin & Howell real estate agency. It was part of the Mission Park and Zoological Gardens often used as an aviary

so far, she had managed to avoid. "I have news."

Francis saw the way he looked at her, his fists tightening.

"News?" She responded, pushing a broom into Francis' hands.

"We? And who is this—if I might inquire? You know the rules about visitors. The zoo is closed to the public, as is Morris Castle."

Placing her hands on her hips she answered him with an intent that he was not used to from a woman. She leaned forward as she spoke, her right hand raised in a brief contemptuous gesture before returning to her hip.

"I know fairly well the rules, Mister Lazlo Zolton." She contemptuously deliberately over-pronounced the 'ton' in his last name as an insult, which it was. "This is my cousin Francis who is visiting after his studies in Europe. He was staying at the Palace Hotel until it was destroyed in the fires. He will be making his bed here in the aviary until he can arrange for funds to be transferred from back east. He will only be staying here for a few days."

"He can't…" The news that he brought caused Lazlo to stop mid-sentence. It changed everything. "Well, I… never mind that now. Crocker and Company has agreed with the city to allow a certain number of refugees to use the park until other facilities can be arranged. What is to be known as *Camp 29* is to be situated over at Mission Park between Church and 18th Street, just on the edge of Glen Park. The zoo will remain closed, as will the castle, except for patrons and friends of the

Crocker Estate, as needed. Since I am the one to determine who is allowed, you are welcome, Mister…I did not get your full name, sir." Lazlo took out a notebook, and small pencil from his coat pocket, looking at Francis for a proper answer.

Francis bowed slightly, giving Antoinette a carefully placed wink. "Francis, Francis Shaeffer Jones, of the Long Island Jones."

Antoinette dug her fingernail into her palm to keep herself from laughing.

Lazlo seemed pleased with the answer, it being obvious that Antoinette's cousin was of a monied background. Crocker Real Estate was reconsidering their opportunities to sell the Glen Park properties as originally planned now that the populace had been uprooted. He held out his hand, less in formal greeting, than to placate Antoinette.

Francis did not take it, returning to sweeping the floor, his strokes too practiced for a gentleman of means,

"After today, anyone who presents you with my card has my permission to stay. I will want to know who and where they are quartered. I almost forgot, we will be taking care of food and the necessary provisions as soon as everything can be arranged. I'll be in touch as soon as I know the specifics." He tipped his hat and left.

Curious, Quinn peeked in the door, his plumb of colorful feathers fluttering, the multiple eyes on his colorful feathers warding off Lazlo's evil spirit. Sensing the nature of the man the peacock often pecked at Lazlo's legs, this time being no exception.

As soon as they heard Lazlo's 1904 Matheson Touring Car sputter away Antoinette burst into laughter. "You are a complete scamp—a scamp beyond reproach." She practically leapt into his arms. They kissed as they danced freely about the aviary.

Quinn followed as they stepped outside the castle, the three gazing from the hillside to see what was left of San Francisco. Columns of smoke still rose from the ashes. Where streets and stately buildings had once been lay a graveyard of deep rubble and broken dreams and aspirations. They could barely make out where the streets and boulevards had once been—where just a week before five hundred and twenty blocks and thousands of buildings had once stood.

"I wonder how many people will be coming," Francis wondered. He had no idea how many people had lived in the city prior to the fires, nor how many camps there were. San Francisco was smaller than St Petersburg, Russia, but he understood the magnitude. In St. Petersburg, the homeless had covered the city like locusts.

Antoinette took his hand. Below there were just one hundred and twenty-seven homes spread out on one side of Mission Park. Glen Park, on the other side, remained vacant undeveloped hillsides, and dunes. She pointed. "Over there, that is where the camp will be. See, there are already people there. Soon there will be hundreds more." They could see small groups of people, most on foot, dragging their few possessions, working their way in their direction.

"Thousands," Francis finished, "perhaps more." His Adam's apple rising with his sigh.

"How will we be able to feed them all?" Antoinette had always thought of Glen Park as her little sanctuary, even though she was one of five caretakers. She doubted that any authority she had would extend over Mission Park. Mission Park had no caretakers,' and it would not surprise her if the city had granted authority over it to Crocker Real Estate. What would become of her quiet little oasis. You could not call it much of a zoo anymore, most of the animals were gone. In the last few months, she had been the only one left to take care of the zoo. The other caretakers were friends of Lazlo Zolton, men she did not trust, who were lazy and frequently absent from their duties. "I'm glad you are here," she told Francis as she squeezed his hand, careful not to hurt it. "Are you going to stay, at least for a while?"

Francis squeezed back whispering that he would.

LI

Li Fengzhang wept.

Despite his yearnings to become more western, Li Fengzhang's fate was intricately tied to the people and commerce of a place that now was no more. Chinatown, with all its faults was now nothing more than charred memories. He felt that all was lost, that when his father passed away, he would be alone and destitute in a place that did not want him. How could one be so hated, despised, and invisible at the same time. As he stood overlooking the devastation of the city, he was unaware of the power politics that were stirring, that Chinatown might rise again from the ashes anew.

Many of his brethren had fled the city, those that remained in San Francisco were not treated kindly. If not for the watchful eyes in Washington D.C., and the Empress-Dowager of China, the fate of the Chinese people remained uncertain, ultimately, they were rounded up to protect them from themselves.

Without any consultation with the Chinese 'The General Relief Committee' proposed to gather all Chinese in the temporary camp at the Presidio. On April 26, a committee comprised of Abraham "Abe" Ruef; James D. Phelan; Jeremiah Deneen; Dr. James W. Ward, president of the Health Commission, and Methodist minister were appointed to take charge of the question of the permanent location of the Chinese. The debate was both hot and heavy, Abe Ruef and James D. Phelan were arch enemies. Their common ground was abiding racism and hatred for the Chinese. Their plan was to move Chinatown to Hunter's Point. Move them to the cities fringes so civilized commerce can rebuild on the valuable land where Chinatown once thrived. There were already Chinese fishing villages throughout the mudflats, 'what's a few more', went one argument. One problem was that the area already had huge sanitation issues, and the estimated number of Chinese to be moved there was simply unknown.

Telegrams sent by the war department to General Funston about the pending arrival of the Chinese consul-general from Washington was one of the deciding factors in the quick establishment of a committee to "assist" the Chinese. The Committee on the Location of Chinatown began, with the help of General Funston, to concentrate the few Chinese left in San Francisco in preparation of moving them to Hunters Point. But more politically astute members of the committee were concerned that San Francisco, ridding itself of the Chinese, would also lose its profitable Asian trade. With all of Chinatown destroyed, many of its inhabitants fled to Oakland, other cities in the East Bay, or huddled in the refugee camp at the west end of the Presidio. The committee did not anticipate stiff resistance from the government of China.

Chow-Tszchi, first secretary of the Chinese Legation at Washington arrived in Oakland within a few days to meet with China's consul-general in San Francisco. They, in turn, met with Governor Pardee in Oakland, and told him of the Empress-Dowager's displeasure with the plan, and that the government of China would build its consulate in the heart of old Chinatown.

The events governing the future of Chinatown were unknown to Li Fengzhang whose fortune about to change due to a fellow merchant he had only met twice. Look Tin Eli had owned the old Sing Chong Bazaar. Like Li, Look Tin Eli saw the future of Chinatown as not becoming more Western in appearance but more Asian, more exotic. A cultural exchange and a place where East and West could meet on more common ground.

Facing an uncertain future, Li Fengzhang returned to his father to tell him the news that Chinatown was gone and would never be part of San Francisco again.

"Who told you this?" His father asked with sorrowful eyes. "I do not believe that such a thing can happen." After a few moments of silence, he turned to his son, writing down a name, and said, "Find this man, he has eyes for the future. Ask him what must be done."

"How do I find him?

"This I do not know. Now, leave an old man to rest his weary eyes. The news you have brought weighs heavily on my heart."

Priscilla Cody waited for Li in the little sunroom that sat facing her back yard and garden.

"He is resting," Li whispered, though his father would not be able to hear them from across the garden.

"What will you do now?" Priscilla asked as she politely gestured for him to sit, while offering a spot of hot tea.

Li had more questions than answers. He folded the piece of paper that his father had given him placing it in his pocket. The name *Look Tin Eli** already forgotten. He would not look for this man, how could he, in a Chinatown that no longer existed. The records of land and property ownership, names and birth records of the Chinese had all been lost to the great fires.

They talked while the tea remained untouched, growing tepid. Priscilla cautious to not ask questions that she knew he did not want to face just yet.

The Japanese housekeeper came in quiet slippers. His face told her that he did not bring good news. He bowed deep and respectfully to Li Fengzhang. "I was checking to see if your father might need something, a blanket perhaps." He could not hide an uncomfortable sigh. "It is with great sorrow that I must unfortunately inform you that your father has passed. He was old, and his time had passed." He glanced at Priscilla, maintaining his bow of respect. "Was he a Christian man?"

"NO," Li answered, now feeling utterly alone.

"I shall see that he is made presentable. One moment please.

---

*Look Tin Eli, a Chinatown resident who had been born and raised in Mendocino County. Eli spoke in fluent English with more intelligence than most of the politicians in office and proved to be a savvy negotiator with one foot in both worlds. Eli and fellow businessman Wong G. Yow worked with white architects to rebuild Chinatown, favoring tourist-friendly flourishes, including Pagoda-style buildings that weren't there before, and narrow streets and alleys to accommodate a higher population density.

LII

Sergeant Huckleberry Freeman strolled to the top of the sand dune that separated him from the ocean and the site he and Malarkey had set up camp for the last few days. The earthquake, their flight through the city of flames, all seemed as if they had happened in another lifetime. He had had that same feeling a time or two back in his army days. He did not have to look back now to know that his shit-hauling days were over. There was one thing that he knew that hadn't changed, the chaos. There would be more people, longer lines, less sanitation, and less tolerance for each other. To an old black man like him that did not sound exactly enticing. But here he was thinking of doing just that, going back. It was not the blowing sand, or the cold fog that grated on his nerves or chilled his bones. He guessed that he and Malarkey had more food and coffee then some of the wealthiest men that were pitching their tents back on the grassy side of the dunes. Not one person had bothered them, not one had raised an eyebrow or given a cold hard stare at a black man being where he ought not to be. That was just it, where was he supposed to be?

"What are you doing standing out here in the chilly wind, waiting for a damned gull to shit on your black shiny head?" Malarkey asked having quietly followed Freeman.

The frothy, blue-green waves breaking one after another, after another, were hypnotic, restful, reminding the old buffalo soldier of the rhythmic clop-clop-clopping of a protracted line of calvary horses slowly trying to reach the horizon. He watched as each wave reached the tide line and slowly rolled back into the churning ocean water. A lone gull hovers over the last breaking waves, searching, then veering off to deeper waters. Huckleberry did not look away from the rhythmic waves, taking no offense from Malarkey's comment as he pondered what the good Lord had brought down the road to mark this day as being different then the thousands that he had lived through in what seemed like another lifetime.

He was seeing things through different eyes these days. Liam Malarkey was a white man that he neither hated nor feared. The thing that made him laugh was that he considered Liam Malarkey this white man to be a friend—that was one good thing the good Lord had brought down the road to him. "Malarkey, I was just thinking that it just might be time for us to go back." He turned and looked his new friend straight in the face. "Now wait a moment and hear me out. We can't stay here on these bleak wind-blown sand dunes forever. Hell, come a day or two more, one or the both of us will go stark raving nuts with the sand blowing this way and that, the whistle in our ears." He turned and looked at Malarkey for a reaction. The one he got he did not expect.

"I was wondering when you'd open up," he answered. "You lost your sass sometime yesterday, and I haven't heard complaint number one about my coffee. You and I both know I can't make a pot of coffee worth a hill of beans."

"You got that right."

"So, you say you want to go back. Where? What is there worth going back to; kids hopping and hollering, long lines and bad chow—if you can find it? The stench? Everyone belly-aching about how their world has ended, and nobody doing diddly-squat about it. Me, I do not want no part of it, old man, I for one thought that if anyone could see the dark side of their welcoming us, it would be you. Go back?" He paused to adjust his thinking. "You said that we ought to be going down that road looking for opportunity. Well, that is just what we ought to do. Go forward, not back, until opportunity kicks us both in our asses, and says, 'Wake up you fools, don't you see an opportunity when it's a knock'in at your door.'"

"What if opportunity is waiting for us back there?" He nodded towards the far side of the dunes where smoke still lingered. "If you listen, you might hear the voices of the lost, beneath the pounding of the surf, we're thinking about leaving behind us."

Liam Malarkey raised both hands in surrender. "Given a little time, and I mean this much," he held up two fingers about an inch apart, "I say that we head south towards Las Angeles. I heard once that Las Angeles can be spelled the same as opportunity." He tried to spell it aloud for emphasis "…o…p…p… e…"

"I had Buffalo Soldiers who could spell better than that."

"I'm not bragging."

LIII

A tall man, stooped, not much older than Alphonso, looking far worse for the wear, fidgeted, and groaned, as they waited in line. After a while, he introduced himself speaking with a strong Scottish accent, "Angus, Angus Willkie Humes, and you, sir?" Leaning on his cane, he swatted at a swarm of over-aggressive flies while waiting for his morning meal. He looked at his pocket-watch, then at the position of the sun. "Damned gadget has not worked right since the day I got it. I don't know why I continue to carry it." The man just wanted to pass the time while waiting, needing something to keep his spirits up.

It only took a discreet glance for Alphonso to determine what was wrong with the watch. It was dented showing rust at the base of the hour hand. *Better to buy a new one than try to fix that one,* he thought. Alphonso did not feel much like talking, preferring his own silence. After the man had tried to engage him for the third time, he just shrugged his shoulders saying, "I'd wish you good luck but there isn't any around today."

The Scotsman sputtered, "Awa' an bile yer heid," looking to those around him for support that he had been insulted, or at least slighted, after he had been the one to extend the courtesy.

Alphonso left the queue with a tightly tucked smile thinking he had rendered some minor injustice to a penny-pinching

Scotsman, who he was not inclined to befriend or extend a polite word to. He returned empty-handed to the tent that he and Katie now shared, feeling remorse that he had not brought her something to eat. He knew that when he looked into her eyes, he would see her pangs of conscience for Lea, Morgan Piff, the others, who were all hungry.

There was nothing to be done but try again.

The high sun suggested that it was somewhere around midday when he returned to the never-ending food line. When he arrived, there were already hundreds of people. Word soon passed down the line that the army had not delivered enough food; never-the-less, they still waited. It did not matter who was to blame, especially when blame could not fill their bellies. The system had yet to function with any sense of reliability, with no promise of when it would. Half a day wasted, Alphonso simply gave up, hungry, his thoughts mired within a bleak swamp of despair.

This had been the third day in a row the commissary had run short leaving vast numbers of the homeless to wonder where their next meal would be coming from. He had heard that the larger camps, further in the park, and at the Presidio, were faring better. The army issued families with children, and the elderly, tents, cots, and blankets at the end of the first week. The larger Church groups managed the actual distribution under the watchful eye of the military which allowed for an orderly layout of the neighborhoods, many by church or religious designation. The largest neighborhood, nearest the food and medical facilities, accommodated the Catholics. Ethnic neighborhoods sprouted here and there, but ultimately it was more important to have a tent of your own, versus having neighbors who spoke the languages of your birth. Single women often shared quarters with each other, single men often had to fend for themselves sleeping in the open just outside the main campsites. Each tent was numbered, that number their identification for food and other necessities. The single men had no identification numbers which led to a certain amount of chaos, their rumbling bellies just as hungry as Alphonso's was, and he had a number. While servant women were tolerated, those with children with no husband to speak for them, were scorned. Scoundrels, prostitutes, and riffraff's returned to the ashes left of the city to find or build whatever shelters they could.

The stench, and the flies were as unforgiving as the over-flowing privies that served the masses. Hell had bubbled over when the city had been devastated by the fires. Now the devil seemed to be laughing at them.

Through all their trials and tribulations, the people inhabiting the camps were mostly polite; at least that was something.

The morning had been cold just as it had been the day before, and the day before that, the fog sometimes not retreating until late afternoon or not at all. Discontent was growing in the camps; the army slow to respond. The churches, meaningful caretakers of the hungry and downtrodden, could only promise that the army was doing the best they could under the circumstances. Half of the privies were over-flowing, the army, once-again, slow to respond—who could blame them, it was a horrible job. The trash, mostly assorted cans, seemed to sprout like too many dandelions—only not so pretty.

Alphonso and Katie took a daily walk together, which offered something different from the narrow confines of their crowded campsite and the endless lines that occupied so much of their time. So far, they had not dared to venture to the top of the hill to gaze through the fields of cemetery plots at the smoldering ashes of the city. They knew that the time would come but for now just getting through one day at a time was enough to bear. He admired her fortitude. She was not one to complain but the hard living was aging her, the aches, and pains more meaningful with each day. Mr. Piff frequently brought them a smile as he raised hell with the devil regarding the infirmities that all to rapidly replaced his long-lost energies of youth.

Their usual walks were deeper into the park, away from the stench and crowds that made an unwanted circus of their lives. The day was without a breeze, nary a leaf stirred, the all-pervasive stench of the camp settling in for a long day's abuse. They ventured nearer the Presidio, finding a camp that they had not seen before. There were five large tents, widely spaced, an expensive touring car, parked near each. There were five men, all wearing gray bowler hats, with full shirted frock coats with broad lapels, a badge on each, standing guard near each tent. There were four more guards just outside the roped off area surrounding the encampment. Pinkerton men, Alphonso guessed, he had seen them before guarding the banks and other financial institutions.

"Someone, almost as important as the Pope, has set up here; must be a general?" Katie whispered as she pointed with her eyes towards the largest tent where they could see a man wearing a white apron cooking over an actual stove. There were more stoves close to each tent, none currently lit.

"Roast beef, with lots of pepper and salt," sighed Alphonso paying more attention to the aromas in the air than the plush nature of the encampment.

"With fresh rosemary," added Katie, her mouthwatering. Perhaps we could…"

"Ask for some," Alphonso finished their shared thought as he too could almost taste the roasting meat.

"With asparagus," Katie anguished, as she took four short steps closer to the rope barrier.

"Afternoon, Ma,am, I'm afraid that you will have to go back to where you came from." A bull of a man, who looked like he might be able to bite the head off a pit-bull without having to chew and swallow, tipped his hat as he moved in front to block their path. The man did not smile, his beady black eyes searched the grassy area behind them for any additional intruders.

"Oh, we wouldn't want to interrupt the general. I am sure that he is a terribly busy man with much on his mind. We just…"

The man was no fool, knowing full-well that it was the aroma of the roast beef that had drawn them near.

"Perhaps if we could just speak with the general for a brief moment." Katie tried to take another step forward, the guard not allowing it. A second guard approached from where he had been standing closer to the field kitchen. He had a kinder demeanor, more polite, that of a gambling man who used a derringer rather than a fist. Of all the men guarding the campsites it was immediately evident that he was the one who held all the cards.

"The General…" Alphonso interrupted.

"There is no General here, Sir…Ma'am. These are private quarters and without an invitation I must ask you to leave."

"What's the problem here, Sam?" The other guard asked."

"Nothing, boss. These good people were just asking directions." He answered as he raised a ham-hock sized hand pointing back towards were Alphonso and Katie had come from. "The main camp is that way, about half a mile."

The wealthy had it better, one presumed, but what happened inside their larger more accommodating tents could only be guessed at. Alphonso and Katie had ventured towards the area where the wealthy presided and were turned away by men they thought to be Pinkerton Men—men who often had a hand in railroad disputes and range wars. The area, nick-named 'Top Hat' by Katie, remained as allusive as their mansions had once been. Unlike most who, had been burned out and rendered homeless, the well to do, affluent set were not exactly put out, their privacy guarded, food plentiful, as was drink and fine tobaccos. The stench and trash of the surrounding camps did not affect them as it did the rest of the populace. One noted inconvenience was the lack of young female household servants to tend to their daily whims and needs. These underpaid servants had their own lives to worry about.

As did Alphonso and Katie.

"Alphonso, I've been thinking," Katie took his hand as they stopped beneath a shady Elm tree.

"As have I." He answered with a gleam in his eyes.

"About what?"

"I had forgotten what it feels like to be in love. I'm not sure, that I ever have…been in love…I mean. Grazia and me, we were so young…"

Katie pressed a finger gently to his lips as she looked into his eyes, understanding. "I know. We'll give it some more time, it has only been a few weeks, and so much has happened." She felt his lip tremble, the light in his eyes fading.

"No, my dear Alphonso. I do have feelings for you, good and wonderful feelings. Feelings I thought that I might not ever feel again. I'm not going anywhere except with you, my love." She brought her hand back touching her own face realizing what she had just done." With a laugh that preceded her kiss and their embrace she said. "There, I've said it, and while I did not intent to, I'm glad

I did." After a long lingering moment, they gently pulled apart, except for their hands as they continued their walk. "But where shall we go. We can't just stay in this horrid camp forever?"

"No, we can't, and we won't"

"But we have no money, nothing but our tent, and that belongs to the army; doesn't it?" She stopped, wondering if he might have an answer.

He had not really heard her, his attention now fixed on a woman who knelt next to a wooden crate just outside a small group of tents that had separated from the main camp due to the crowding.

She dropped his hand wondering why, at this moment, he was looking at another woman, a younger, pretty one at that. She had thought better of him.

He felt her hand slip away He saw her concern but did not understand why. "Wait one minute, I have an idea." Taking her hand back in his he quickly approached the woman practically dragging Katie with him. "Excuse us ma'am, is that a sewing machine that you have there?"

A toddler cried, startled at the strange man's approach. A little girl, four, or five years of age, grabbed hold of her mother's skirt, hiding her face, thinking herself invisible to the approaching strangers. The woman soothed her daughter's fears as she answered. "It is, but I fear that it has seen its last days; broken it is, and I have no parts with which to fix it.

"B'fhéidir gur féidir liom cabhair a fháil," He recognized her accent and responded in the language of the Irish he had often served back at the watchmaker's shop. She looked puzzled, not understanding the Irish, she being second or third generation. "Perhaps I can be of some help," he replied, this time in English.

The woman stepped back, gathering up her frightened toddler, while pulling her daughter nearer. "Quiet, children, the kind gentleman, only wishes to help."

Katie watched with pride as he quickly isolated the problem. "I can see what the problem is. There is a tiny gear here," he pointed where neither woman could see.

"It has come loose. I have a tool which I shall fetch and return shortly. I will have it fixed and working almost as good as new in no time at all."

On their way back to their tent to retrieve his watchmaker's tools he told Katie, "There must be hundreds of sewing machines, watches, and such, that will all be needing repair. When we met outside what was left of the shop, where I once worked, I had managed to salvage a tool belt. I have the tools needed to repair these things. As for parts, we can salvage from those that are beyond repair, to fix those that are. It will be a small start, but a start never-the-less, and we shall have the means for our future."

With that, she spun him around, surprising him with a kiss that tasted of love, admiration, and of hope, that for a while had almost slipped away.

Katie rested in their tent while Alphonso returned to fix the ailing sewing machine. Her thoughts fluttered in a dozen different directions. One thought bothering her she could not shake off; that he shouldn't become a traveling repair man, the chances of being robbed were too great.

LIV

"Good God almighty," exclaimed Liam Malarkey as he reigned in his horse stopping the wagon just as the field of tents came into view.

"Where did they all come from," Muttered the old buffalo soldier as he spat from his seat on the wagon into the dust that now rose from what had once been a grassy field. *So many people, too many,* he thought. "You ever seen a herd of buffalo. I mean a big one you can count from sunrise to sunset, and the next day through. Now, that was something to see; of course, their mostly gone now. They could turn a great green prairie into a wasteland of brown grass nubs in no time flat. Oh, the grass would grow back all right just as it will after a prairie fire scorches the earth. Those buffalo were a force of nature…" He paused, looking once again towards the horizon where the road disappeared, only to keep on going to yet another horizon. "They're gone now…the buffalo." He whispered.

"They were something to behold. Yes sir, they were something to behold, but that was back in a time that will never come again our way. "He took a pinch of tobacco as he studied the camp for a moment. "For once the government has kept its word. They said they would be bringing in enough tents to take care of everyone that needs one. But this…" The once green expanse of Golden Gate Park now choked with white army branded tents pitched a few feet from where they were to as far as they could see, and beyond. There were hundreds, thousands of tents, all lined up in neat tidy rows, each row staked out properly by the engineers as if one day they might suddenly be replaced by wood and brick to become a city as mighty as San Francisco had once been. Dust, smoke, and the rubbish that marked civilized progress filled the air and any ground between. "Where did they all come from? Where there that many people in San Francisco?"

"I guess there were, and I'll bet that at least half of them have picked up whatever they had left and moved on." He chuckled a little beneath his breath. "The buffalo smelled better than this."

"You don't say," acknowledged Malarkey. He didn't cotton much to people. "It is a powerful sight, and a right powerful smell.

"I guess they haven't dug enough latrines yet. You and me, we had a swim or two in the ocean but most of these folks haven't had a bath in a month of Sundays." A swarm of flies descended around them in greetings.

"Well, it's up to you?"

Huckleberry Freeman waved away the flies as he digested the vision of the enormous refugee camp in front of them. It seemed doubtful at best that they would be able to find his friends, his family, in the sea of humanity that had turned the green grass brown. The field of white was more than a white canvas, it was filled with white folks, who would not take with any kindness and a generous heart, his presence. Beneath what had been all her beauty, San Francisco had been as sinful and treacherous as the Comanche Indians that once ruled the west. There would be no place for an old black man here. "I guess I've done seen enough, we might as well be moving on."

"Change your mind about Montana?" Asked Malarkey, knowing what the answer would be anyway.

"Winters in Montana are too long and too cold. I've been pondering Southern California, down near Mexico. I hear that a place called Las Angeles is warm and an up-and-coming place."

"I've heard different, that it's a dirty shanty-town with more oil wells than common sense. Hell, I overheard a couple of fellas talking back at the café a couple of months ago that Las Angeles County is flat running out of water."

"San Francisco ain't much better. Surrounded by water and always looking for that next glass to drink. Not all roads lead a fella to where he might want to go."

"Ha…" Malarkey mused. "Judging by the smell of this place the last of the water might just have been used up to fight the fires." He swatted uselessly; he too had become bothered by the buzzing pesky flies.

"You ever been up Sacramento way? Sacramento is not a bad place, except in the summer when it's hot as hades on a fiery afternoon." Huckleberry, who had the reigns, clicked at the horse. "Git! We got places to be, that are a lot better than this."

"One place is too cold, another too hot. The earth here, rears up and kicks you in your ass, another place hasn't any water.

Why don't we just keep looking down the road until opportunity gets in our god-damned way." Malarkey said.

"Sounds good to me." He looked at the endless lines of tents, the people, and the squaller, thinking that anywhere must be better than this.

LVI

Sargent-Major Wilcox looked at his orders and scratched his chin. Where was he to get a hundred skilled carpenters, men who could build a highly crafted structure like the ones that used to crown San Francisco's hills. His orders said specifically that he was not to recruit them for the army. They were to be the master-craftsmen who would lead the legions of carpenters, plumbers, and electricians that were arriving daily to rebuild the city. Their first task would be to build dozens of single room occupancy hotels to house the mostly single men, many who were rough around the edges, men the army wanted to keep out of the civilian camps they now oversaw. Bars, cathouses, and cheap john accommodations ripe for bubonic plague were already rising from the ashes of the Barbary. The army's task would be made all that much more difficult if the thieves and ruthless shanghaiers beat them to the punch.

LVII

Efah was a young woman without much social or physical charm. For years she had been intimidated and told that she was good-for-nothing and never would be, by Maude Perkins, the cruel domineer of orphans and frightened little boys. Maude had been one nasty bitch with nary a kind word or action for anyone unless it benefited herself. Having finally found the courage to take flight from *Maude's School of Reprehensible Bitchiness,* Efah was desperate to find her own place in society. Unfortunately, she had been a good student with Maude as her role model. While the others did their best to accept and welcome Efah, she very quickly became as insufferable and demanding of everyone and everything as Maude had. The harder Efah tried the wider the gap became until finally she was told in no short terms to move on. Evicted by unanimous consent Efah tried to find a home in neighboring camps. Everyone had heard of Efah, she had become a pariah.

Efah volunteered to help in the field kitchen knowing that some kitchen helpers were provided with shelter because of their early morning hours. It did not take long for her to be shunned from the mostly catholic dominated kitchen for planting seeds of mistrust and discord.

In time, she found a Rabbi who took her under his wing, soon falling under the spell of her unerring bitchiness. In the Rabbis' eyes Efah just needed a little guidance; unfortunate the paths she chose always seemed to lead down the wrong road. Efah, unwilling to listen or take advice from anyone, finally forced the rabbi's hand. "What has she done now," the rabbi asked as he eyed the faces of the women as they scurried about the bakery doing their best to avoid Efah.

It took a moment for Father Hanlon to find the right words. A catholic priest turning to a rabbi for advice was not something he did every day. *Still,* he thought, *these are extraordinary times.* "Efah, took it upon herself to distribute the flour. Yesterday she so infuriated the post commissary sergeant that this morning we received no flour at all," explained Hanlon who had decided that the rabbi needed to know the truth about Efah. "The sergeant did not exactly use diplomatic words in suggesting that we could all go to the flour warehouse to get what we need rather then he waste one more moment working with that *shiksa*."

The Rabbi fell silent for a moment tucking his smile beneath his beard. "The good sergeant said *shiksa,* did he?"

"*Shiksa* would be a term of respect compared to the words he actually used." He responded, returning the smile he knew that the rabbi was doing his best to suppress.

The rabbi gazed thoughtfully across the room at the empty shelves that should be filled with their daily flour rations. Finally, he said, careful not to be overheard,

"It is easier to contemplate whether or not a flea has a bellybutton then how to get Efah to listen to anyone—in particular, a rabbi. She is a difficult young woman…"

"Feeding the masses is difficult at best. God, in his wisdom, has provided enough challenges without adding Efah. Too much salt ruins the soup." The priest added, his eyes seeking a remedy from the Rabbi.

"The sergeant said *shiksa,* did he? Well, something must be done." The rabbi parted with a whimsical smile.

"I have been wondering if Efah is actually a Jew, is it possible that in truth she is catholic, and belongs with your flock?"

Father Hanlon gave thought to the matter. "I very much doubt it; however, the life of a cloistered nun might suit her. The mystery of the contemplative life is woven tightly with the mystery of the Incarnation. This mystery finds an especially vivid expression in the life of a cloistered nun, where a woman chooses to spend her whole life within the walls of a monastery, hidden from the world for the sake of intimacy with God."

"I have heard it said that silence is a woman's best garment. Unfortunately, our Efah is not exactly stylish." The rabbi sighed. "In Yiddish, Efah means darkness and gloom. He smiled knowingly. "Never-the-less I will speak with her."

LVIII

Hatti was livid.

Fact or fiction, it did not matter, the rumor was as disheartening as if a second earthquake had struck. She was not a woman to let her emotions over-rule her judgment but this was too much. She had learned from the tittle-tattle telegraph among the women the camp community that the fickle wind that brought what might be good news rarely lasted while the siren that brought unwelcome news changed as it passed from person to person, rarely benefiting anyone. She had heard it now three times—more—that Efah was no longer working at the bakery. Was this good news or sad news?

Efah had found work in the main flour warehouse at the Presidio. While the army guarded the thousands of pounds of life-giving flour, it would be Efah who would oversee the distribution of flour into the camps. The army kitchens still had flour for bread and cooking, but never enough. The daily rationing of flour to individuals for their own baking purposes was now up to Efah. Why? Who would make such a foolish decision? Hatti adding some well-chosen curse words, more frequently uttered by rough dock workers than women of stature—not that her opinion was highly sought. She was after all a harlot, though not common by any measure.

Hatti had long since grown weary with the lines at the field kitchens. All things considered the food was not bad, never good, bread often in short supply as the camp populations had grown. Flour from the army warehouse was a staple for the home bakers who had procured and rehabilitated stoves from the ruins of the city. It being easier to barter home-made bread then to wait in lines for the poor-quality bread occasionally found in the field kitchens. There were times that she regretted having dined at some of the best restaurants in San Francisco with her gentlemen friends, promising herself that she would never again take a satisfying meal for granted.

"Where the hell did you get that?" Hatti exclaimed as she and Katie returned from a long morning of waiting for what turned out to be a breakfast of cornbread, pork fat, and beans. Real meat, chicken, and meat both, were becoming as rare as bread. She was looking at a fire damaged Montgomery Ward wood and coal burning stove that Dimitri had retrieved from the ruins of a house.

Dimitri would often disappear for hours at night leaving the others to wonder if he had a secret lover, none daring to raise the specter that he was part of a secretive Masonic temple. This fear was put aside when he returned with items that looked beyond repair but with his skills and patience he would repair and barter or sell them for things that made their lives a little better. How could this simple saint be a clandestine masonic monster? The beat-up and dented stove, looking well beyond repair, was the largest item he had drug back to camp.

"That is a waste of time, my friend," Piff chortled, though secretly he wished Dimitri the best. There had been a time when he had been more than a little handy with his hands but from where he sat now the old stove was nothing more than a piece of junk that somehow had not been rendered into a piece of melted slag by the intense fires.

"You just sit there and watch what happens, old man. If I can't fix it—and I will—then we'll just turn it into a nice shiny table once I finish sprucing it up." Dimitri responded as he took an old rag from his hip pocket test the grime. The grime won.

"It sure would be nice if you can get this old stove to where it can bake a loaf of bread again. The pitiful excuse for a field kitchen mismanaged by the army is getting worse by the day." Hatti whined. "I've all but given up dreaming of a hot plate of short ribs with black barley and mushrooms. For the life of me, I can't remember if it was just a few months ago or years since I enjoyed a succulent New England lobster with drawn garlic butter."

"Oh, I wouldn't dare think about what you must have had to do for the price of that kind of meal," Katie scolded good-naturedly. "I've never seen a lobster yet alone tasted one. Why I…"

"Fatback and fresh sourdough bread, yes sir, I'd like to have some of that just once more before I meet my maker.

Did I ever tell you about the time I won me the price of a dinner at Delmonico's?" Piff held up his shaky hands as if he were showing off the legendary fish that got away. "The steak was this big," his hands exaggerating the size, "and it came with some asparah-geese, and some of those little potatoes" he bragged, winking at Alphonso who was practically drooling with all the talk about tasty food.

"Irish Soda Bread honey-glazed lamb and olives, which is what I would like," Dimitri grinned. "I had it once in Ireland and have not had it since, best damn bread on God's green earth. If I do say so myself." His attempt at putting on an Irish accent fell laughably short.

"You get this stove working and I'll make us all a nice batch of cornbread muffins." Katie promised.

"With what?" Groaned Hatti. "We can't even get a pound of flour around this place. It's depressing."

"Speaking of being depressed, outside of going to the privy Leah has not left the tent in days. All she does is pet Purplepaws."

Hatti concurred. "We are all hungry and she has little appetite, and she is looking rather pale."

"We need to get her out of this dreadful camp. The poor dear has lost everything, her grandma, home, everything she has known." Katie looked around their campsite thoughtfully. "Somehow, we need to get her out of this place, somewhere where she can play. Somewhere where children can…"

Voices.

A female Tower of Babel stole their attention as a troop of women stormed into the camp sounding and looking as if they were on an earthshaking mission. A diminutive woman, forty-ish who looked as if she had once been a dancer led the way,

"Come on ladies, we have work to do." Four of the women each grabbed Hatti and Katie by their elbows spinning them around in the direction they had just come from. "We have had enough, and we are not going to allow the army to run the field kitchens any longer. We are going to let the Commanding General know who the real boss is around here. Right ladies?!"

"Right." This echoed several times with resounding certainty…

"Count me in." Piff toned as he rolled his wheelchair forward. Putting women back in the kitchen was all right by him. The food here was worse than he had experienced back in the Sierra gold camps.

Katie broke free from her escorts grabbing Piff's wheelchair from behind. Come on Piff, you old poop, it's about time we went on an adventure."

"Damn toot'en," replied the old man cracking a large mostly toothless grin as he waved his cane about. "Remember the Alamo. "With a sheepish look on his face he turned back to Katie saying," Where the hell are we are going, anyways?"

"We'll know when we get there." She looked for Alphonso to join them.

He in turn turned his eyes and good intentions towards Dimitri and his wayward stove. "Not this time, Katie, there is work to be done here."

Dimitri, seeing a few attractive women hoping that one or two might be single, put down his mallet, joining the parade.

Alphonso, scratching his head at Dimitri's betrayal quick-stepped next to Katie. "I hope you know what you are getting us into?"

"Not a clue, love, not a clue."

LIX

"Please stay for just a while longer." Priscilla Cody said. "I think that your father would have appreciated what I have to say. "First, let me ask you something. What are your plans now?"

Li Fengcheng shook his head not having an answer, still in shock at his father's passing. He had planned to stay in San Francisco for as long as his father needed him. Now, he did not know if he should stay or go. There was no thought of returning to China. He had no one else in America except for his father and now he was gone.

Pricilla knew from the look on his face that he was a man adrift with neither a family nor a place to be. She also knew that he was a man who had long rebelled against the limitations placed on him for being Chinese. "Have you even been to Hawaii," she asked?

He shook his head no.

Our church mission has had a long-term interest with Asian immigration to the islands. Low wages and unfair labor conditions have created an atmosphere that has about reached a breaking point between the field laborers and the plantations, especially with the Chinese, Japanese, and Korean workers. Porta Rican workers are being recruited as strike breakers.

Our missionaries are trying to find a peaceful, if not amicable settlement, on behalf of these hard-working laborers. There has been a long-term mistrust by the Chinese of their white supervisors." She saw that she now had his attention. "Allow me to get straight to the point. You are Christian, of Chinese decent, and well versed in western ways. I know that you are fluent in Cantonese. What we are looking for is an ombudsman, an intelligent man of good character, who can act on our behalf to help these poor people who are trapped in a world that frankly needs to change. We can offer a small bungalow which is located on mission property on the big island, all of the necessities of life, and an allowance equal to what our other missionaries receive elsewhere around the world." She paused, looking for a reaction. "You would not be acting as a Christian missionary, but as I said earlier, you will be an ombudsman helping to bring both sides together."

Li rose and walked to the window where he remained silent for a few moments then turned saying. "Right now, I am needed by my father's side to say good-by. When I return, I will give you my answer."

Priscilla found a folded piece of paper where Li had sat. Written on it was the name: *Look Tin Eli.*

---

*After the 1906 San Francisco earthquake and fire destroyed Chinatown, including the Russo-Chinese Bank, Look Tin Eli became "the public face of the post-quake rebuilding of Chinatown". As general manager of the Sing Chong bazaar, he articulated a vision of post-quake Chinatown as an "ideal Oriental City". Already a skilled negotiator, he secured substantial loans from his Hong Kong and Canton partners for the rebuilding and persuaded Chinese merchants to hire western architects to rebuild Chinatown in an "Oriental" style in order to promote tourism and social change.

LX

Francis DeGeorgie was clearly on edge, pacing back and forth in front of the castle. At first, Antoinette was amused but the longer it lasted the more she came to understand that something was really bothering him. Even Quinn, who had taken a liking to Francis, noted his distress, pacing him step for step, ruffling its feathers which did not distract Francis from his emotional journey.

Behind on her chores she left him in Quinn's watchful eyes. She left him alone to sort things out.

An hour later Francis found her cleaning the monkey cage. Tongue-tied and awkward he did not know how to say what he needed to, so he blurted it out, making things worse. "I'm leaving first thing in the morning."

Antoinette dropped the broom she had been sweeping with turning towards him, tears already sparkling in her eyes. This was totally unexpected and beyond what she thought their relationship was about. Yes, they were new lovers, not yet intimate, but something she had been thinking about. "Leaving? Why? I…I don't understand. I thought we…?"

Francis' heart skipped a beat as his Adam's apple bobbed in search of something to say. He realized that he had hurt her unknowingly and did not know how to fix it.

"I…I, no I'm not leaving. I'll be back, I think. I mean…" He reached out for her.

She pulled away. Anger and panic blinding her to what he was trying to say. All she heard, as he stammered and stuttered, was that he had just announced out of the clear blue sky, that he was leaving her. *WHY?* She shouted it, only in her head, so loud she might have woken the man in the moon, who shared her angst with Francis, from the dark of night on the far side of the world.

Seeing Antoinette pull away from him as she became more enraged, Quinn gave Francis two sharp pecks on his chins causing him to stumble back outside the monkey cage. Knowing how dangerous a peacock can be when provoked Antoinette slammed the cage door shut. "No, no Quinn, it's all right, Francis is not hurting me." She stroked his long neck just where he liked as she calmed the big bird down. Then, as both realized what had just happened and how stupid they were both being, they stopped and looked at each other with sad eyes.

A slight nervous smile teased Francis's face.

"It's not funny!

That caused him to laugh as he rubbed first one chin and then the other.

Enjoying his neck massage, Quinn batted his eyes, cocked his head, giving Francis a silly 'who me?' expression.

"Antoinette, what I wanted to say is that I am planning I on leaving tomorrow to see if I can find out what happened to my friends back at the tent camp. It is something that I just must do. It's a long walk and I don't even know if they're there. It could take some time to find them. I don't know when I'll be back, it could be days or weeks even." He felt better for saying it, worse because he did not want to leave her, afraid that for whatever reason he might not see her again.

She looked at him, eyes ablaze with determination. "Francis, I will not take no for an answer. I am going with you."

"No! *It is a long walk.* I don't even know where I am going."

She brushed Quinn away with a final pat sending him scurrying. "The zoo will have to do without me for a while, someone else will have to earn their pay for a change. Just give me a moment to pack a few things."

Twenty minutes passed and Francis could wait no longer. All he had were the clothes on his back, so he was set to go. He called her name one last time having decided to leave without her, hoping that if he ever saw her again, he would be forgiven. When he reached the little bridge over the creek she was waiting with a wagon.

Quinn followed to the edge of the park then watched as they disappeared over a knoll.

LXI

Nothing was going right. Efah threw up her hands in exaggerated despair searching for someone, anyone to blame for a lengthy list of her own incompetence's. Soldiers and civilians alike faded into the dusty shadows of the warehouse finding the smallest, seemingly important task to avoid Efah, the storm goddess of darkness and gloom. Efah's wrath could scorch the whitewash from the walls had there been any. The day started with six wagonloads of flour that were expected but had not arrived. The scale for weighing the flour for distribution had broken and there was no replacement—that and a dozen other foul-ups. Efah knew that it was a personal plot against her, raging eternally, her demons flying carnivorous monkeys.

It did not take long for everyone to leave the flour warehouse, echoes of Efah's rage clearly heard from a block away. "You can't fool me, you lazy, useless idiots. God damn it, I will not be blamed for this. You hear me! If there is no flour you are to blame. You are all a bunch of lazy, good for nothing…"

"A little Jewish woman should not be using language like that," murmured one of the soldiers guarding the front doors to the warehouse.

The duty sergeant in a field tent across the way, heard the commotion and seeing the sudden exodus of mostly women marching away from the warehouse, rose from his desk and huffed. "What the hell and darnation is going on here, and why haven't you gone inside to deal with it?" He barked as he yelled at the soldiers. The three soldiers just shook their heads, embarrassed that they were intimidated by Efah.

The sergeant pushed open the door just enough to see inside. Closing the door quickly, he shared a look with the soldiers. "Efah," he uttered her name as if were a curse word seasoned sailors rarely used. "Well, there are two things we can do now. Shoot her and put her out of our misery; no, I thought not, I have little zeal to explain why we shot her to the Major who has never had the pleasure of meeting the screw. No one enters until she has calmed down." He sighed." I'll go and see if I can find the Rabbi.

By the time they reached the flour warehouse the protesters had grown to fifty or more, mostly women, the only men were the three soldiers guarding the large wooden door. Piff. And Dimitri and Alphonso who hung reluctantly behind the mob of angry women. All had something to say, angry voices drowning each other's voice from making any sense. There was no consensus as to what to do next. No leadership other than from those at the front of the mob who had no plan other than having arrived first.

The soldiers knew their orders, no one was to get into the warehouse until the sergeant returned. While it was a cool morning the men quickly developed an itchy nervous sweat in their wool uniforms as they stood their ground against the women. They were as clueless as the women in how to resolve the standoff, until a barrage of over-ripe tomatoes rained down on them.

"God damn it, that's the last straw." Wiping tomato from his face, one of the soldiers who had taken the worst of the deluge raised his bayonet menacingly.

"Careful, Al, remember that these are ladies not looters."

Three more tomatoes blitzed Al who almost stumbled, eye stinging from the acidic tomato juice. "That does it, fix bayonets, there aren't any ladies on the field today."

Seeing the bayonets as the real threat most of the women quieted and backed away.

"What do we do now, Sarge?"

Al was still fuming. "If any of them comes at us we gut them."

The soldiers looked at each other, each thinking almost the same thought, *you've got to be kidding me.*

—

"I don't like what I'm seeing here. Alphonso took a long hard look at the situation. "Those boys are getting riled and just might start to shoot. One shot and more soldiers will be coming to back up their own. It won't matter if their women, there will be a massacre."

Dimitri, who was not afraid of a fight, figured the odds and had to agree. "What few men are caught up in the fracas will be the first targets."

Alphonso took a step back without realizing it. "That's you and me."

Dimitri put a firm hand on Alphonso's shoulder. "And the old man?"

At first, Alphonso had trouble seeing where Dimitri had pointed; the woman in front of him too tall. For some unknown reason the women began moving slightly to the left. There, now I see the old goat, over with Katie and Hatti." His heart skipped a beat as he saw that they were up front, at the flash point of the crowd. His first instinct was to push his way through the crowd and drag them out of there but thought better of it after a moment's reflection. Two men, aggressively approaching the soldiers, especially one the size of Dimitri, might just spark the violence they dreaded.

"We go." Dimitri squeezed his shoulder as a signal that he was going to get the women out of there.

"No, not now," Alphonso answered with more bravado than an old man who had never really raised his hand in anger against another. "I have an idea." He said, stopping the big Greek in his tracks. Hurriedly, he scratched a note on a piece of paper that he had pulled from his shirt pocket, tipped his hat to a woman immediately on front of him. "Would you please pass this forward to the old man in the wheelchair? It is very important."

At first she seemed hesitant but seeing the old man in his wheelchair she passed the note forward telling the woman ahead of her where it needed to go.

"What are we going to do; storm the citadel, murder or hold the guards hostage for a few pounds of flour?" Katie asked as she looked at the faces around her. They looked like they wanted to do just that. Katie did not have to guess who would come out on the losing end.

"I'm game," Piff chimed in. "I haven't had this much fun since the labor strike of 1883…or was that back in eighty-eight. It doesn't much matter…" He raised his cane as if he was leading a charge at Bull Run. "Soldier boy, you just wait until I get my hands on you." He looked up at Katie. "What did they do to chafe our behinds?"

Katie just smiled, Piff was a piece of work, one of a kind. When the dust settled it had been pioneers like Morgan Piff that had made San Francisco golden. She did not see the note that someone had stuffed in the old man's free hand as it fell to the ground like an autumn leaf. The heat of the moment grew hotter when a second and larger group of women led by Mary Kelly.[*] That sent the sergeant scurrying back to his tent where a rider was dispatched to the Presidio with a written message that trouble was at hand.

---

[*] Kelly's entry into public activism began in July 1906, over a necessity of domestic life—food. Fed up with long lines and inadequate food supplies, she led about one hundred disgruntled refugee women to relief headquarters to demand flour for their hungry families. In a decisive victory over red tape, the women left with fifty bags. Within days, their success inspired an event known as the "Flour Riot"—angry women stormed the main relief warehouse and made off with two thousand pounds of flour. Rather than seeing themselves as thieves, the rioting women accused the relief committee of hoarding donated supplies that actual event occurring several months later.

"What did you write on that note?" Dimitri," asked Alphonso."

"Fresh johnnycakes and bacon back at camp." Alphonso laughed wishing it was the truth. "I thought that it would get Piff's attention. Katie, too."

Dimitri looked quizzically, his stomach unconsciously rumbling. "Johnnycakes, you say?"

"The flour to make them is in there," Alphonso whispered as he pointed towards the warehouse. It was obvious that no one was getting near the flour inside. The soldiers had their orders, and the duty sergeant was the meanest son-of-a-bitch in the army. Still, the thought of fresh johnnycakes with syrup puckered the imagination.

While they quietly discussed the best cakes they had ever had, practically smelling the smoked bacon Piff, Hatti and Katie had moved.

Katie saw that they were not going to get into the warehouse by mob rule, it would take some deviousness.

The warehouse was part of an old barn finished off by a large military tent. The barn faced the protesters, the tent making up the rear mostly out of sight and vulnerable. There was no entryway at the back, but cloth was no match when it came to a sharp knife. Neither women had one. Piff did.

—

Efah's unhinged behavior could have put her in Agnew's Insane

Asylum had anyone noticed and protecting the flour wasn't more important. But she was alone, raving at the shadows, sure that all the evils in the world were there to taunt her. She sat in a white mound, turning wildly from one side to another throwing handfuls of flour at the apparitions she could not see. Just because she could not see them did not mean that they were not there. They were there…she screamed words that no longer made any sense. The voices she heard were real, they were coming to embarrass her in front of the whole world. For once she had amounted to something. God had given her the flour, without the flour there would be no bread, without the bread people would starve. She could not, would not let those who taunted her have the flour.

Suddenly she understood.

She filled her apron with as much flour as it would hold, powdering herself from head to toe until she was made of flour, a cloud of white marking her path as she rose and followed the voices.

The sun blinded her as she stepped outside the protective womb of the warehouse. In the unforgiving brilliance of the sun, she could not tell who friend or foe was; the soldiers, women, all of them, lemurs rising from ancient times to take what was hers.

Everyone fell silent, staring at a mad woman.

"You want it, come and get it. I can't stop you." She wheezed the fine powdered flour dust chocking off her breath, restricting her lungs. She was light-headed, intoxicated though she did not drink. Reality becoming as blurred as her vision as she cocked her head looking back into the warehouse. "I can you know…I can stop you. If there is no flour to be had, you can't take it, now can you."

The soldiers looked at each other, the threatening women who now practically surrounded them, then back to this one mad woman: Efah.

A banshee in white, Efah turned and fled back into the warehouse, slamming and bolting the door behind her.

—

A slit was cut through the cloth just big enough for Katie to duck through. The front doors to the barn were closed leaving only a few kerosene lanterns to light the interior. Where there should have been tons of flour stacked ceiling high in white bags there were only twenty or thirty bags of flour waiting to be bagged. Hatti followed leaving Piff outside, his wheelchair unable to gain traction in the loose straw that covered much of the rough cedar planked floor.

"Is that all of it," whispered Hatti? There were numerous storage bins tucked in the dark shadows of the warehouse; most appearing empty. The air smelled nutty sweet, like a fully grown wheat field. The floor little snow drifts mixed with straw in places trampled into hard lumpy tracks by horse drawn wagons and human footprints. The roiling noise of discontent outside echoed of an approaching storm as all else was still. Beams of sunlight penetrated the gaps in the barn framing as flour dust sifted down from the rafters above. The residue on her tongue tasting of fresh grain, raw almonds and old pennies.

To their right on the other side of an old horse stall a kerosene lantern flickered and moved as if someone was carelessly waving it about. Who? It doesn't matter, Katie thought as she picked a ten-pound flour bag off a stack. It's weight, though light for the moment, would become troublesome when she had three, four, and more of them.

"Here, give me that," whispered Hatti as the dust in the air became a thin coating of wallpaper paste on her tongue creeping down her throat. She grasped the flour sack quickly carrying it to the slit in the tent where Piff waited. "How many can you carry on your lap? She asked. He took the bag awkwardly in his arthritic hands plopping it on his bony lap, raising four fingers.

She brought him six.

Delirious, Efah weakly tossed more flour into the air, itty-bitty fireflies danced before her eyes. She struggled to breath, each breath drawn through a straw with an elephant on your chest with hundreds of tiny feathers tickling her airways all at the same time. Fire ants replaced the feathers as her breathing became more difficult. Close to passing out she saw a tall slender woman, perhaps an angel coming for her. Her last thought oblivion as the lantern slipped from her grasp.

Hatti saw movement in the shadows then froze in place when she saw that it was Efah. Her heart pained for a troubled woman raging against her demons. She wanted to reach out…

Katie pulled her back. "Get out, the flour dust is explosive!"

Two of the flour bags were jolted from Piff's lap as Katie used everything she had to spin him around forcing his wheelchair over rough ground. Hatti added her strength to add a few more yards before a tremendous WHOOOMP a pressure wave bowled them over. The roof to the old barn exploding as the cloth tent making up the rest of the flour warehouse vanished in a brief but brilliant burst of flame leaving some of the beams that had supported it all to burn.

"What the hell and darnation was that?" Piff sputtered from where he sprawled on the ground next to the wheelchair, its wheels still turning. He was as white as a ghost, one of the flour bags having torn open.

Katie and Hatti just looked at each other as they realized how close they had come to meeting the same fate as Efah had. The buzzing in their ears muffled all sound as they struggled to their feet. Silent laughter slipping from their lips as they took in the ghost of Morgan Piff. The old man was still talking and for once they couldn't hear a word. Katie laughed, pointing at Hatti's worn and tattered evening gown, now scorched with a few burn holes, its former eloquence now toast.

Others were not as fortunate.

Caught in the explosion one of the soldiers suffered burns and life-threatening injuries as he was blown through the air plowing through some of the nearest protesters as if the women were bowling pins. Those left standing, as soon as they got their wits about them, fled in all directions, panic-stricken cattle caught in a violent thunderstorm.

Lance Corporal Jacob Jurinek who had been sitting in for the

Duty Sergeant watched the events unfold from the sergeant's field tent. His only injury a sprained wrist as he fell backwards in his chair when the huge white-yellow explosion all but leveled the warehouse. As he surveyed the carnage, counting the wounded, and watched the women scurry out of harm's way, one thing that caught his attention was an over-turned wheelchair near where the rear entrance to the warehouse had been. The cloth having burned away gave him a clear view as two women, one tall and shapely, helped an old man back into the wheelchair and then wheel him back towards the cypress tree forest that grew along the edge of the Presidio. His hunch, and he would report it as so was that they were somehow responsible for the destruction of the flour warehouse.

—

Leah napped in their tent, Purplepaws played with some string in its cage, when the explosion jolted her awake. More startled then scared she called out: "Katie?

Hatti?" When she got no answer, she crawled to the tent flap where she could see outside. The camp was deserted though there were plenty of people about all looking north to where a plume of smoke was rising. Grandma Traudle, an old woman in the neighboring camp who always kept an eye on Leah when the other women were absent, spotted her and came over. "Nothing to worry about, dearie, something exploded just over the hill. We are in no danger here."

Rumors were flying widely throughout the larger camp

As elements of the 14th Calvary rode at full gallop towards the plume with enough urgency to cause speculation that the massive refugee camp was under some sort of attack.

Liam Malarkey pulled his wagon over to the side of the road as the calvary stormed past. "I haven't seen something like that since the Indians up Dakota way were stirring up a hornets' nest. Old Huckleberry, nodded his head as he coughed from the dust, leaning over the side of the wagon to spit he said. "Well, I'll be damned, will you look at that," as he saw Leah just across the way.

Malarkey did not know Leah from any other little girl.

"As soon as the dust settles we'll get back on the road. What the hell are you gawking at?"

"Leah, is that you there?" Huckleberry called out joyfully.

Leah did not hear him, but she did see the old black man sitting hunched over on a wagon. Tears came to her eyes, she had sorely missed him. She thrust Purplepaws basket into grandma Traudle's hands as she practically flew towards the wagon.

"Oh, happy days. Child I thought that I was never going to see your smiling face again." Huckleberry said with a grin larger than his face as he lifted her up into the wagon.

Grandma Traudle gawked in surprise as she watched Leah slip into the welcoming embrace of the old black man. Originally from Germany, living in a mostly German neighborhood, she had met few men of color. That one now cradled Leah in his loving arms just wasn't done. "Mein Gott, was ist aus dieser welt geworden?" She muttered, her face paling. It did not take long for a small gathering of men from Traudle's camp to draw near, each feeding another's intolerance for this kind of mixing of the races.

All good German Lutheran Men from St. Mathew's Church, they did not see themselves as prejudiced, nor did they see themselves as intolerant—this type of abomination just couldn't be allowed.

A stout brawny man shadowed by two of similar size stepped menacingly towards the wagon. "Schwarzer mann, you will give the little white girl to us now, or we will hang you from that tree." He moved closer. Saying to the white man sitting next to Huckleberry. "What are you doing with this schwarzer mann? Have you no shame. Get down before we hang you too."

Through the corner of his eye, he could see two men running from the German encamp with a stout rope. "You had better do what they say, Huck. I think they mean business."

Leah heard and clung tighter. "No, I want to stay with you."

The only thing worse than being threatened with hanging was feeling Leah hugging him as tight as she could with tears in her eyes.

"Have it your way old man," Malarkey said as he cracked his whip to jolt the horse and wagon back onto the road. Before he could say "Get," two of the men reached out grabbing the horse's harness, the horse rearing, as Risky was yanked from the wagon landing with a loud hard thump on the ground.

Before he could catch his breath a large working man's boot came down just hard enough on his chest to let him know that he was not going anywhere.

"Have it your way, there is enough rope for the both of you."

Grandma Traudle came to fetch Leah down from the wagon. Placing Purplepaws basket just inside the backboard she held both hands up, her eyes telling Leah that she had no choice. "Come child, there will be some hangings today, not something for a little girl's eyes."

"Not today there won't." It was Dimitri. He and Alphonso had just returned to camp. "I suggest that you remove your boot from this man before I use mine to kick your ass back across the Rhine.

With trepidation Alphonso took the reins from the men who had stopped the wagon, the two men stepping back, not from any fear of the much smaller Italian but the sheer size of Dimitri.

Huckleberry Freeman let lout a long slow breath of relief.

Leah understood what had almost happened saying to Grandma Traudle. "Go away. I hate you." The look in her eyes paining the older woman. Without another word she turned determinedly back towards the Germans' camp; the men following.

Everyone within viewing distance turned their attention from the explosion and the rising smoke plume to the contest of wills around the wagon. Most could care less if there was a black man involved. The boring routine of camp life had been broken. As their attention returned to the smoke and whatever had happened on the other side of the hill some of the women protesters trickled back into camp. The news quickly spreading of the destruction of the flour warehouse. While gossip changed as quickly as the wind, it soon became clear that somehow Katie, Hatti, and Piff had been involved.

Dimitri helped Liam Malarkey to his feet, eying what looked like a stove beneath the tarp on the wagon.

Alphonso took Leah from Huckleberry asking if she was all right. She nodded but still hung on, not sure if the world was safe for the old black man yet.

"You had better get down now, Leah, us men folk have got some figuring to do." He looked around the campsite wondering where the women were. And Piff?

Meow.

That got Leah's attention.

Dimitri and Alphonso were wondering the same thing.

Malarkey introduced himself shaking Dimitri's hand. "I can see why those gents did not want to spar with you." Alphonso did the same.

"Now that all the introductions have been made and everyone has danced to the fiddle music why don't someone ask this old nigga how he's doing. Damnations, I came this close to being hung."

"I will, how you, Huckleberry. We thought you had gone south for the winter." It was Katie smiling up at him.

LXII

No sooner than the two women and Morgan Piff returned to camp than word filtered down through the gossip mill that the army was looking for two women and an old man in a wheelchair for sabotage in the burning of the flour warehouse. They were not saboteurs, but they knew that it would not belong before the thousands of hungry people living in the tent camps came looking for them. The wagon was loaded with what few things they had managed to acquire since the great quake and fires had taken everything away. They wanted to take one of the tents until it was agreed that Dimitri's tools were more valuable. Walking alongside the wagon with Huckleberry driving, and Piff at his side, they made their way back up through the cemeteries where they took a moment to try to remember the way it had been. San Francisco, a city that had been in a hurry to become the golden gate of wealth and men's dreams, settling instead for greed and depravity. Here and there buildings were being raised in what was left of the city. The ruins a dark scar that would take some time to replace.

Piff broke their silence: "She was something to behold in her

---

The story goes that after the 1906 earthquake a state of martial law was proclaimed in the city by mayor Eugene Schmitz. This is actually an urban legend, and no evidence exists to support the claim. According to the legend, though, the mayor had issued a blanket KILL order (supposedly written in all caps) to police officers and the military.

day. I wonder if she will just fade away to become a forgotten village like Yerba Buena?"

Malarkey reached out petting the horse's haunch, a yellow blade of wild grass perched between his lips. "I've never liked cities; too many people, too many rules. Once you have been touched by this place you can't forget her. What was that you said Huckleberry about looking down the road?"

Huckleberry smiled as he looked around at his new family. "Never stop looking down that road…you never know what…"

"Francis?" Hatti exclaimed.

"Where on earth have you been? And who is that with you?" Katie interrupted.

No one had noticed the wagon as it approached from the south until it drew up next to them. Smiles, laughter, and a hundred questions greeted Francis and Antoinette as if they were family coming to visit for the holidays. What they did not know was that Francis and Antoinette were the one's bearing gifts.

Foot-weary, everyone climbed aboard Antoinette's wagon, and they headed down the road to find their futures.

AT THE END OF THE ROAD

On a late August afternoon Leah Carmichael paused to look at the billowy wall of white cotton candy fog as it edged its way over the Twin Peaks towards Noe Valley. It was late August and a pleasant seventy-eight degrees in the city. She was old now and had grown up with the city. She and San Francisco had grown up and grown old together. She did not know how many people were left who had been there when the earthquake had knocked the old girl down. That was seventy years ago, but oh the memories: Glen Park, once upon a time an oasis with a zoo had become her home becoming a neighborhood just over the hill from the grand dame of them all—San Francisco.

She had grown up in a boarding house run by Katie and Alphonso. Hatti found her own road which led her to a place called Hollywood where she established a dress shop for women who had too much money to spend. Sergeant Huckleberry Freeman lived another eight years until he was reunited with his Buffalo Soldiers plot at the Presidio.

Old Mr. Piff expelled his last breath in the middle of a tall-tale four days after their arrival at the zoo. Quinn seemed to have enjoyed the old man's company.

Dimitri helped build many of the Queen Ann Victorians that still flourished and had become just as famous as the cable cars.

Liam Malarkey opened a neighborhood café which was just down the road from Glen Park. Shortly after Huckleberry passed on, he just up and disappeared, some say that he had a score to settle in Montana. The café he left for Leah.

Francis and Antoinette married and had two children.

He died in 1934, his body found in an alley on the waterfront. Leah suspected that he had been murdered in retaliation for his union activities.* Antoinette moved to Denver to be near her daughter who worked at the Denver Zoo.

Leah married David Carmichael, a young law student.

They were young and foolishly in love. He died during the great influenza epidemic in 1919. After that she never remarried, always being too busy, but never too busy to not look down that road where she can still see that old buffalo soldier watching for that next opportunity.

---

*The 1934 West Coast Waterfront Strike (also known as the 1934 West Coast Longshoremen's Strike, as well as a number of variations on these names) lasted eighty-three days, and began on May 9, 1934 when longshoremen in every US West Coast port walked out. The strike peaked with the death of two workers on "Bloody Thursday" and the San Francisco General Strike which stopped all work in the major port city for four days and led ultimately to the settlement of the West Coast Longshoremen's Strike. .The result of the strike was the unionization of all of the West Coast ports of the United States.

It's estimated that at least 3,000 people died in the 1906 earthquake and fires with 500 city blocks devastated. No one really knows how many may have perished in Chinatown. Around 250,000 residents were left homeless, while the estimated damage climbed to $500 million (over $10 billion today). The death toll remains the most significant loss of life from a natural hazard in the history of California. By 1909 the city been mostly rebuilt and proud to show off what she had become at the Panama—Pacific (World's Fair) held there in 1915.

www.ingramcontent.com/pod-product-compliance
Lightning Source LLC
Chambersburg PA
CBHW051417290426
44109CB00016B/1339